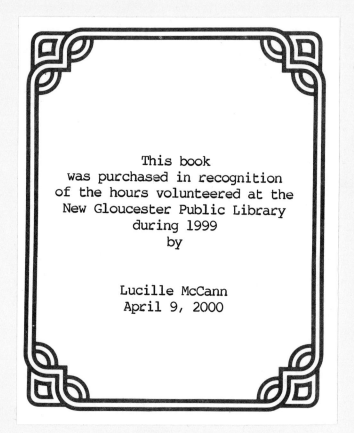

Easy Roses

FOR NORTH AMERICAN GARDENS

Easy Roses

FOR NORTH AMERICAN GARDENS

TOM CHRISTOPHER

READER'S DIGEST ASSOCIATION, INC.

Pleasantville, New York / Montreal

A READER'S DIGEST BOOK

Produced by STOREY COMMUNICATIONS, INC.

PRESIDENT **M. John Storey**
EXECUTIVE VICE PRESIDENT **Martha M. Storey**
PUBLISHER **Pamela B. Art**
CUSTOM ACQUISITIONS DIRECTOR **Deirdre Lynch**
PROJECT MANAGER **Linda G. Conway**
COVER DESIGN **Betty Kodela**
BOOK DESIGN **Betty Kodela** and **Leslie Noyes**
PRODUCTION ASSISTANCE **Eileen Clawson, Jen Rork, Mark Tomasi**
PHOTOGRAPHY MANAGEMENT **Laurie Geannelis, Mary Brott, Laurie Figary**

Reader's Digest General Books

VICE PRESIDENT, EDITOR-IN-CHIEF **David Palmer**
MANAGING EDITOR **Christopher Cavanaugh**
EDITORIAL DIRECTOR **David Schiff**
DESIGN DIRECTOR **Sandra Berinstein**
DESIGN DIRECTOR **Henrietta Stern**
SENIOR EDITOR **Carolyn T. Chubet**
SENIOR EDITOR **Don Earnest**
SENIOR EDITOR **Delilah Smittle**
TRAFFIC COORDINATOR **Diane Hoffman**
CONTRIBUTING DESIGNER **Diane Lemonides**

The credits and acknowledgments that appear on page 225
are hereby made a part of this copyright page.

Text Copyright © 1999 Thomas Christopher
Copyright © 1999 The Reader's Digest Association, Inc.

Christopher, Thomas.
    Easy roses for North American Gardens / Tom Christopher.
        p.   cm.
    Includes index.
    ISBN 0-7621-0123-7
    1. Rose culture–United States.   2. Rose culture–Canada.
3. Roses–United States.   4. Roses–Canada.   I. Title.
    SB411.C545   1999
    635.9'33734'0973–dc21   98-30638

❧ To my mother, June Christopher, whose fascination with plants and gardens filled my childhood and who remains my inspiration ❧

Many people and many organizations helped with the writing of this book. Two deserve special mention. Bill Welch, the epitome of southern graciousness, shared most generously his legendary gardening skills. Special thanks, also, to Mike Ruggiero of the New York Botanical Garden, who took time out from teaching me the arts of angling to share with me the secrets of his success as a rosarian.

The American Rose Society, an organization to which every rose gardener ought to belong, provided invaluable information and contacts. I also owe a great debt to the library of the New York Botanical Garden, whose librarians are the most helpful and knowledgeable it has been my good fortune to meet.

Every one of this book's regional consultants — Jim Adams, David Earl Bott, Trevor Cole, Robert Downing, Donna Fuss, Peter Haring, Clair Martin III, and Kathy Zuzek — deserves special thanks for the insights they provided, and for their patience in answering my seemingly endless questions.

Finally, I would like to thank my editor, Linda Conway, for her skill and her tactful, cheerful determination to get it right, no matter what it took. Working up to her standards wasn't easy, but the results have been gratifying.

Contents

THE EASY PLEASURES
OF EASY ROSES

*Gardeners are rediscovering roses. One of the oldest of garden shrubs,
the rose has also traditionally been the favorite, the "Queen of Flowers." Archaeologists have
found evidence in the Middle East that the cultivation of roses began at least 5,000 years ago, and sheer
numbers testify to this plant's popularity:* Modern Roses 10, *the American Rose Society's
registry of roses, recognizes some 15,000 distinct species and cultivars.*

The reason for the appeal of the rose is simple. No other hardy garden shrub can offer the same combination of continuous flowering and such an astonishing range of color and fragrance. Besides, roses are inextricably bound into our memories of good times. Roses are the flowers we give to loved ones; it's a rosebud we pin to the lapel when we get married.

Yet for a generation, fewer and fewer of us have grown roses in our gardens, and with good reason: roses, or at least the roses found in most garden centers, were too difficult to grow. They were fussy plants, magnets for pests and diseases. These were shrubs with a serious dependency, demanding weekly spraying with a cocktail of toxic chemicals. In addition, during spells of dry weather, they needed twice-weekly watering and monthly feedings with specially formulated fertilizers. And then there was the winter protection: in the fall the bushes had to be half-buried, so that the dormant twigs would survive until they could be dug up again in spring. Even loyalists admitted that growing roses had become more a calling than a hobby.

But this is changing. A revolutionary collection of roses has emerged over the past few years, and with them a new style of rose gardening. These are *easy roses* — roses that are easy to grow and easy to like. They are redefining not only how roses are cultivated, but also how they are used in the garden. Most important, these plants are making roses a source of pleasure again rather than a frustration.

The hardiness and self-sufficiency of easy roses has helped them escape the isolation of a traditional rose garden. Here, they mingle comfortably with a tangle of perennial and annual flowers: larkspurs, snapdragons, dianthus, and alyssums.

What Makes Roses Easy?

Just what is an "easy rose"? It is a garden shrub that is as easy to grow as an azalea, lilac, or dogwood. Easy roses are shrubs that are naturally resistant to diseases and pests. There are easy roses for every North American soil and climate, and they thrive with no more care than one annual pruning, an occasional feeding, and perhaps a weekly watering during a drought.

Are these shrubs some special race of roses? No. On the contrary, they are remarkable for their diversity. As a group, easy roses include dozens of different species and hundreds of distinct named hybrids (or "cultivars," as the plant breeders call them). What's more, membership changes from region to region: a rose that is easy in the East may not be easy in the West and vice versa. That may sound confusing, but with the help of this book, you will soon find it a simple matter to identify the types of roses that will prove easy to grow in your garden.

You'll find these roses are not only easy to grow but also easy to fit into your garden design. That's because their genetic diversity gives them a corresponding diversity of beauty. The easy roses include shrubs and climbers of every imaginable size, from midget bushes a few inches (cm) tall to giants that can climb 30 ft (9m) up into a tree, if allowed. The blossoms range from tiny circlets of five petals to huge puffs 5 in (13cm) or more across, and in them is found every hue except pure blue. In addition, many of the easy roses furnish not only flowers but also handsome foliage and colorful fruits. These shrubs are an asset to the garden year-round.

One more virtue you will find among the easy roses: because of their diversity, they are easy to work into any type of garden design or landscape. Depending on the roses you select (the Gallery of Roses [Chapter Three] will help with that process), you can wreathe a fence or clothe a wall, blanket a sunny slope, add backbone to a flower border, or run them down your property line to enclose the backyard with a thorny, intruder-proof hedge.

Where the Rose Went Wrong

Are these easy roses the results of some special breeding program? Many of them are. As long ago as the 1920s some perceptive nurserymen realized that garden roses had begun to develop down the wrong track.

In fact, the unfortunate turning point had come a couple of decades earlier, when rose breeders had begun to focus all their efforts on a single strain of shrubs, the hybrid teas. The first of the hybrid teas, a rose called 'La France', had appeared on the market in 1867, and it had a lot to recommend it. It was a husky, sturdy shrub that bore large and fragrant silvery pink blossoms. Most important, it bloomed in repeated surges ("flushes," as they are called by rosarians) right through the growing season, from late spring into fall. It was what the breeders described as "everblooming," and that term alone made 'La France' a great success with home gardeners.

There was a reason for their enthusiasm. Previously, the roses that could withstand winter weather in most of Europe and North America had been more or less seasonal in their bloom. That is, they bloomed heavily for several weeks in early summer and then sparingly or not at all through the rest of the summer and fall. This does not mean these older roses bloomed less than hybrid teas. Actually, many of them produced *more* blossoms during their brief season of flowering than the typical hybrid tea rose produces in the course of a whole season. Still, these earlier garden roses were seasonal shrubs, and with the appearance of an "everbloomer," they suddenly seemed passé.

So by the turn of this century, hybrid tea roses — the offspring of 'La France' and a few close relatives — had swept most other types of roses out of the nurseries and out of most gardens, too. Even when other everblooming competitors appeared — the new floribunda and grandiflora roses — they

The climbing miniature rose 'Jeanne Lajoie' shinnies up a lamppost in this rock garden, while 'Nozomi' spreads a foam of white flowers in front.

never rivaled the hybrid tea in popularity, and in fact they were basically derivatives, sort of hybrid-hybrid teas. The hybrid tea type of flower, which remains the only rose sold at most florist shops today, had become not only the ideal but really the only acceptable kind of rose. The color might vary, but the profile of the rose had to be the same: a long, stiff stem and a pointed, tulip-shaped bud that opened to a tightly packed, many-petaled, expansive blossom.

Rose breeders achieved this uniformity through inbreeding, by crossing and recrossing a relatively small group of closely related roses. Whereas once any type of wild or garden rose had been potential material for the creation of new roses, breeders now focused relentlessly on this single race, whose members were spectacular and consistent but also fatally inbred. Different climates and soils require different kinds of plants, but now there was only one kind of rose. When it turned out that hybrid tea roses were especially susceptible to a variety of fungal diseases, that meant that *all* roses were susceptible. To grow roses now, you had to spray.

If hybrid teas didn't like the conditions in your garden, you had only two options. You could give

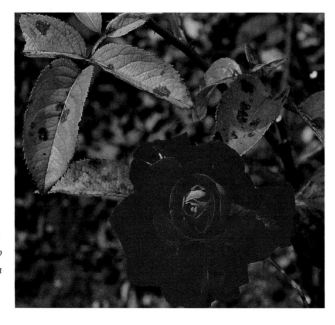

Blackspot-infected foliage is an all too common condition among hybrid tea roses.

up roses altogether, or you could accept the fact that you would have to replant on a regular basis. Even if hybrid teas did like your garden, they often behaved little better, because in the course of the inbreeding, most of the rose's natural vigor and adaptability had been lost. Gardeners could give the best care, and yet in most parts of the U.S. and Canada they might look forward to losing 25 percent or more of their plants each winter. Roses were on the way to becoming in truth what angry gardeners already labeled them: "expensive annuals."

Gardeners in northern regions were particularly dissatisfied. Hybrid teas were largely descended from hardy European garden roses, but included in their bloodlines were some frost-sensitive roses from subtropical Asia. It was these ancestors that gave them their everblooming habit. As a result, hybrid tea roses are not reliably hardy where winter temperatures drop below 0°F (−18°C). In colder regions, if these roses are to survive the winter, they must be dug up in late fall, laid on their sides, and buried entirely until spring.

New Roses from Canada

Not surprisingly, it was Canadians, the gardeners farthest to the north, who were the first to demand something better. Agriculture Canada, the department of agriculture, became active during the 1920s in collecting hardy (if unspectacular) native Canadian wild roses and crossing them with a mix of wild roses from northern Europe and Asia and some conventional garden roses. This produced a collection of hardy, handsome shrubs named after Canada's first nations: 'Mohawk', 'Cree', 'Chippewa', and so on.

Probably because these were seasonal roses that bloomed only in early summer, they never made much headway against the hybrid teas. But a second round of releases that appeared in the late 1940s and 1950s — "prairie roses," with names such as 'Prairie Maid' and 'Prairie Youth' — did

This red climber, 'Henry Kelsey', one of the ultra-hardy Canadian explorer roses, withstands winter temperatures as cold as –40°F (–40°C). Also resistant to fungal diseases, this rose blooms throughout the summer.

rebloom through the summer and so managed to carve out a niche for themselves in their native land. In the end, though, it was the "Canadian explorer roses," a group of hybrids bred in part from a superhardy Asian species, *Rosa rugosa*, at an experiment station in Ottawa, that made a reputation for the Canadian rose breeders in the United States. Named for Canadian pioneers such as Henry Hudson and William Baffin, these are being adopted as outstandingly easy roses all over the northern United States as well as in Canada.

Easy Roses in the United States

While Canadian breeders were introducing their prairie roses, a young American named Griffith Buck had started breeding his own roses at Iowa State University in Ames. He, too, crossed modern garden roses with ultrahardy wild roses such as *Rosa blanda*, a native prairie rose, and hardy garden roses of primitive types.

The seedlings Buck raised from these crosses were planted out into an open field. There he grew them not only without protection from winter weather but also without chemical sprays. For Buck had another goal besides cold hardiness: he also wanted to restore a more general vigor and disease resistance to his roses.

Because the hybrid teas demanded so much special care, gardeners had taken to segregating them from the rest of the garden. Roses had come to be planted all together, to make the constant spraying, feeding, and watering more convenient. Buck, however, wanted to return roses to the garden at large.

Today his roses are helping to make this happen. In 35 years of work, Buck introduced 85 new roses. For the most part, these remarkable roses were ignored at the time of their release onto the market. Gradually, however, word about them spread among gardeners across the northern United States and Canada. Although Griffith Buck died in 1991, sales of his roses are starting to boom.

Rose Survivors

These efforts to develop new and hardier roses continue today. Yet many other easy roses, though unfamiliar to most modern gardeners, are actually quite old. Some of them are centuries old.

These are members of a group that the American and Canadian rose societies have dubbed "Old Garden Roses." Living antiques, they all belong to types of roses developed before the appearance of 'La France', the first hybrid tea rose, in 1867. Because they date back to before the era of inbreeding, these antiques offer a much greater genetic diversity than modern roses. This means that within their ranks are roses adapted to soils and climates in which hybrid tea roses do not flourish.

Not all of these garden antiques qualify as easy roses, but many are outstanding, time-tested survivors. Many, in fact, survive today only because of their natural persistence. Nurseries dropped these old roses from their catalogs to make room for hybrid teas; then gardeners followed suit, replacing the old standbys with the glamorous newcomers. Often the only specimens to survive were those that grew unattended on abandoned homesites and in old cemeteries.

There these forgotten roses received no care — no feeding, watering, pruning, or spraying — and yet in spite of it all, the best of them continued to grow and bloom through the decades. Today, thanks to a growing interest in garden history, nurserymen have collected cuttings from many of the survivors and are again offering them for sale. Historians enjoy these roses for their nostalgia; resourceful gardeners favor them as some of the easiest roses of all.

Roses for Your Region

The most important lesson the old roses have to teach is that easy roses are regional. The survivors that Texans discover by abandoned ranch houses are likely to be China roses or tea roses (the everblooming ancestor of the hybrid teas). These wouldn't have survived the first winter in a New England burying ground. There the survivors are more likely to be rugosa roses or gallica roses.

Clearly, roses are a group of tremendous natural diversity, and each member of that group is best adapted to a different climate, a different kind of soil, and a different sort of habitat. Discovering what sorts of roses are best suited to the conditions in your garden is really the most important step you can take toward ensuring that your roses will always be easy roses.

Of course, every garden is unique, and in Chapter One you will find help in identifying and dealing with the unique aspects of your plot. But if each garden differs in the details from its neighbors, there are also broad similarities that link the gardens throughout a region. We have identified seven such general regions within the United States, with Canada making an eighth. In part, what defines these regions is geography, but equally important is the complex of environmental conditions.

Often different regions share some important characteristic. The Southwest and the Southeast, for example, both enjoy mild winters. But there are also crucial distinctions. Whereas summertime in the Southwest is hot and dry, in the Southeast it tends to be hot and humid. This humidity fosters the spread of fungal diseases, so that roses that are prone to them are difficult to grow without excessive spraying. Yet in the arid atmosphere of the Southwest, these same roses may remain disease free and behave as truly easy roses.

Left: What makes a softer, more inviting entrance to a garden than a rose-covered arbor? The hardy, self-sufficient nature of easy roses makes this most attractive garden feature a thoroughly practical one, too.

Meet the Consultants

To help sort out the regional differences and advise on adapting cultural techniques to suit the local conditions, we have called on eight expert rose growers — one from each of the seven regions in the United States and one from Canada. These are all gardeners with a broad experience of growing roses. All share the belief that roses should be easy.

To get the most benefit from these experts' advice, though, you will need to add a bit of interpretation. That's because your garden is unique. Kathy Zuzek can counsel you on selecting roses that won't mind a bitter midwestern winter, but if you live at the western edge of this region, where summers are hot and dry, you should also heed the advice of David Earl Bott, or even Clair Martin. For in the end, you will be the expert on what makes a rose easy for you.

Mid-Atlantic

Jim Adams

Washington, D.C.

As curator of the Herb Garden at the National Arboretum, Jim Adams cultivates "useful" roses — species and cultivars whose petals were used as a source of perfumes or for scenting soaps and salves, as well as roses whose hips have been harvested as a source of vitamin C. Given the long relationship between gardeners and roses, the list of roses that meet this utilitarian criterion is longer than one might think: 100 species and cultivars.

Because so many of these roses belong to the older European types such as the moss roses (the oldest of these date back at least to the 17th century), the Herb Garden at the arboretum enjoys its peak of bloom in late spring and early summer. The garden would offer relatively few flowers for the rest of the season, were it not for the com-panion plants — larkspurs, columbines, lilies, phloxes, and the like — interplanted among the roses. Unfortunately, although these perennial flowers prolong the garden's display, they also block the air movement around the roses. This promotes the spread of the fungal rose disease blackspot, which is the most serious challenge for a rose grower during the hot and usually humid Washington summer.

Jim Adams is replacing the more aggressive spreaders among the companion plants with flowers that form more compact clumps and so do not encroach on the roses. He's feeling his way to a new style of rose gardening, moving roses out of the traditional segregated beds. He is also a realist, however. The use of chemical sprays is minimal at the National Arboretum, where a new style of pest control, Integrated Pest Management, is practiced. This means that Jim sprays his roses in March with a mixture of sulfur and lime, and then not again until the arrival of hot weather and a forecast of several days of rain (a type of weather encouraging to blackspot), when he may spray again with neem, an extract of a tropical tree that protects against blackspot and insects.

A more satisfactory solution, from Jim's perspective, is the planting of modern English roses in beds that lie outside the Herb Garden proper. English nurseryman David Austin has created these roses over the past 30 years by crossing antique types with modern roses. By doing this, he has produced a race of bushes with the modern everblooming habit that preserves the attractive shrubbiness of the old garden roses and their greater variety of flower forms. These English roses also have proven disease resistant in Washington and are well adapted to the often chilly but rarely frigid local winters.

Jim Adams believes that acceptance of imperfection is essential to easy rose growing. Gardeners must move away from the excessive use of pesticides. As they do, they must accept that roses will suffer some damage. The roses can still be beautiful; they just won't be flawless. But that's only natural.

Midwest

Kathy Zuzek

Excelsior, Minnesota

As the scientist in charge of developing new landscape trees and garden shrubs at the Minnesota Landscape Arboretum, Kathy Zuzek is on the front line of the quest for easy roses. In fact, because this kind of rose is of such interest to the public, what began as just one part of her work has come to occupy nearly all of her time.

Currently, Kathy has 3,000 to 4,000 rosebushes planted out in a field for evaluation. Some of these are roses that she and her coworkers have hybridized themselves. Many are roses from other breeders that seem promising but have never been tested in Minnesota. Kathy has the most complete collection of Dr. Griffith Buck's roses, for example. All of Dr. Buck's original collection at Iowa State University was destroyed after his death in 1991. Fortunately, his widow was able to furnish the Minnesota Landscape Arboretum with duplicates. Now Kathy is working with wholesale nurseries to return the best of the Buck roses to the catalogs.

These same mass-market catalogs often horrify Kathy, however. She sees roses in them that are described as "hardy" even though she knows they are not hardy in the Upper Midwest. But "the gardening public here doesn't know that," Kathy explains. "They read 'hardy,' and they are going to order those roses."

Like roses, Kathy adds, rose diseases are regional in their adaptation. She knows that differences in climate can affect a particular rose cultivar's susceptibility to a disease, and she theorizes that different strains of the same pathogen may afflict certain regions of the country. Although a particular rose may be hardy to the strain of some fungal disease commonly found in one region, it may not be resistant to a strain found in another region. Powdery mildew, for instance, is not a serious problem for Kathy's roses in Excelsior. When she visited Toronto, Ontario, though, she was "appalled" to see how prevalent this disease was on the roses there.

Rocky Mountain West

David Earl Bott

Bountiful, Utah

"I don't remember any time when I *haven't* grown roses," says Earl Bott, "except for when I was in the Army." By age 12, he had taken over the care of his mother's rose garden; that was 60 years ago.

Today Earl grows some 500 rosebushes in his one-quarter-acre (.1ha) yard, and although he's retired, he also manages the ordering, potting, and maintenance of the 5,000 roses sold annually at a local nursery. In addition, he regularly inspects Utah's three public rose gardens, which serve as testing sites for new roses for the American Rose Society.

"Roses are very special in Utah," Earl explains. The state's first pioneers, the Mormons, came with the mission "to make the desert blossom as a rose," and they brought the first bushes with them in their wagons. Rose hedges are extremely popular, and roses are being used more and more as ground covers. Even condominium owners and apartment dwellers commonly raise miniature roses in tubs.

Rose growing in the northern desert has its special challenges. Sudden frosts and intense winter cold threaten tender cultivars at the state's higher elevations, and in many areas the soils are alkaline. A dearth of natural rainfall makes irrigation essential; drip-irrigation systems are popular but can concentrate the salts from the water to a toxic level in the soil.

Earl travels all over the country as a judge of rose shows, and he often brings roses home with him. He's found that roses that thrive in other regions often "just won't even hardly grow here." Plant the right roses, though, and it's easy to realize the pioneers' dream.

Southeast

Peter Haring

Shreveport, Louisiana

Long Island, New York, is where Peter Haring learned to grow roses, and the move he made to Louisiana in 1980 has required some adjustments. In Shreveport, summer heat is more of a challenge to his rosebushes than winter cold, though the occasional late-spring frost can wreak havoc. Humidity makes fungal diseases an ever-present threat during the growing season.

As past president of the American Rose Society, Peter stays in touch with growers throughout the country, and he strongly emphasizes the importance of local experience. How local is local? Well, he notes that the soil in his yard near the Red River is dense, heavy clay, while the soil at the headquarters of the American Rose Society just 17 mi (27km) away is porous and sandy. This means that drainage is a primary concern when he's caring for the 400 roses in his yard, but drought is more of a threat at the society's headquarters, where Peter manages the 300-rose Hudson Garden.

Location, Peter agrees, plays a critical role in determining which roses are easy. When he gardened on Long Island, old garden roses were a special enthusiasm. He was a pioneer in reintroducing these hardy antiques to fellow members of the

American Rose Society back in the 1970s. Nevertheless, Peter has gradually weeded most of them out of his Shreveport garden; with their European origins, the old garden roses typically require more winter cold than northern Louisiana can provide. Yet surprisingly, the gallica roses, which are among the most cold hardy of the old garden roses, grow well in his new garden.

Southwest

Clair Martin III

San Marino, California

A textbook of roses is how curator Clair Martin envisions the rose gardens at the Huntington Botanical Gardens. With 1,800–2,000 different species and cultivars, this is one of the most comprehensive collections of roses in the country. This makes Clair's garden a mecca for rosarians, which in turn enriches his experience. Often he learns about the roses from their hybridizers, and he has the opportunity to discuss antique roses with the same experts who rescued them from obscurity.

Though a beautiful spot for a stroll, Clair's rose beds are designed as much for education as for display. For a rose lover, perhaps the most interesting area is the one-acre (.4ha) "study plot," where Clair has grouped roses by type, arranging them by the date of origin. Here, at a glance, the visitor can see the development of a dozen or more classes of roses in a sort of living history museum. Though not open to the public, this study plot reaches the average gardener through

catalogs: from the bushes here, Clair supplies material for propagation to nurserymen in search of rare roses.

One of Clair's challenges as a rose grower is to supply his hardier roses with the period of dormancy they need. Because winter temperatures rarely drop below freezing in San Marino, Clair has to put his roses to sleep himself. In September he stops fertilizing, and in mid-January he prunes the bushes back by one-third to one-half to stimulate a springlike renewal.

Are there roses that Clair cannot grow in San Marino? Some of the most cold-hardy roses do not like his climate, so Clair is inclined to leave the growing of these roses to northern gardeners. He believes that growing roses should be simple; that's why he grows the roses that grow well.

Northeast

Donna Fuss

Hartford, Connecticut

Elizabeth Park Rose Garden in Hartford, Connecticut, is where Donna Fuss learned to love roses. The oldest municipal rose garden in the U.S. (it was founded in 1904), this planting boasts 15,000 roses of some 700–900 cultivars. Donna loved to visit the park as a child, and later she and her husband-to-be courted there. Today she serves as the rosarian, not only supervising the maintenance and development of the collection but also conducting tours and workshops to introduce the public to the pleasures of rose growing.

Donna's collection at home, which she shares with her husband, Mike, grew within a few years from an initial planting of five bushes to a total today of 250 plants of 240 different types. As founders of the Connecticut Rose Society, Donna and Mike keep busy advising novices on rose growing. Donna also consults on a professional basis for private clients.

It is the contrast of the two gardens — the grand one at Elizabeth Park and the smaller one at home — that Donna finds most interesting. A good number of the original plantings at Elizabeth Park have survived, which provides invaluable insight into the kinds of roses that flourish in southern New England. Still, Donna finds that the roses that thrive at Elizabeth Park sometimes do not grow well in her yard at home; climate and soil change significantly with a distance of just a few miles (km).

Northwest

Bob Downing

Portland, Oregon

"There are a lot of roses out there," says Bob Downing, "and you have to select carefully. But you'll find good roses you can grow without much care." He ought to know — as curator of the Portland, Oregon, public rose gardens, Bob manages the care of 20,000 rosebushes of roughly 800 different cultivars. His major responsibility, the International Rose Test Garden, has as its mission the evaluation and display of new roses from all over the world, and Bob has planted 200 new cultivars there in the past two years alone.

Portland calls itself the "City of Roses," and its mild winters mean that an exceptional variety of them can be cultivated. Still, late-spring frosts can be a problem, killing the new growth that, according to Bob, doesn't have the "natural antifreeze" that roses produce in their tissues as they enter dormancy in the fall. In addition, the drying winds that sweep through the test garden's exposed hillside site in winter can cause considerable damage.

In the valleys east of San Francisco where Bob grew up, the crucial factors in successful rose growing are protection from the burning afternoon sun and regular irrigation. In the cloudy Northwest, roses need all the sun they can get, and improving the drainage of the heavy clay soil with doses of compost or sphagnum peat moss and organic mulches is essential. When it comes to rose cultivation, Bob says, "I spend my time on soil preparation. That's where the magic is." At home he grows only self-sufficient roses, and because he takes special care with the planting, he has to fertilize and spray only twice a year.

Knowing your soil is basic, Bob emphasizes. Annual tests are a cornerstone of his maintenance program. In the test garden, he has found that the soil is naturally high in phosphorus and potassium, so instead of fertilizing with the 5-10-10 formula commonly recommended for roses, he uses a slow-release turf fertilizer that is rich in nitrogen but relatively poor in the other two major nutrients.

Canada

Trevor Cole

Kinburn, Ontario

Trevor Cole "wrote the book" on roses — literally. As former curator of the Dominion Arboretum, Canada's national arboretum in Ottawa, he supervised the rose collection there and was author of Agriculture Canada's bulletin on growing roses.

Though he was born in Britain and trained at the Royal Botanic Gardens at Kew, Trevor has been a Canadian for 30 years. His work for the Canadian government began with studies of the adaptability of native plants including roses for use in gardens. His subsequent experience with roses has been broad. At the Dominion Arboretum, the rose garden includes collections of hybrid tea and floribunda roses, rose hedges, old garden roses, shrubs, and climbing roses.

Perhaps it is Trevor's international background, but he definitely advises gardeners not to define their region solely by national boundaries. Coastal British Columbia, for example, shares the temperate, moist climate found along the coast of the United States' Northwest. So he advises his countrymen in British Columbia to consult the regional tips of Bob Downing, as well as his own.

As a gardener of Canada's east, Trevor is a fan of the hardy shrub roses, because he finds them "so much less work and so much more reliable." In contrast, his opinion of conventional hybrid tea and floribunda roses as garden plants in most Canadian climates is not flattering. Years ago, when these roses were virtually all that was available to the home gardener, Trevor recalls advising novices to regard roses as annual flowers. If mounded with soil, your rose *might* survive the winter, and if it did, that was a bonus.

However, the increasing availability of Canadian-bred hardy roses such as the explorer rose series has persuaded him that he can recommend roses as long-lived shrubs. He warns, however, that the shopper must pay attention to whether the rose is growing on its own roots or has been grafted onto a rootstock of some other kind of rose. A rose, he points out, is only as hardy as its roots.

Agriculture Canada, and especially the Central Experimental Farm in Ottawa, have a long history of rose breeding, dating from the early 1920s when William Saunders, the Dominion Horticulturist, introduced the rugosa hybrid 'Agnes' that is still available today. This work was continued by Miss Isabella Preston (probably better known now for her work on lilacs) who introduced several rugosa and glauca hybrids.

The breeding work that resulted in the explorer roses was begun at the Central Experimental Farm, and Trevor was responsible for the public display of these deservedly popular roses.

Chapter One

ROSES FOR EVERY GARDEN

Bill Welch had given up on roses. He had grown up with them. As a teenager, he had worked
in a garden center in his native Houston, Texas, where he helped to sell "oh, thousands" of the latest
introductions — "hybrid teas and floribundas, mostly." He'd spent his wages on bushes that he brought
home to try in the family garden. But his plantings didn't thrive. The roses he brought home from work
rarely lived more than a couple of years, and more often behaved "like expensive annuals," Bill recalls.
These off-the-rack roses couldn't tolerate the heat and humidity of a Gulf Coast summer, a
season when the air drips moisture and yet rain might not fall for weeks or even months.

So Bill lost interest in roses and didn't return to them for 20 years or more, until he confronted the challenge of landscaping the small rural yard of a weekend retreat, a turn-of-the-century farmhouse he had bought in Rayburgh, Texas, 80 miles (130km) north and west of Houston. By then (1980), Bill had a doctorate in landscape architecture and was a senior member of the Department of Horticulture at Texas A&M University. One of his professional projects was identifying new sources of color for Texas gardeners and nurserymen — azaleas, camellias, peonies, and so many other landscaping standbys of the rest of the country don't do well in the central Texas climate and soils.

At work and at home, Bill wanted the same thing: a shrub that would flourish locally with a minimum of care and yet offer flowers, lots of them. That's when he remembered roses — another kind of roses.

A Success Story

Bill recalled a shrub his aunt Edna had called 'Old Blush'. She had planted this bush as a hedge at her home in Rosenberg, Texas, where it bloomed 11 months out of the year. Many of these pink-flowered shrubs still survive, he notes, 45 years after his aunt moved away. 'Old Blush', Bill discovered, was a rose from 18th-century China that had come into Texas with the first Anglo settlers.

There was a more recent discovery, too: a red-flowered rose that Bill had found blooming on Christmas, 1980, in the abandoned garden of his wife's grandmother, Maggie. Bill never identified the proper name of that rose — it is sold as "Maggie" today — but he did establish that it, too, had some Chinese ancestry and that it seemed to belong to an antique breed known as Bourbon roses (*see pp.*62–64). The cuttings he brought back to central Texas rooted readily and flourished, making expansive shrubs that could be easily trained as climbers.

Bill began haunting old cemeteries. A couple of generations ago, he explains, it was the custom to plant your mother's favorite flower by her grave, and often this flower was a rose. All the care a shrub got in such a setting was an occasional cutting back with a string trimmer or scythe. If a rose continued to thrive despite this neglect (and many did), it obviously suited Bill's needs.

He also helped found a group that became known as the "Rose Rustlers," a band of enthusiasts who went into the countryside looking for rose survivors in old farmhouse gardens and next to abandoned homesteads. The cuttings that this group "rustled" were taken home and rooted, and then grown in various locations to evaluate their viability as garden plants.

In short order, Bill realized that he had solved two problems. He had found roses that liked Texas, and in the process he had identified a spectacular low-maintenance shrub for his weekend garden. His finds accumulated around his farmhouse until he had a cottage-garden planting with some 75 bushes. These thrived under a regime of a light pruning in spring, a feeding with a balanced fertilizer in early winter and again in spring, with a dose of ammonium sulfate in August to replace the nitrogen that central Texas's torrential rains washed from the soil. (Currently, Bill prefers cottonseed meal or alfalfa meal as a rose food, though he still uses the ammonium sulfate in late summer.) New plantings were watered as regularly as Bill could manage on his irregular visits, but after the first season for a rose, it had to rely on nature for its irrigation.

ORGIN THADUS
SEPT. 9, 1879
NOV. 5, 1918

When searching for roses adapted to your region, a visit to the local cemetery is a useful first step. Beside the headstones you will find rosebushes that have, commonly, survived decades of neglect. These are roses that like the local climate and soil.

The collection of Texas-loving roses that Bill amassed included many antiques. There were China roses, tea roses, Noisettes, Bourbon roses, and others of even more obscure old-fashioned breeds. But as a collector, he was never doctrinaire. He would take a cutting from any rose that had proven itself by thriving in neglect, and among his recent "discoveries" was a shrub of the 1977 Dr. Griffith Buck rose 'Carefree Beauty'™.

A visit to Bill's cottage garden became a pilgrimage, and the roses that he and the other rustlers collected became standards of the Texas nursery trade. They have sparked a renaissance of rose growing in the Gulf states. For, as Bill's aunt Edna could have told him, roses can be tough, persistent, and practical plants — even in a Texas summer.

What We Can Learn from Bill Welch

Bill Welch's experience is a rose-gardening success story — but is it a blueprint for other gardeners to follow? Yes — and no.

The way in which Bill tracked down roses that liked his garden might well work for you; it's always wise to find out what plants have a record of success in your neighborhood. But heirloom plants are not the solution to every gardening situation. As you will find by exploring the Gallery of Roses (Chapter Three), there are also many outstanding modern roses. Many of these were bred to succeed in specific conditions. Griffith Buck's "prairie roses," for example, were bred in the Upper Midwest to flourish in that region's climate, and an Iowa gardener will quite likely find that the Buck roses perform as well as or better than any heirloom rose.

By sharing cuttings of "Maggie" with local nurserymen, Bill Welch has succeeded in making this "lost" treasure available to gardeners all over the South.

The really important part of Bill Welch's success is not the particular solution he developed, but the way in which he solved the problem. He did something very simple, yet it's something that very few gardeners have the good sense and humility to try. Bill Welch let his garden tell him what to plant.

Most gardeners do the opposite. They begin their landscaping by thumbing through catalogs or by visiting the local garden center. They look for plants that

---

Southwest — Clair Martin III
HUNTINGTON BOTANICAL GARDENS, SAN MARINO, CALIFORNIA

REGIONAL CHALLENGES:
- Summer heat can be intense.
- Inadequate rainfall makes continual irrigation essential.
- Warm winters do not provide the period of winter dormancy and chilling required by some classes of roses.

REGIONAL ADVANTAGES:
- The growing season lasts almost 11 months.
- Mild winters result in almost no frost damage.
- Dry summers protect roses against fungal diseases, especially blackspot.

MOST TROUBLE-FREE ROSES (BY CLASS):
Tea roses, China roses, Noisette roses, David Austin's English Roses (modern shrubs); floribunda and hybrid tea roses perform especially well in this region.

MOST TROUBLE-PRONE ROSES (BY CLASS):
Rugosa roses and hybrid rugosas do not perform as well in this region as in colder ones because of lack of winter dormancy.

WORST DISEASES:	*WORST PESTS:*
Mildew and rose rust	Thrips, aphids, and spider mites

appeal to them, and then they explore ways in which they can impose these plants on their sites. Often they succeed, but usually at a considerable cost.

Maybe the plants they choose turn out to need more moisture than their gardens naturally provide — so the gardeners install irrigation systems and spend their leisure time mending leaks and unclogging sprinkler nozzles. And when the plants still languish, the gardeners have to install windbreaks to block the arid winds that dehydrate their unnatural landscaping. Winter freezes the moisture in the soil, increasing the stress on the plants, so every fall the gardeners are obliged to cover the plants with burlap or evergreen boughs, or to heap soil around their bases so at least some bud survives to send up a shoot the next spring.

Rose gardeners are the most notorious perpetrators of this brand of "success." North American gardens range from subtropical to subarctic. Yet the greatest honor a rose can win in the United States is to be chosen as an "All-America Rose Selection" by a nursery industry group of that same name. In fact, there is no such thing as a rose that is suited to all of North America. Your success as a rose gardener begins with recognizing that. Instead of listening to nursery associations, you must learn how to listen to your garden and make it your partner in selecting roses. The matters of climate, exposure, soil, and likely pests and diseases all must be taken into consideration.

Climate

This is the factor that more than any other should dictate your rose choices. You can modify other aspects of your garden, though if you are smart, you will choose to work with them rather than against them. You cannot change local climate, and although you can compensate for it, this requires continual effort. Choose to fight the climate, and you will not have easy roses; in fact, you will end up with extremely difficult roses.

To help you with your rose selection, this book divides the United States into seven climatic

---

Northwest — Bob Downing
INTERNATIONAL ROSE TEST GARDEN, PORTLAND, OREGON

REGIONAL CHALLENGES:
- Dry winds in wintertime can desiccate roses when the soil is frozen, causing dieback.
- A "false spring," a prolonged thaw in late January or February, can cause roses to break dormancy, leaving the new growth very vulnerable to spring frosts.
- Acid rain can lower soil pH beyond optimal range.
- Abundant rainfall makes fungal diseases such as blackspot a constant threat.

REGIONAL ADVANTAGES:
- Regular, abundant rainfall year-round makes irrigation unnecessary.
- A drop in rainfall in the summertime, combined with moderate temperatures, moderates the humidity and helps curb fungal diseases.

- Soil pH is generally acceptable, naturally in the range of 6.3–6.8.
- Mild winters allow the cultivation of a wide range of roses.
- Nine-month growing season promotes strong, vigorous growth.

MOST TROUBLE-FREE ROSES (BY CLASS):
Most classes of roses will survive in the temperate northwestern climate. Disease-resistant hybrid teas and floribundas thrive here, as do many of the antique classes.

MOST TROUBLE-PRONE ROSES (BY CLASS):
Heat-loving roses such as the China roses survive but do not flourish. The constant rainfall in the coastal regions makes any rose susceptible to fungal diseases a poor choice.

WORST DISEASES:
Blackspot and powdery mildew

WORST PESTS:
Spider mites, caneborers, and thrips

A cold-hardy shrub rose brightens this September garden in coastal New England. The nearby ocean helps roses thrive by moderating the seasonal temperature swings that typify northern climates.

regions: Northeast, Mid-Atlantic, Southeast, Midwest, Rocky Mountain West, Northwest, and Southwest. Although it includes many different climates, Canada is treated as a single region because the single greatest challenge throughout all but the extreme west is the severity of the winters.

What exactly is climate? It's a way of describing the weather conditions that prevail in a region. It's the batting averages for local rainfall, winter cold and summer heat, and intensity of sunlight. Put these particular characteristics together, and you will have a general profile that is your climate.

Depending on the region in which you live, different aspects of climate may seem more or less important. For example, gardeners in the Northeast and most of Canada tend to worry most about winter cold, because that is the greatest threat to their plants. In New York or New England, or in British Columbia and the eastern provinces of Canada, you can usually depend on adequate rainfall, and the summer temperature rarely rises to a level that is fatal to the more popular garden plants. But a particularly severe freeze in winter often causes extensive damage. So when northeastern and Canadian gardeners speak of a plant's "hardiness," usually they are referring to its tolerance for cold.

This, incidentally, is a prejudice that has been passed along to the U.S. Department of Agriculture (USDA). That organization publishes the "Plant Hardiness Zone Map," which uses the average local winter low temperatures to divide North America into 11 zones. When a nursery catalog describes a plant as "hardy to zone 4," that means the plant will survive winter temperatures as low as −20° to −30°F (−29° to −34°C), temperatures experienced in the area marked zone 4 on the USDA map. That zone comprises an area that includes most of northern New England, the Upper Midwest, and a band of land just inland from the Atlantic and Pacific coasts of Canada, as well as the northern and high-altitude areas of the Rocky Mountain West.

Outside of the eastern provinces of Canada, British Columbia, and the northeastern United States, however, other aspects of the weather may be more critical than winter cold to the survival of plants. For example, in the prairie regions of the Midwest and central Canada, where droughts are common, the average rainfall may be a more important consideration.

Information about local climate is easy to obtain. In addition to the USDA Plant Hardiness Zone Map and the Canadian Plant Hardiness Zone

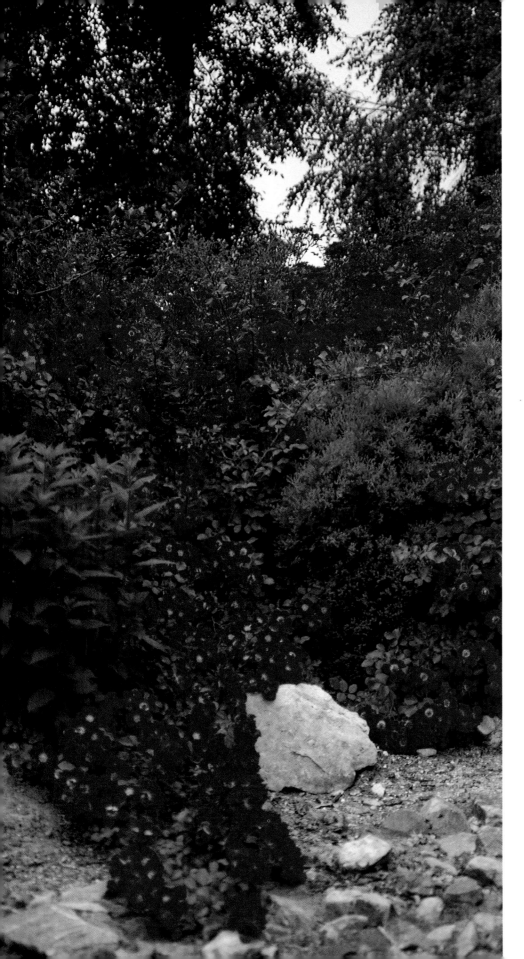

Map, information about other aspects of climate and information specific to your area can be obtained at your local public library, or in the U.S. through the local office of your state's Cooperative Extension Service. (Look in the state and county listings in your telephone directory for the number.) In Canada contact Environment Canada.

From these sources, you may actually get more information than you want. Sorting through all the data is simple enough, though. What you need to extract are just the following basics.

Average lowest winter temperature: Because winter lows are the basis for the USDA plant hardiness ratings, and those ratings are the criteria by which the nursery industry recommends plants, identifying the average low temperature for your area is the first step toward assembling a local climate profile. Check the USDA and Canadian Plant Hardiness Zone Maps on pp.208–209; these will provide you with an average winter low for your area. Be sure, however, to check local weather records, too, since local conditions can affect winter temperatures dramatically.

If you live on a mountain, for example, the rise in altitude may make winters in your garden colder than in the surrounding region. In general, a climb of 1,000 feet (305m) causes an average drop in temperature of 3°F (1.5°C); this means that a garden on a high hill may belong to a colder climate zone than one on the plain below.

Nearness to a body of water such as a lake or river can also affect winter temperatures. Water collects heat during the summer and releases it in the winter, acting to moderate the temperatures in its vicinity. A lakeside garden may rate a full climate zone warmer than the surrounding countryside.

Because water absorbs and retains heat so well, a water feature such as this stream or a pond can significantly affect your microclimate. Nearness to any body of water has a tempering effect on the local climate, making a garden more hospitable to roses. In the North, water moderates winter cold, while in the South it reduces summer heat.

Summer heat: This can play a central role in determining which roses thrive in your region. In fact, gardeners in the southeastern United States more often speak of summer hardiness than they do winter hardiness.

To appreciate this perspective, compare the climates of the Texas Panhandle and the Pacific Northwest. Over much of these two regions, the average low temperatures in wintertime are similar: about −10°F (−23°C). But summer temperatures in the Panhandle regularly soar to 110°F (43°C), while in the Pacific Northwest they rarely rise above 90°F (32°C), and near the coast they stay considerably cooler. Most of the antique garden roses developed in Europe, such as the gallica roses or Bourbon roses, grow to perfection in the Pacific Northwest. In the Panhandle, they dry up in the summer heat, behaving like Bill Welch's "expensive annuals."

Unfortunately, the USDA did not take summer heat into account when it set up its zones of hardiness. *In this book, when discussing plant hardiness in terms of USDA zones, we will specify not only the northernmost zone in which a plant will survive but also the southernmost one.* In that way, you will know the whole geographical range of each type of rose. As summer temperature is not as critical in Canada, only the minimum hardiness zone is specified.

Rainfall: The total amount of precipitation that falls in your region is important when you select plants. So also is the seasonal pattern of rainfall.

Throughout much of the Southwest, for example, not only is rain scarce but it also is highly seasonal. In Tucson, Arizona, more than half of each year's small budget of precipitation falls in a series of brief, violent storms during the weeks between July 1 and September 15. During the rest of the year, months may pass without significant rainfall. This means that roses must be irrigated regularly in Tucson throughout most of the year. In addition, this seasonal pattern of rainfall ensures that the atmosphere remains bone dry for months at a time. Such conditions discourage the spread of blackspot, the fungal disease that is the scourge of many types of roses, particularly hybrid tea roses.

In humid climates, such as that of the southeastern United States, most hybrid tea roses must be sprayed continually if they are to remain free of blackspot. Throughout much of the Southwest, the dry atmosphere provides natural protection from this affliction. Where hybrid tea roses need spraying, they most definitely are not easy roses. But in the Southwest, they are, especially if the gardener installs a drip-irrigation system.

Rocky Mountain West — David Earl Bott
BOUNTIFUL, UTAH

REGIONAL CHALLENGES:
- Soils are excessively alkaline, possibly needing treatment with sulfur to add iron and magnesium.
- Frost damage and winter kill occur at higher elevations.
- Low rainfall makes continual irrigation essential.

REGIONAL ADVANTAGES:
- Low humidity discourages fungal diseases.
- Winter cold reduces insect pest populations.

MOST TROUBLE-FREE ROSES (BY CLASS):
Alba roses, gallica roses, damask roses, and other antique classes of northern European origin; miniature roses and shrub roses — David Austin's English Roses — are very slow starters but perform well once established.

MOST TROUBLE-PRONE ROSES (BY CLASS):
Any classes that cannot tolerate severe winter cold; climbing roses do not bloom as well as in milder regions.

WORST DISEASES:
Crown gall, blackspot, and powdery and downy mildew

WORST PESTS:
Spider mites, caneborers, and thrips

SUNLIGHT INTENSITY TABLE

| CITY | SUNLIGHT (BTUs/DAY/SQ FT ON A HORIZONTAL SURFACE) | | | |
	MARCH	JUNE	SEPTEMBER	DECEMBER
FAIRBANKS, ALASKA (latitude 64°49'N)	860.5	1970.8	699.6	20.3
SEATTLE, WASHINGTON (latitude 47°27'N)	992.2	1909.9	1211.8	239.5
BISMARCK, NORTH DAKOTA (latitude 46°47'N)	1328.4	2173.8	1441.3	464.2
GRAND JUNCTION, COLORADO (latitude 39°07'N)	1622.9	2625.4	1957.5	793.4
WASHINGTON, D.C. (latitude 38°51'N)	1255.0	2080.8	1446.1	594.1
LITTLE ROCK, ARKANSAS (latitude 34°44'N)	1335.8	2091.5	1640.6	701.1
LOS ANGELES, CALIFORNIA (latitude 33°56'N)	1729.5	2272.3	1898.1	901.1
BROWNSVILLE, TEXAS (latitude 25°55'N)	1505.9	2288.5	1774.9	982.3
MIAMI, FLORIDA (latitude 25°47'N)	1828.8	1991.5	1646.8	1183.4

Adapted from Edward Mazvia, *The Passive Solar Energy Book*
(Rodale, 1979)

Sunlight: The quality of sunlight varies markedly from one region of the country to another. In general, the intensity of sunlight increases as you move south. Likewise, the thinner, clearer air found at higher altitudes in the Rocky Mountain West does much less to filter the sunlight than do the moister, dustier atmospheres of the Northeast, Midwest, or Northwest. Denver may lie on roughly the same line of latitude as Philadelphia, but in terms of the intensity of sunlight, it is much closer to Cairo, Egypt.

Some roses that originated in cloudier northern regions (many of the old garden roses from Europe, for example) do not thrive in the more intense light of the Southeast, Southwest, and Rocky Mountain West unless given some shade in early afternoon to midafternoon, the time of day when the sunlight is most intense. In at least one case, however, the opposite is true. British nurseryman David Austin's English Roses, a group of shrubs that he bred to combine an old-fashioned look with a modern reblooming habit, are handsome roses in the Northeast and Northwest. But they are *spectacular* roses in the Southwest, as regional consultant Clair Martin of the Huntington Botanical Gardens has proven. In Clair's garden near Los Angeles, the English roses commonly grow to two to three times the size they attain in David Austin's nursery, and the bloom is correspondingly more abundant.

Microclimate

Once you have identified the key points of the regional climate, it's time to focus on your own backyard. In almost any garden, you will find features that modify the normal local climate. Often the effect of these features is substantial — significant enough that they should influence your choice of roses.

If you are planting a rose into a flower bed that runs along the south side of a fence or wall, for example, you should keep in mind that such a site receives direct sunlight all day long and that the man-made backdrop will trap and reradiate solar energy. This boosts the temperature in that microclimate, so any rose you plant there must be heat tolerant. If you are setting a rose into a foundation planting that lies under an overhanging eave, remember that the overhang will block most rainfall, so the rose you select should be drought tolerant.

Microclimates can be very small, but they may also take in a whole yard. Because cold air is heavier than warm, it settles into low spots. So a garden at the foot of a hill is likely to be extra cold and to suffer frosts earlier in the fall and later in the spring than the gardens of neighbors up the hill. In the East, exposure to sea breezes reduces humidity in the summer. A garden that enjoys this advantage is

Cold air runs downhill like water to collect in any depression at the slope's foot. Similarly, a hedge running across a slope works as a dam to trap cold air.

likely to be a particularly healthy home for roses.

In looking for microclimates, the gardener should watch for the following features:

Boulders or outcroppings — These create pockets of shade and can shelter roses from the prevailing winds, helping protect the plants against dehydration and both heat and cold.

Fences or walls — Features that shade and block the wind, they also act as solar collectors on their south and west sides. Northern gardeners will find roses planted on the sunny side of a wall or fence to be less prone to winter damage. Southwestern gardeners will find these structures useful in protecting roses from dehydrating winds.

Ponds, pools, or streams — Like the larger bodies of water discussed previously, these tend to moderate the climate, cooling the area around them in summer and keeping it warmer in winter.

Asphalt driveways — These trap sunlight's heat and block the infiltration of rainfall to create hot, dry microclimates.

Woodland edges — Blocks of trees cast filtered shade along their edges, creating a good habitat for roses in the South. They also cool the air, creating a more temperate microclimate.

Hedges — Hedges draw moisture and nutrients from the soil around their roots, leaving the earth poor and dry. In areas where humidity is high, hedges increase the risk of fungal diseases by blocking the winds that would otherwise help to keep rose foliage drier and that would blow away fungal spores. On the other hand, hedges are very effective windbreaks, which can be an advantage in areas where roses need shelter from cold winds or from hot, dry winds.

Midwest — Kathy Zuzek
MINNESOTA LANDSCAPE ARBORETUM, EXCELSIOR, MINNESOTA

REGIONAL CHALLENGES:
- Intense winter cold (−25° to −30°F [−31° to −34°C]). Even hardy roses may suffer considerable damage if they are types that are slow to enter dormancy in the fall.
- The short growing season can prevent fall rebloom among some of the old classes of roses, such as the autumn damasks.

REGIONAL ADVANTAGES:
Soil pH is typically close to ideal, between 6.5 and 7.5. Relatively low humidity discourages powdery mildew. There are no Japanese beetles.

MOST TROUBLE-FREE ROSES (BY CLASS):
Alba roses, gallica roses, shrub roses; "I don't like categorizing by class — there are good and poor cultivars in every class."

MOST TROUBLE-PRONE ROSES (BY CLASS):
Hybrid tea and floribunda roses; "They only survive if protected from winter temperatures. These roses must be tipped into trenches and covered with soil and leaves or straw in the fall and during winter."

WORST DISEASES:
Blackspot, powdery mildew, anthracnose, and cercospora leaf spot

WORST PESTS:
Stem girdler, mossy rose gall, and aphids

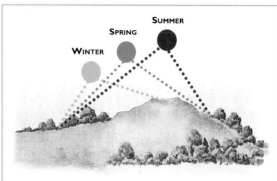

In the northern hemisphere, sunlight comes from the south, and so strikes south-facing slopes more directly, delivering more intense radiation. The angle of the sunlight also varies with the season.

Permeable barriers such as an intermittent board fence or hedge are more effective at protecting roses from wind than solid barriers. By filtering the wind, permeable barriers reduce its energy without creating air turbulence. Snow fencing can provide an inexpensive temporary windbreak.

Exposure

This term refers to the orientation of the garden — the direction that it faces — and to its openness to the weather. These two factors can have an important effect on the climate within the garden and therefore may influence the choice of roses.

If a garden lies on a north-facing slope, for example, it will receive less sunlight than a garden on a south-facing slope, and so it will remain cooler in summer and colder in winter. Likewise, a garden that faces west will tend to be hotter than an east-facing garden, because the afternoon sun is stronger.

Openness to the wind can be an advantage or a disadvantage. In the Southeast, this kind of exposure will help to keep roses disease free, but it will also increase the need for irrigation because the wind will dry the garden. In the North, exposure to the wind will increase the threat of winter damage, and the gardener should be sure to plant extra-hardy roses. In the Southwest, exposure to the wind is likely to prove fatal, for no matter how fast you apply water to the roots, the rosebush won't be able to deliver it to the leaves as fast as the arid desert wind draws it out through the surface of the leaf.

Topography can also affect the character of a garden. Because water runs downhill, a hilltop garden will almost always be drier than one at the foot of a hill. That's why in the North, roses in a hilltop garden will be more prone to winter damage, because winter's dry winds nip the buds and canes as much as the cold temperatures do. In such a situation, you should plant only roses recommended as winter hardy in a zone to the north of the one in which your garden seems to lie.

A final word about exposure: remember that roses are sun-loving plants. Most require at least six hours' exposure to direct sun to thrive. You will find some roses described as shade tolerant in this book, but that term is relative. It means that the rose in question will tolerate a period each day when overhanging trees or some other obstruction lets only dappled sunlight reach it. Shade-tolerant roses, for example, will adapt well to the intermittent but intense sunlight they will receive among well-spaced, high-branched mature pines in the South. If, however, you place a rose among your ferns, the shrub may survive, but it will be an easy target for diseases and pests and will bear few flowers.

Soil

The quality of your soil is just as important as climate or exposure in dictating what types of roses will feel at home in your garden. For that reason, you should get to know your soil thoroughly before you begin selecting roses.

Of course, you can also change your soil to suit the needs of the plant. You can enrich a sandy soil with sphagnum peat or compost, and you can use these same organic "amendments" and maybe a dose of coarse sand to loosen and lighten a heavy clay soil. In cases of an extremely sandy soil or a really sticky clay, you may have no choice. Changing the character of your soil is a laborious, expensive process, and in many cases the effects are only temporary. And if you skimp by reforming only the pocket of soil into which you plant a rose, what you create is just like a potted plant — the rose roots won't venture out beyond the transformed soil.

That constricted root system won't be able to forage for nutrients and moisture, and to keep the rosebush healthy, you'll find yourself watering and fertilizing constantly.

In most cases, a transformation is unnecessary. Among the thousands of different types of roses on the market, there are shrubs adapted to a wide range of soils. You may end up adjusting your soil to improve the growth of your roses, but if you plant intelligently, your work will be a fine-tuning rather than a rebuilding.

The first step is to investigate what sort of soil is native to your garden. The best way to do that is to have the soil tested. In the U.S. contact your local Cooperative Extension Service office. For a modest fee, the Extension Service will provide a preaddressed box in which you place a sample of soil; then you mail it to the state lab. In Canada contact an agricultural university or private soil laboratory (a list of labs is available through your provincial Ministry of Agriculture). Be sure to request a complete soil profile, one that includes information about the soil type and organic matter content. A test of this sort costs more, but otherwise all you will get back is a prescription for what you must do to make the soil acceptable to a generic rosebush.

To collect a representative soil sample, excavate holes 6 in (15.2cm) deep in several spots throughout your planting area. Cut a uniform slice off the side of each hole, mix the slices in a clean plastic bucket, and take your test sample from this.

For the rose grower, the following points of the soil profile are the most important.

The importance of pH: A number that usually falls somewhere between 4.0 and 8.5, the pH is a reading of the relative acidity or alkalinity of your soil. The lower the number, the more acidic the soil; the higher the number, the more alkaline the soil. The pH is important because rose roots cannot absorb nutrients from a soil that is too acidic or too alkaline. For most roses, a soil pH anywhere

Southeast — Peter Haring
AMERICAN ROSE SOCIETY, SHREVEPORT, LOUISIANA

REGIONAL CHALLENGES:
- Summer heat is intense.
- Warm, humid climate promotes blackspot.
- Thrips are a prevalent pest in summer, and spraying roses with insecticides encourages spider mites.
- Late spring frosts, occurring after roses have emerged from winter and often damaging reemerging foliage dormancy and new growth, can cause considerable damage.

REGIONAL ADVANTAGES:
- Winters are mild, so protection from cold is unnecessary.

MOST TROUBLE-FREE ROSES (BY CLASS):
China, tea, and shrub roses (including David Austin's English Roses); Noisette and hybrid musk roses do extremely well.

MOST TROUBLE-PRONE ROSES (BY CLASS):
Most of the old garden roses that originated in Europe, including alba, centifolia, damask, and moss roses. Rugosa and hybrid rugosa roses do not thrive except in coastal areas.

WORST PESTS	*WORST DISEASES*
Spider mites	Powdery mildew and blackspot

between 5.5 (moderately acidic) and 7.0 (neutral) will produce good results.

If you live in the West or Southwest, or even parts of the Southeast such as central Texas, you may find that your soil is distinctly alkaline and that its pH is higher than 7.0. One way to cope with this is to plant China roses and tea roses that have been grown on their own roots (for an explanation of this, see p.39). These two classes of roses are more tolerant of alkalinity than most other kinds of roses, and they thrive in soils whose pH lies in the range of 7.5–8.0. If you are planting grafted roses into alkaline soils, make sure that they have been grafted onto the rootstock known as 'Dr. Huey', since this, too, is alkaline tolerant.

If you wish to plant other kinds of roses, or if your soil is more alkaline than 8.0 (which is unlikely), you will be obliged to adjust your soil's pH, adding sphagnum peat or sulfur to reduce the alkalinity. The amount of these remedies will vary with the type of soil and the intensity of the alkalinity, but your soil test results will include a detailed prescription.

You should realize that this treatment is not permanent, since alkalinity will gradually seep back into your garden from the surrounding soil. And be sure to check the pH level of your tap water with your water company (or have it analyzed if it is well water or if you live in Canada). If it is alkaline (it is likely to be, since the water in reservoirs and wells is filtered through the local soil), you will restore a small measure of alkalinity to the garden every time you irrigate. In any case, you should retest the alkalinity of your soil every year or two. You can perform this simple test with an inexpensive kit available at your local garden center.

Raised beds such as those seen here are invaluable for growing roses in problem soils. In areas of dense clay, a raised bed provides essential drainage. Where saline tap water tends to poison the soil, a raised bed's superior drainage helps natural rainfall to wash out toxic salts. By mixing lots of compost or sphagnum peat into a raised bed, you can also provide superior growing conditions where soils are sandy and poor.

In the Northeast or Northwest, your soil pH is more likely to be too low — that is, too acidic. You can correct this by digging in ground limestone. Again, the amount of limestone you must add will vary with the type of soil and the degree of acidity, and the best prescription is the one you will receive with the test results. Acidic soil also requires periodic retesting, especially if you live in a region afflicted with acid rain. Continual use of chemical fertilizers will also tend to acidify the soil.

Soil type: This is the second piece of vital information a soil test will provide. Depending on the coarseness of the individual soil particles, your soil may be classified as clay (very fine particles), silt (fine particles), or sand (coarse particles). Most often a soil is some combination of these three types of particles and will be classified as a hybrid, such as silty clay or sandy clay. Or the soil may be a more balanced blend of clay, silt, and sand known as "loam."

Any sort of loam is fine for any kind of rose. If your soil is sand or clay, however, you will have to adjust either your planting or your gardening. You can "fatten up" very sandy soils by digging in generous doses of compost — layer it on several inches deep and mix it in with a power tiller. Or you can plant species roses (*see pp.*127–132), wild type roses that are naturally adapted to sandy soils. You'll find descriptions of two such roses, *Rosa spinosissima* and *R. virginiana*, in the Gallery of Roses (Chapter Three). Most of the hybrid rugosa roses also thrive in sandy soils. In addition, any of the roses described as tolerant of poor soils in the Gallery of Roses will grow reasonably well in sandy soils.

Pure clays — so-called heavy soils — present a more serious problem. Their tiny particles may pack together so tightly that they become impenetrable to air and water. Rose roots cannot thrive in such an environment. If you want to plant roses in an area of dense clay, you should plant them in a raised bed in which the natural soil has been mixed with coarse builder's sand and compost or sphagnum peat: one part soil to one part sand and one part peat or compost.

Organic content: This will be the low number of your test results, since organic matter typically makes up 5 percent or less of garden soil. However, organic content plays a critical role in the health of the soil. This is the fraction of the soil that keeps it open to air and water and helps it retain moisture and nutrients. The organic portion of the soil is also what supports the bacteria and fungi that fill healthy soil, and these in turn help control the populations of soilborne diseases and parasites. For all these reasons, roses planted in soil rich in organic matter will be healthier than roses planted in poorer soil.

Northeast — Donna Fuss
Elizabeth Park Rose Garden, Hartford, Connecticut

REGIONAL CHALLENGES:
- Fungal diseases (blackspot and powdery mildew)
- Winter cold

REGIONAL ADVANTAGES:
- "Connecticut Valley soils are some of the richest in the world."
- Summers are relatively cool.
- "We as the growers have a rest — unlike California, where gardeners have to care for roses year-round."

MOST TROUBLE-FREE ROSES (BY CLASS):
Rugosa roses, modern shrub roses, old garden roses (gallicas, albas, and the like), ramblers, miniature roses

MOST TROUBLE-PRONE ROSES (BY CLASS):
Hybrid teas (both shrub types and climbing teas), grandiflora roses, floribunda roses

WORST DISEASES:
Powdery and downy mildew, blackspot

WORST PESTS:
Japanese beetles and aphids

Aim to keep your soil at an organic content of 5 percent. If the test reveals a lower organic content, dig in several inches of organic material, such as autumn leaves, composted bark, or even sawdust, together with a sprinkling of five pounds (2.3kg) of 5-10-5 fertilizer for every 100 sq ft (9m²) of bed. Do this in the fall and let the bed sit until spring before planting, so that the waste can decompose.

This is not a permanent fix, since the organic part of your soil will gradually be devoured by the soil bacteria and fungi. In fact, in warm, humid climates such as in the Southeast, a dose of organic matter will disappear from the soil in a few months. To maintain organic content at an adequate level, cover the soil around your rosebushes with an inch (2.5cm) of some organic mulch such as shredded bark. As this decays, earthworms will draw it down into their burrows and so continually nourish the soil.

Soil fertility: These readings from the soil test will help you determine the amounts and kinds of fertilizers you should apply to your roses. Guidelines for a fertilizer program should be included in your soil test results. If they aren't, your local Extension agent can help you interpret the results and design your own program. In Canada contact a private soil laboratory.

There is one major nutrient that you should watch for in particular: phosphorus. It does not wash into or out of the soil as easily as the other major nutrients. This means that in phosphorus-deficient soils, it is particularly important to dig this nutrient (in the form of superphosphate or as part of a balanced fertilizer) into the soil at planting time. But it also means that phosphorus can gradually accumulate and eventually reach levels at which it blocks the roots' absorption of minerals such as iron and magnesium, which also are essential to plant growth. There is a special risk of this buildup with roses, because most fertilizers labeled as "rose foods" contain a high proportion of phosphorus. In older gardens — ones that have been treated with commercial fertilizers for many years

CLASSES OF ROSES

- **ALBA ROSES:** An antique group of roses best adapted to cool climates.
- **BOURBON ROSES:** Another antique class best adapted to moderate climates such as those of the Mid-Atlantic region, the lower Northeast, the Northwest, and milder parts of eastern Canada.
- **CENTIFOLIA ROSES:** A hardy antique class from Europe best adapted to cool climates such as those of the Northeast, Northwest, Midwest, and Rocky Mountain West. Some centifolias do perform well in the Southeast and Southwest, however.
- **CHINA ROSES:** An antique class that originated in Asia; best adapted to the Southeast and Southwest.
- **DAMASK ROSES:** Hardy European antiques well adapted to cooler climates but flourishing also in the dry Southwest.
- **FLORIBUNDA ROSES:** A modern class that is moderately winter hardy and performs well from the more temperate parts of the Northeast, Midwest, Rocky Mountain West, and Northwest down to the upper Southeast. Floribundas flourish in the Southwest.
- **GALLICA ROSES:** Cold-hardy European antiques; a good choice for the Northeast, Midwest, Rocky Mountain West, Northwest, and eastern Canada, these roses perform well in the Mid-Atlantic region, too.
- **GRANDIFLORA ROSES:** Modern roses best adapted to temperate climates such as the lower Northeast and Midwest (up through USDA zone 6, Canadian zone 7), the Northwest and Mid-Atlantic states. The grandifloras flourish in the arid Southwest and the milder parts of the Rocky Mountain West, and a few cultivars perform well in the upper Southeast, too.
- **HYBRID MUSK ROSES:** A 20th-century class that is both cold and heat tolerant, winter hardy in the North to USDA zone 4 (Canadian zone 5), and a star in the Southeast, Mid-Atlantic region, and the Southwest.
- **HYBRID PERPETUAL ROSES:** European and American antiques that perform best in temperate climates from the lower Northeast (USDA zone 5, Canadian zone 6) to the milder parts of the Rocky Mountain West. Hybrid perpetuals tolerate summer heat in dry climates but do not as a rule perform well in the summer heat and humidity of the Mid-Atlantic region and the Southeast.
- **HYBRID RUGOSA ROSES:** Among the hardiest of roses, the hybrid rugosas tolerate frigid winters and hot summers.

This is the best class for the upper Northeast and Midwest and the colder regions of the Rocky Mountain West and Canada. These roses do not flourish in the Southeast and Southwest.

- HYBRID TEA ROSES: Spectacular performers in arid, temperate regions such as the Southwest and the milder parts of the Rocky Mountain West. Good for the Northwest, too, but not reliably winter hardy in the upper Midwest and Northeast and most of southern Canada. They are disease prone wherever summers are hot and humid.

- MINIATURE ROSES: Winter hardy in the northern regions to USDA zone 6 and Canadian zone 5 (farther north where these natural dwarfs remain covered by snow). Excellent in the Southwest and in the cooler, airy microclimates of the Southeast.

- MODERN SHRUB ROSES: A catchall class that includes roses of many different kinds. Look for the strains adapted to your region — for instance, Dr. Griffith Buck's shrub roses or Agriculture Canada roses for cold northern regions.

- MOSS ROSES: Cold-hardy antiques good for the Northeast, Midwest, Rocky Mountain West, Northwest, and much of Canada. Acceptable in cooler parts of the Southwest. Disease prone in the Mid-Atlantic region and the Southeast.

- NOISETTE ROSES: An antique class of roses that flourishes in the Southeast, Southwest, and the Mid-Atlantic region.

- POLYANTHA ROSES: Excellent roses for the Southeast and Southwest, Mid-Atlantic region, and Northwest; temperate parts of the Northeast, Midwest, and Rocky Mountain West, and warmest regions of Canada.

- PORTLAND ROSES: An antique class that is exceptionally durable in cool climates and acceptable in the Mid-Atlantic region. Problematic in the Southwest and the Southeast.

- SPECIES ROSES: Wild type roses; there are species roses that flourish in every region of North America.

- TEA ROSES: An old-time favorite in the Southeast and Southwest. Not winter hardy north of the milder part of the Mid-Atlantic region.

- CLIMBERS AND RAMBLERS: Another catchall class composed largely of long-caned roses drawn from other classes, such as climbing tea roses and climbing floribundas. Refer to the Gallery of Roses (pp.138–145) to identify types suited to your region.

— a soil test may reveal that you should switch to a phosphorus-free fertilizer, such as ammonium sulfate or blood meal.

Drainage: The ease with which water passes through your soil is also crucial to the health of roses. With the exception of the species rose Rosa palustris (see p.129) roses will not tolerate "wet feet." That is, they need soil that accepts water easily but also lets it drain away promptly.

Laboratory tests do not address the matter of drainage, but you can easily determine this yourself. Dig a hole 6 in (15cm) across and 1 ft (.3m) deep. Fill it with water and let it drain. Then refill the hole. If it takes more than a couple of hours for the water to drain away the second time, your soil has a drainage problem. Your options at this point are to plant R. palustris or to grow your roses in raised beds or containers.

Pests and Diseases

One of the most important characteristics of an easy rose is that it is pest and disease resistant. Yet disease and pest resistance is regional, because no rose is resistant to all such enemies. Even if a given cultivar is immune to the entire selection of problems endemic to one region, there is sure to be an insect, fungus, or bacterium somewhere else to which that rose is susceptible. Indeed, one region's trouble-free rose may be another region's problem child.

That's why it's important to identify your region's pests and diseases. You'll find help with this in our consultants' comments on regional problems. For a more local perspective, you can join the American Rose Society (ARS, P.O. Box 30,000, Shreveport, LA 71130) or The Canadian Rose Society (CRS, 10 Fairfax Crescent, Scarborough, ON M1L 1Z8) and contact one of their consulting rosarians. These are expert rose growers from every region of the United States and Canada. The ARS and CRS can put you in touch with the rosarian living nearest to you.

The Right Roses for You

You've analyzed your garden and identified the challenges your roses will face there. At last, you can start choosing your plants. But before you head to the nursery or reach for your catalog, you should do just a little more homework.

There is a secret to singling out the easy roses from the multicolored masses out in front of the

garden center. There are thousands of rose cultivars — individual roses with names such as 'Peace' and 'Tiffany' — to be found in North American nurseries, and choosing one or two from this mass may seem like an overwhelming task. To simplify the choice, before you shop, identify the breeds of roses that are guaranteed to thrive in your garden. By eliminating all other roses, you can reduce your potential choices to a more manageable selection of cultivars. At the same time, you can eliminate most of the bad choices. By selecting only from breeds that you know will thrive, you will make rose selection a fail-safe process.

A Breed of Roses for Every Grower

When you are choosing a dog to herd sheep, to retrieve, or to guard your house, you don't go down to the pound and select any puppy at random. Instead, you choose a puppy from a breed that has been bred for the purpose you have in mind. In this respect, roses are like dogs.

Actually, rosarians started with a much more varied breeding stock. Whereas all dogs descend from either wolves or jackals, roses may descend from any of some 200 species of wild roses. These wild roses each inhabit a different environmental niche; there are roses that naturally thrive on mountain peaks, on the arctic tundra, in meadowlands and prairies, on beaches, in swamps, even in subtropical forests. Modern garden roses usually derive from some marriage of different species. Your job is to select the one that includes the right mix for your garden.

Rosarians have simplified this process by organizing roses into family groups. Roses that descend from the same group of parents and/or show similar characteristics are grouped into a "class." The American Rose Society recognizes 56 different classes, but many of these are based on fine distinctions that are of little interest to home gardeners. We will focus on just 21 classes here. These are

Most roses prefer full sun, but a few types (see the list on p.41), such as the 'New Dawn' seen here, thrive in partial shade.

listed on pp.36–37, and with each one are recommendations concerning that class's adaptation to the various regions of North America.

Twenty-one classes may seem like an intimidating array, but remember this: because many of the classes do not flourish in your region, you'll end up making your rose selections from perhaps half a dozen at most.

For detailed descriptions of each class, turn to the Gallery of Roses (Chapter Three). There you'll find the various classes covered in alphabetical order (with the exception of Climbers and Ramblers, which come at the end of the section), with notes about each one's characteristics, its use in the garden, and selections of the best cultivars.

Anatomy of a Rose: Rootstocks and Own-Roots

One last point you should keep in mind when you shop for roses: when you buy what looks like one rose, you actually may be buying two. In fact, most roses you will find at the nursery are propagated by grafting. That means that the glorious-flowered garden rose has been reproduced by taking a bud from it and grafting it onto the roots of some tough "rootstock rose."

It is possible, however, to root a *cutting* of the garden rose so that the roots and aboveground

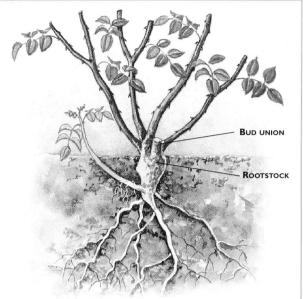

BUD UNION

ROOTSTOCK

Success with grafted roses depends on recognizing that such a bush is actually two plants. The ornamental rose that you admire is joined at the bud union to a genetically distinct rootstock. The proper level for planting, with the bud union above, at, or below the soil surface, varies with the climate.

growth are all of one piece; such plants are called "own-root roses." But it is far more common to propagate by grafting, because this method produces a marketable bush more quickly. In addition, grafting can offer specific advantages to the knowledgeable gardener.

For example, many garden roses do not flourish in alkaline soils, so if you grow them as own-root,

Mid-Atlantic States — Jim Adams
THE NATIONAL ARBORETUM HERB GARDEN, WASHINGTON, D.C.

REGIONAL CHALLENGES:
- Fungal diseases (blackspot and powdery mildew) are prevalent.
- Soils are excessively acidic.
- Rainfall is irregular — summer droughts are common.

REGIONAL ADVANTAGES:
- Winters are mild.

MOST TROUBLE-FREE ROSES (BY CLASS):
Rugosa roses, moss roses, David Austin's English Roses

MOST TROUBLE-PRONE ROSES (BY CLASS):
Hybrid tea roses and China roses

WORST DISEASES:
Powdery mildew and blackspot

WORST PESTS:
Rose slug and Japanese beetles

When dusky red, semidouble blossoms burst forth from a formerly pink-flowered rose it's not a miracle — it's trouble. A sucker has sprouted your garden rose's rootstock, the old, red-flowered climbing rose 'Dr. Huey'. If not removed, it will soon smother the hybrid rose grafted onto the rootstock's top.

they will not be easy roses in a garden with alkaline soil. But 'Dr. Huey', a popular rootstock, does thrive in alkaline soils. Graft an alkaline-hating rose onto 'Dr. Huey', and you'll have a lovely bush that looks the way you want and actually likes your soil. Other rootstocks are resistant to nematodes, plant parasites that lurk in the soil in some regions. Grafting onto resistant rootstocks protects roses that would otherwise be easy targets.

Rootstocks can also pose problems for the unaware. Many different types of roses are used for this purpose, and commercial growers, for obvious reasons, generally select the type that grows best in their nursery fields. 'Dr. Huey', because it likes dry,

alkaline soils, is the favorite rootstock among commercial growers in Arizona and southern California, where such conditions prevail. 'Dr. Huey' is good for them, but it's not good for you if you garden in the moist, acidic soils of the Northeast or Northwest. In addition, 'Dr. Huey' is sensitive to cold and is likely to die if soil temperatures drop to 20°F (−7°C). If the rootstock dies, the top dies, too, and this makes 'Dr. Huey' a poor rootstock for northern gardens.

Following is a list of rootstocks with descriptions of the strengths and weaknesses of each. Consult this list and identify the rootstocks suited to your garden. When you shop for roses, accept only plants grown on those rootstocks. If your local nurseryman doesn't know the rootstock of his roses, ask him to check with his supplier. Mail-order nurseries should be able to furnish this information over the telephone.

'Dr. Huey' — Grows well in dry, alkaline soils; dislikes acidic soils and is cold sensitive. A good rootstock for southwestern gardens and milder parts of the Rocky Mountain West.

'Fortuniana' — Nematode resistant; it is well adapted to hot climates. The best rootstock for the Southeast; a good rootstock for the Southwest.

Rosa canina — Very cold hardy but sends up many suckers that can overwhelm the garden rose

---

Canada — Trevor Cole
KINBURN, ONTARIO

REGIONAL CHALLENGES:
- These vary from region to region within Canada, but except in coastal British Columbia, winter cold is the greatest threat to roses.
- Alternate freezing and thawing characterize the winters throughout much of the eastern provinces, and this can promote winter damage.

REGIONAL ADVANTAGES:
- Severe winters reduce populations of many insect pests.
- Dry climates prevalent in the western provinces discourage fungal diseases.

MOST TROUBLE-FREE ROSES (BY CLASS):
Shrub roses, especially those bred by Agriculture Canada

MOST TROUBLE-PRONE ROSES (BY CLASS):
Climbing roses and ramblers (subject to extensive winter damage), hybrid teas, and floribundas

WORST DISEASES:
Varies throughout country; blackspot and mildew in southern Ontario

WORST PESTS:
Aphids, Japanese beetles, and chafers

ROSES FOR SPECIAL CONDITIONS

FOR PARTIALLY SHADED SITES:
'Alba Maxima' (alba)
'Ballerina' (hybrid musk)
'Cécile Brünner' (polyantha)
'Celsiana' (damask)
'Constance Spry'® (modern shrub — English)
'Cornelia' (hybrid musk)
'Danaë' (hybrid musk)
'Fimbriata' (hybrid rugosa)
'Frühlingsmorgen' (modern shrub — Kordesii)
'Gloire de Dijon' (climber)
'Golden Showers'® (climber)
'Goldstern'® (climber)
'Henry Kelsey' (climber)
'Iceberg' (floribunda)
'Lavender Lassie' (hybrid musk)
'L. D. Braithwaite'® (modern shrub — English)
'Madame Hardy' (damask)
'Martin Frobisher' (climber)
'Mermaid' (climber)
'Mister Lincoln'® (hybrid tea)
'New Dawn' (climber)
'Red Cascade' (miniature)
Rosa banksiae lutea (species)
R. glauca (species)
R. woodsii fendleri (species)
'Rose de Rescht' (damask)
'The Fairy' (polyantha)
'Thérèse Bugnet' (hybrid rugosa)
'Veilchenblau' (climber)
'William Baffin' (climber)

FOR DRY, SANDY SOILS:
China roses
Hybrid rugosa roses
'Radiance' (hybrid tea)
Rosa setigera (species)
R. spinosissima (species)
R. virginiana (species)
R. woodsii fendleri (species)

FOR EXPOSED, WINDSWEPT SITES:
Agriculture Canada roses (modern shrub)
Dr. Griffith Buck roses (modern shrub)

FOR SEASIDE GARDENS:
Hybrid rugosa roses
Rosa banksiae lutea (species)
R. nitida (species)
R. sericea pteracantha (species)
R. spinosissima (species)
R. virginiana (species)
R. wichuraiana (species)

budded to it. Not used by American growers but is sometimes present on European roses imported by Canadian nurseries and then exported to American customers.

R. *multiflora* — Tolerates acidic soils, cold winters, and nematodes; does not thrive in alkaline soils. A good rootstock for the northern United States and Canada.

Given the advantages of grafted roses, why would anyone wish to grow roses on their own roots? Well, there can be an advantage to having the whole bush be one type of rose.

In really cold climates, a hard winter may kill a rosebush all the way back to its roots. Commonly, though, the underground part of the plant will send up new shoots the next spring. With a grafted rose, this new growth will be shoots of rootstock; the garden rose budded on top has been lost. With an own-root rose, new growth from the roots will be shoots of the same garden rose that you planted.

This ability to resprout from the roots gives own-root roses an extra ability to withstand all sorts of calamitous injury to the top growth. The landscape service may run over the rose with a lawn mower or slash it with a string trimmer, or a deer or rabbit may slip into the garden to graze on your roses. The own-root roses may recover; the grafted roses certainly will not.

Roses for Special Conditions

Some microclimates, soils, and exposures are particularly challenging to roses, and in such conditions species and cultivars that normally thrive locally may not perform well. Four of the most trying situations are considered at left, and for each a list of roses that will succeed is included. Beside each rose's name, the name of the class to which it belongs is noted, to make the task of locating this rose in the Gallery of Roses (Chapter Three) easier.

Chapter Two

NEW ROLES FOR THE NEW ROSES

Isolationists. That's an odd label to pin on gardeners, but it's what most of us are when it comes to roses. Traditional roses demanded so much special care that gardeners ended up planting them all together in their own isolated garden. It made sense. With all the spraying and special protection that traditional roses demand, it was just simpler to group the floral invalids together so that they could all get their treatment at the same time. As a result, roses rarely fraternized with other garden plants and so had little role in the larger landscape.

*B*ut roses are changing, and now we gardeners have to change the way we think about them. There's no reason to isolate roses anymore. On the contrary, as garden and landscape shrubs, the new easy roses are too useful to waste.

Take a rose such as 'Carefree Wonder'™: forget the name and consider it simply as an anonymous garden plant. Here's a compact shrub 4–5 ft (1.2 –1.5m) tall and wide with attractive, disease-free foliage. It thrives with almost no care, just the once-a-year feeding and trimming you might give your azaleas. Except, unlike your azaleas, this shrub bears its large, lightly perfumed flowers through the summer and into the fall. Surely, there are plenty of ways you could use such a plant in the garden.

Indeed, because there is such variety among roses — this group of plants offers shrubs of many sizes and shapes — it's hard to imagine a niche in which roses cannot serve. That, for some, is the puzzle. There are so many roses, how do you choose the best one for each spot?

Actually, that's easy, too. You have already begun the process by developing a palette of roses that thrive in your climate and your garden. To select from that the right rose for any given spot is partly a matter of consulting your garden again. Check the spot you intend to plant: What size and shape of shrub will it accommodate? What color of rose will harmonize with other flowers and foliage in the same area?

Consider also the purpose the rose will serve. Is it going to be a ground cover to spill down over a sunny bank? Or a colorful accent to give some structure to a flower bed? Or will the rose climb a wall to soften the harsh lines of masonry?

Obviously, each of these uses demands a different sort of rose. To make an effective ground cover, a rose must have flexible canes that grow outward rather than up, and it must make a dense mat of foliage. An accent shrub should be upright and compact, and of a size to preside, but not tower, over neighboring perennials and annuals. A climber needs long, flexible canes, but it should not be as dense as the ground-cover rose. And the climber needs to be extra cold tolerant, since its canes will spend the winter above the snow, where they are at the mercy of the wind.

To simplify the task of selection, see the lists of roses suited to various uses and applications on pp.47–53. But before you skip to those lists, you should spend a little time exploring the aesthetic and personal side of selecting a rose for your garden. Just because a rose fills a niche neatly doesn't mean it is the best rose for the spot. It's the best rose only if it works well in partnership with the rest of the garden — and if it pleases you.

Flower Color

This is the characteristic that most gardeners check first when selecting a rose. Too often, in fact, the color of the flowers is the only consideration. Keep in mind, though, that the glorious hue of the petals may be that rose's only virtue. Often a spectacular success in this department will persuade a breeder to propagate and sell a new rose that is an otherwise mediocre, or even poor, shrub.

Experts on garden design are full of tips on blending and managing colors. Ultimately, though,

The white floribunda rose 'Iceberg', a bushy, upright shrub, fits this cottage garden nook perfectly. The snowy white of its flowers works with the blue of the lobelia (Lobelia erinus) that edges the bed, to give this corner a cool effect even in summer.

such choices are personal. Your neighbor may think that a certain mix of colors clashes, but you may find it exciting. It's your garden. Following are some rules of thumb that you may find useful.

For soft, delicate effects, you can count on the old-fashioned roses. The hues of their blossoms most commonly run in shades of pink, red, white, and cream. A century ago, there were few yellow roses hardy in the North, and even among the southern roses, the teas and Noisettes, one did not find the brilliant metallic oranges and yellows common now among the modern hybrid teas and floribundas.

If you lack confidence in your ability to manage contrasting colors, you can work within a single range of hues. A scarlet rose isn't going to clash with the pink and red flowers around it.

When planting a rose as an accent in a border of perennials and annuals, consider the effect of a contrasting color. An orange rose, for example, will galvanize a planting of blue flowers, just as a yellow rose will bring to life a purple border or a red rose will enliven a sea of green foliage.

If you aim for a more subtle effect, combine harmonious colors: reds with pinks or purples, yellows with oranges or greens, blues with greens or purples.

Formal versus Informal Plantings

Before selecting a rose, consider the style of your garden. Is it an easygoing, irregular tapestry of colors and textures? Or does it follow a more carefully structured, geometric design? Your choice of roses should reflect and reinforce this look.

In general, compact and mounded shrubs such as the polyantha roses (*see pp.*123–125), the floribundas (*see pp.*71–76), or the compact rugosa hybrids such as 'Rotes Meer' or 'Snow Owl' (*see pp.*87–92) work better with a formal garden style, while loose, expansive shrubs such as the hybrid perpetuals (*see pp.*85–86) are more at home in an informal setting. The species roses (*see pp.*127–132), in particular, rarely look comfortable in a formal

setting; their artless simplicity shows up best in a naturalistic setting, such as the edge of a meadow or a wildflower garden.

Some roses can be either formal or informal, depending on how they are grown. The Noisettes, for example, and many of the Agriculture Canada roses can be left alone to form sprawling shrubs, or their canes can be tied to a trellis to turn them into mannerly climbers. The at-ease shrubs clearly belong in an informal setting, while the restrained climbers integrate easily with a formal design.

Season of Bloom

Although the beauty of the rose's foliage and fruits is welcome, most of us cultivate roses primarily for their flowers. So it is essential to understand the when and how of each cultivar's flowering when you select a rose for the garden.

Rosarians divide roses into two basic groups: *remontant* (repeat blooming) and *nonremontant* (once-blooming). Remontant roses are roses that produce blossoms repeatedly through the warm-weather months. Some of these roses flower in "flushes" — that is, they bear their flowers in bursts, with blossomless periods in between. Many of the older remontant roses, the antique types

Bold contrast lends a vibrant energy to this planting of miniature roses: pink 'Child's Play', orange 'Pride 'n' Joy', and yellow 'Rise 'n' Shine'.

The soft pink of the centifolia 'Rose de Meaux', one of the once-blooming "old garden roses," stands out among the stronger colors in this mixed garden of roses and perennials.

from the last century, really produce only two major flushes of flowers, one in late spring or early summer and another as the heat subsides in early fall. Modern everblooming roses, however, come close to being just that: they flower more or less continuously from late spring or early summer until cold weather settles in in late fall or winter.

Nonremontant roses, the once-blooming sorts, are those that bear their entire crop of flowers in a period of several weeks in late spring or early summer to midsummer. This group includes most of the wild type, or species roses native to North America and Europe, as well as most of the older classes of garden roses that were bred from them. The alba roses and the gallica roses, for instance, are nonremontant.

The repeat-blooming habit was introduced with the roses from Asia in the late 18th and early 19th centuries. These roses were frost sensitive, and they passed this tenderness to the classes of repeat-blooming antique roses that were bred from them. The tea roses and China roses often are not hardy where winter temperatures drop much below the freezing point (USDA zone 7, Canadian zone 8, and north). Even those antique classes that derive from crosses of Asian roses with European or North American ones — the Bourbon roses, for example — are not as cold hardy as the once-blooming sorts. This is a fault that has been corrected by modern breeders, so the gardener can now enjoy roses such as Dr. Griffith Buck's shrub roses, which combine an everblooming habit with exceptional cold hardiness.

Still, it is a common mistake for gardeners to insist on growing only repeat-blooming roses. Remember when making your selections that a more prolonged season of bloom does not necessarily translate into more flowers. When one English rose fancier, Norman Young, kept records of the numbers of flowers his roses bore, he found that his hybrid perpetual roses, an antique class that repeats only intermittently, produced 95 percent of their flowers during a few weeks at the end of June. Yet during that period, the average hybrid perpetual rose actually bore more blossoms than its hybrid tea neighbor did over the course of a whole summer and fall.

If your goal is a lavish burst of seasonal color, you cannot do better than some of the older, once-blooming roses. When they're in full flower, their effect is overwhelming: the bushes bury themselves with blossoms, and they may perfume the air for 100 ft (30m) around. But when planting these roses, place them as you would an azalea or any other source of seasonal color. Put them where they can be appreciated while in flower, but also where they can fade into the background when the bloom has passed. You probably wouldn't want to make a once-blooming rose the focus of your mixed border, but it would make a fine backdrop for a flower bed.

Thorny versus Thornless

Roses vary considerably in the amount of protection they carry. Some cultivars are heavily armed with needlelike prickles or grabbing, hooked thorns; others produce few or none of these barbs. Common sense suggests that you keep the thorniest roses away from paths or places where children play. Nor will you want to use a really thorny rose as a ground cover, for weeding among its branches will be a bloody business.

There are situations in which thorns are an asset, however. A rose hedge, for example, provides a much more secure barrier if the canes are well armed. Such a hedge is better equipped to protect itself against the neighbor's undisciplined dog, and the postman is less likely to tramp a shortcut through it. On occasion, thorns can even be decorative. In fact, the huge, ruby red thorns of *Rosa sericea pteracantha*, the wingthorn rose (*see p*.130), is the principal attraction of this species rose.

Whenever a rose is unusually thorny or thornless, this fact is noted in its description in the Gallery of Roses (Chapter Three). In addition, you'll find a descriptive note attached to each of the cultivars recommended in the list of roses for hedges (*see p.49*).

Roses for Special Purposes

Every garden is unique, but the challenges that gardeners find themselves facing are not. We want privacy even if we live in a densely built suburban neighborhood. The concrete foundation of our ranch house is just as hard and unappealing as the one on the house next door. And as gardeners, we never have as much space as we want.

There are shared wants and needs. So although it is impossible to predict exactly which roses will

The outsize, ruby red thorns of the wingthorn rose are that shrub's principal attraction. More often, the value of thorns is practical, making a hedge secure against shortcuts.

A cap of roses softens the austere look of this New England stone fence; the thorns give authority to what is otherwise a purely ornamental barrier.

please you, it is possible to prescribe selections that are best suited to satisfying these common design problems. No one can tell you the best rose to plant in the scrap of soil alongside your patio; that depends on what you like. Developing a list of roses that might fit that spot, however, isn't hard. Often, too, in looking at recommendations for one situation, you may come across an idea or information that helps with another. In a list of roses for containers, for example, the patio gardener may find a way to fit more roses and more color into a small space, and in recommendations for rose hedges, another gardener may find a way to order and structure a kitchen garden.

Shrubs for Hedges, Landscapes, and Foundation Plantings

Roses to be used for these purposes must be upright, sturdy shrubs. Ideally, they should be compact growers, too, since that will eliminate the need for constant trimming. Handsome foliage is a plus for roses in these situations, while thorns can be an asset or a liability. A parent of small children, for example, may regard a thorny landscape shrub as a hazard, whereas a property owner intent on defining a boundary or enclosing a garden may appreciate thorns as making a hedge a more secure barrier.

When creating a hedge, you may mix roses of different kinds to create a more varied and interesting look, but make sure the various plants are of a similar size and rate of growth so that one shrub doesn't overwhelm its neighbors. If your hedge is intended as a barrier, you will find that own-root roses (*see p.*39) are best, because any suckers they send up from their roots may be left in place to reinforce the hedge. Suckers from a grafted rose will be shoots of rootstock and will be of a coarse and undesirable type.

Finally, when selecting roses for foundation plantings, keep in mind that the building above typically creates a dry microclimate. It will trap sunlight and work as a solar collector to make the area at its foot extra warm. The building is also likely to block rainfall, and a concrete foundation wicks away water to dry the soil next to it. Any rose used for a foundation planting should be extra drought tolerant.

Compact (3 ft [.9m] tall or less)

'COUNTRY DANCER' (MODERN SHRUB)

'ESCAPADE'® (FLORIBUNDA)

'FLOWER CARPET PINK'™ (MODERN SHRUB)

'HELEN TRAUBEL' (HYBRID TEA)

'HENRY HUDSON' (HYBRID RUGOSA)

'MARIE PAVIÉ' (POLYANTHA)

'ROTES MEER' (HYBRID RUGOSA)

Medium (3–5 ft [0.9-1.5m] tall)

'BALLERINA' (HYBRID MUSK)

'BELLE DE CRÉCY' (GALLICA)

'BONICA'® (MODERN SHRUB)

'CAREFREE BEAUTY'™ (MODERN SHRUB)

'CAREFREE DELIGHT'™ (MODERN SHRUB)

'CAREFREE WONDER'™ (MODERN SHRUB)

'DANAË' (HYBRID MUSK)

'EARTH SONG' (GRANDIFLORA)

'FÉLICITÉ PARMENTIER' (ALBA)

'FIMBRIATA' (HYBRID RUGOSA)

'FRAU DAGMAR HARTOPP' (HYBRID RUGOSA)

'GENE BOERNER' (FLORIBUNDA)

'HAWKEYE BELLE' (MODERN SHRUB)

'ICEBERG' (FLORIBUNDA)

'JENS MUNK' (HYBRID RUGOSA)

'KÖNIGIN VON DÄNEMARCK' (ALBA)

'LINDA CAMPBELL' (HYBRID RUGOSA)

'MARGARET MERRILL'® (FLORIBUNDA)

'MORDEN BLUSH' (MODERN SHRUB)

'MORDEN RUBY' (MODERN SHRUB)

'OLD BLUSH' (CHINA)

'OLYMPIAD'™ (HYBRID TEA)

Rosa spinosissima — SCOTCH ROSE (SPECIES)

'SNOW OWL' (HYBRID RUGOSA)

Large (more than 5 ft [1.5m] tall)

'BASYE'S BLUEBERRY' (MODERN SHRUB)

'FOLKLORE'® (HYBRID TEA)

'FRÜHLINGSMORGEN' (MODERN SHRUB)

'HANSA' (HYBRID RUGOSA)

'JEANNE LAJOIE' (MINIATURE)

'LAVENDER LASSIE' (HYBRID MUSK)

'PAUL NEYRON' (HYBRID PERPETUAL)

The smaller roses make superbly ornamental container plants, and outstandingly durable ones, too. With proper care, a well-chosen rose may thrive for years in a pot or tub.

Rosa sericea pteracantha — WINGTHORN ROSE (SPECIES)

'SAFRANO' (TEA)

'THÉRÈSE BUGNET' (HYBRID RUGOSA)

Roses for Small Spaces, Containers, and Hanging Baskets

The miniature roses (*see pp.*99–103) are obvious choices for these purposes. Although the polyantha roses (*see pp.*123–125) are too big for hanging baskets, they perform well in tubs and large pots and are compact enough to fit into all but the most confined spots.

'CINDERELLA' (MINIATURE)

'FLOWER CARPET PINK'™ (MODERN SHRUB)

'GOURMET POPCORN' (MINIATURE)

'GREEN ICE' (MINIATURE)

'JEAN KENNEALLY'™ (MINIATURE)

'JEANNE LAJOIE' (MINIATURE)

'MINNIE PEARL'™ (MINIATURE)

'NOZOMI' (MINIATURE)

'RED CASCADE' (MINIATURE)

'ROTES MEER' (HYBRID RUGOSA)

'SNOW OWL' (HYBRID RUGOSA)

Spilling down a rocky bank, the shrub rose 'Carefree Wonder'™ (MEIpitac) makes a robust and spectacularly colorful ground cover. One of the hardy, disease-resistant Meidiland™ roses, 'Carefree Wonder'™ is just what the name suggests.

Roses for Ground Covers

Two types of roses work particularly well as ground covers: robust climbers such as the miniature rose 'Red Cascade' or the species rose *Rosa wichuraiana*, and shrub roses with a spreading pattern of growth, such as 'Scarlet Meidiland'™ or 'White Meidiland'™. Each type creates a different effect. The climbers make a neater, more formal carpet, while the shrubs make a more luxuriant but also informal surface with their sea of arching canes. The species roses, as we might expect, are even wilder in appearance. But their rugged tousles of foliage, flowers, and hips are perfectly suited to the contemporary "natural" garden.

This list of ground-cover roses is a sampling of the species and cultivars that perform best under these conditions. A look at the Gallery of Roses (*Chapter Three*), however, reveals many other climbers and shrubs that will adapt to this use.

'FLOWER CARPET PINK'™ (MODERN SHRUB)
'LA SEVILLANA' (MODERN SHRUB)
'RED CASCADE' (MINIATURE)
Rosa nitida — SHINING ROSE (SPECIES)
R. setigera — PRAIRIE ROSE (SPECIES)
R. spinosissima — SCOTCH ROSE (SPECIES)
R. wichuraiana — MEMORIAL ROSE (SPECIES)
'SCARLET MEIDILAND'™ (MODERN SHRUB)
'WHITE MEIDILAND'™ (MODERN SHRUB)

Roses for Interplanting Among Perennial and Annual Flowers

The size of the rose you use for this purpose depends on the height of the surrounding flowers. Among hollyhocks and delphiniums, you'd need a large shrub such as 'Paul Neyron'; among shorter, more delicate flowers, a smaller shrub such as 'The Fairy' is indicated. As a rule, shrubs of compact growth are best because they do not send out long canes to flop down and crush their herbaceous neighbors. Because the surrounding flowers hamper air circulation, fungal diseases are a particular problem for roses in this type of planting, so your selections should be roses of outstanding disease resistance.

'ALEC'S RED'® (HYBRID TEA)
'BALLERINA' (HYBRID MUSK)
'BELLE ISIS' (GALLICA)
'BONICA'® (MODERN SHRUB)
'CAMAIEUX' (GALLICA)
'CINDERELLA' (MINIATURE)
'COMTE DE CHAMBORD' (PORTLAND)
'COUNTRY DANCER' (MODERN SHRUB)
'DEUIL DE PAUL FONTAINE' (MOSS)
'DUCHESSE DE BRABANT' (TEA)
'FLOWER CARPET PINK'™ (MODERN SHRUB)
'FRAU DAGMAR HARTOPP' (HYBRID RUGOSA)
'GOURMET POPCORN' (MINIATURE)
'JEAN KENNEALLY' (MINIATURE)
'L. D. BRAITHWAITE' (MODERN SHRUB)
'MABEL MORRISON' (HYBRID PERPETUAL)
'MINNIE PEARL'™ (MINIATURE)
'MORDEN BLUSH' (MODERN SHRUB)
'NATCHITOCHES NOISETTE' (NOISETTE)
'NOZOMI' (MINIATURE)
'PASCALI'® (HYBRID TEA)
'PAUL NEYRON' (HYBRID PERPETUAL)
'PEARLIE MAE' (GRANDIFLORA)
'QUEEN ELIZABETH'® (GRANDIFLORA)
'ROSENSTADT ZWEIBRÜCKEN' (MODERN SHRUB)
'ROTES MEER' (HYBRID RUGOSA)
'TAMORA' (MODERN SHRUB)
'THE FAIRY' (POLYANTHA)

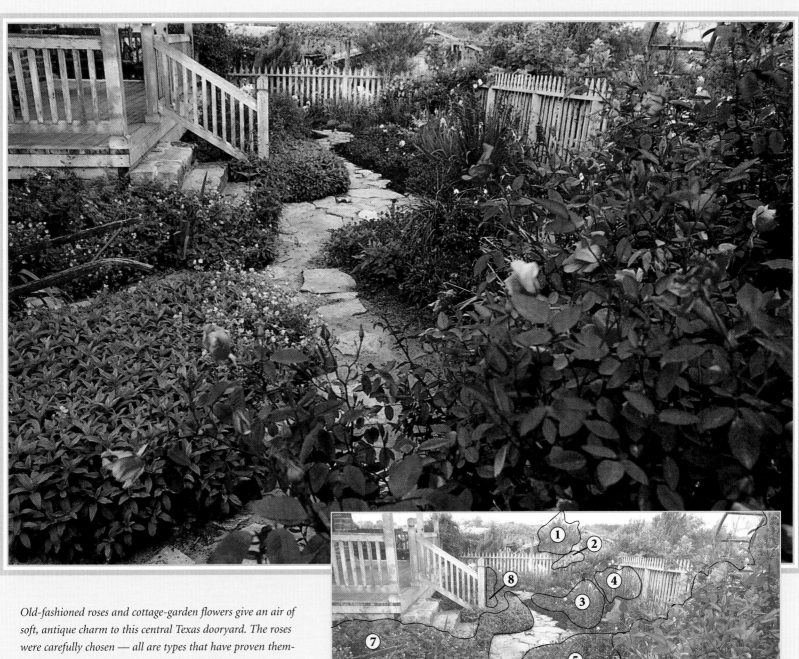

Old-fashioned roses and cottage-garden flowers give an air of soft, antique charm to this central Texas dooryard. The roses were carefully chosen — all are types that have proven themselves in that area as survivors in abandoned gardens and in cemetery plantings.

1. CRAPE MYRTLE (*LAGERSTROEMIA INDICA*)
2. CHINA ROSE 'OLD BLUSH'
3. BEARDED IRIS
4. FOXGLOVE (*DIGITALIS PURPUREA*, BIENNIAL)
5. GARDEN PINKS (*DIANTHUS* SPP., BIENNIAL)
6. CHINA ROSE 'MUTABILIS'
7. BOUNCING BET (*SAPONARIA OFFICINALIS*, PERENNIAL)
8. CHINA ROSE 'CRAMOISI SUPERIEUR'

Roses for Naturalizing

Because they are such healthy, self-reliant shrubs, the easy roses lend themselves to the current enthusiasm for "natural gardens" — gardens in which the aim is to duplicate the easy informality of a wild landscape. Generally, it is the simpler roses with blossoms of a single round of five petals that look most at home in such a setting, although semidouble roses — blossoms with an extra round of petals — can fit in, too, if the flower color isn't too bright and artificial-looking. The form of the shrub itself is important: a looser, gracefully mounded rosebush is usually best suited to a natural setting.

'ALBA MAXIMA' (ALBA)
'ASSINIBOINE' (MODERN SHRUB)
'BASYE'S BLUEBERRY' (MODERN SHRUB)
'DORTMUND'® (CLIMBER)
'FIMBRIATA' (HYBRID RUGOSA)
'FRAU DAGMAR HARTOPP' (HYBRID RUGOSA)
'FRÜHLINGSMORGEN' (MODERN SHRUB)
'GOLDEN WINGS' (MODERN SHRUB)
'HANSA' (HYBRID RUGOSA)

Roses may seem like strange bedfellows for vegetables and herbs, but the results can be striking. Obviously, only roses that thrive without regular spraying are allowed in a kitchen garden.

'MUTABILIS' (CHINA)
'NEARLY WILD' (FLORIBUNDA)
'OLD BLUSH' (CHINA)
'PRAIRIE DAWN' (CLIMBER)
Rosa banksiae lutea — YELLOW LADY BANKS ROSE (SPECIES)
R. *glauca* — RED-LEAFED ROSE (SPECIES)
R. *laevigata* — CHEROKEE ROSE (SPECIES)
R. *nitida* — SHINING ROSE (SPECIES)
R. *palustris scandens* — SWAMP ROSE (SPECIES)
R. *sericea pteracantha* — WINGTHORN ROSE (SPECIES)
R. *setigera* — PRAIRIE ROSE (SPECIES)
R. *spinosissima* — SCOTCH ROSE (SPECIES)
R. *virginiana* — VIRGINIA ROSE (SPECIES)
R. *wichuraiana* — MEMORIAL ROSE (SPECIES)
R. *woodsii fendleri* — SIERRA NEVADA ROSE (SPECIES)

Roses for the Kitchen Garden

In medieval times, roses were valued especially as medicinal plants and were commonly cultivated in the herb garden. Later on, country women included roses in the vegetable garden, because they used the hips as a source of vitamin-rich teas, and the fragrant petals were used to perfume vinegars and jams. Today's fashion for *potagers* — gardens in which vegetables, fruits, and herbs are cultivated in an ornamental design — has encouraged the reappearance of roses in the kitchen garden.

Any rose that is to be planted among your food crops must be highly disease resistant — you do not want to be spraying with fungicides around things you will eat. Since the planting style of kitchen gardens tends to be geometrical and formal, usually a formal style of rosebush is the best choice. The compact shrubs of the gallicas, floribundas, and polyanthas fit naturally into a kitchen garden. The more compact hybrid rugosa roses, such as 'Rotes Meer', not only fit physically, but they also offer the advantage of being "allergic" to chemical sprays — they flourish without applications of fungicide and pesticide and in fact won't tolerate them.

One further suggestion for the kitchen garden: Traditionally, this type of planting was enclosed with a wall or fence to protect the vegetables from cold spring or fall breezes and to provide some shelter from unseasonable frosts. These enclosures also offer an ideal canvas on which to arrange climbing roses.

Attractions Often Overlooked

It's almost a shame that rose blossoms are so spectacular, for the flowers so overshadow the other attractions of these shrubs that gardeners rarely recognize them at all. Yet the beauty of the roses' foliage, fruits, and fragrance can be considerable. Often, in fact, these features are appealing enough that in another kind of shrub they would serve as the main attractions. Besides, even in the South, there are long periods when the most prolific rosebush bears no blossoms. During that time, it is by its other features that a rosebush earns its keep.

Foliage

This is a characteristic that deserves far more attention than it usually gets when you are making your rose selections. After all, it is the most persistent feature of a rose, and although the foliage is not as visually assertive as the flowers, it does as much or more in its quiet way to determine the effect of the bush. The foliage may be fine, almost fernlike, as in the case of the wingthorn rose, *Rosa sericea pteracantha* (*see p.*130); bold, rugged, and creased, like that of the hybrid rugosa roses (*see pp.*87–92); or even hollylike, as in the case of the climbing rose 'Dortmund'® (*see p.*138). Foliage color varies too: the leaves of the memorial rose, R. *wichuraiana* (*see p.*132), are dark green and shiny, while those of the alba rose 'Félicité Parmentier' are gray-green and those of the shrub rose 'La Sevillana'® have a touch of bronze.

Some roses even contribute to the fall foliage show. The prairie rose R. *setigera* is one of the first

The rugosa roses' glossy, rugged foliage makes a dramatic setting for the fat, orange-red hips. Northern gardeners especially value hips because their development seems to enhance winter hardiness.

shrubs to change color in autumn; its leaves turn bronze-red. The leaves of the shrub rose 'Flower Carpet Pink'™ also turn bronze-red before they drop. Hybrid rugosas turn yellow and red, as does the Virginia rose, R. *virginiana* (*see p.*131).

Fruits

The other show of fall is the roses' fruits, or hips. Not all roses bear fruits. Very double roses — roses that bear flowers with many petals in each blossom — tend to be less prolific and as a rule bear few hips. In addition, many of the garden hybrids are sterile. These cultivars are usually the results of crosses of genetically incompatible parents; they cannot produce seeds and so never bear fruits. The shrub rose 'Carefree Wonder'™ is an example of this; although it is a heavy bloomer, it makes no hips. Actually, hybridizers consider sterility a virtue, because when a rosebush bears hips, it tends to stop producing flowers. You can forestall this change of gears by deadheading — snipping off the flowers as they start to wither — before the hips begin to form, but sterility eliminates the need for this kind of maintenance.

Roses that do not bear fruits survive from one generation to the next only because gardeners propagate them, either by cuttings or by grafting. In the wild, of course, roses must depend on seeds to produce the new plants. That's why the species roses (*see pp.127–132*) — roses that were taken directly from the wild — are such reliable and generous producers of hips. The native North American species *Rosa virginiana* and R. *setigera* both spangle themselves with abundant clusters of orange-red fruits, and these, in combination with the plants' fall foliage, make an extraordinary seasonal picture.

The hybrid rugosa roses are, as a rule, champion hip producers, bearing large, fat, almost tomato-like fruits. Sometimes, though, a more modest display is more intriguing, as with the little maroon-black hips of the Scotch rose, R. *spinosissima*.

Fragrance

There is still one more attraction of the rose that is often overlooked. Curiously, this is also the quality above all others that most people respond to instantly. It is fragrance. Catalogs describe in detail the color of a rose's flowers, the size and form of the blossoms, and how regularly the rose reblooms, yet they usually dismiss the rose's fragrance with a word or two, or ignore this engaging characteristic altogether.

There are a couple of reasons for this neglect. To begin with, fragrance is difficult to describe, and one nose often perceives a fragrance differently from another. But fragrance has also come to be overlooked among rose nurserymen because the most commercially successful modern roses, the hybrid teas and floribundas, commonly are lacking in this quality. The classic hybrid tea fragrance,

Fragrance

Rose perfumes are highly variable, with different noses perceiving the same fragrance differently. To one nose, a particular rose may smell like "spice," while to another it smells "fruity." In addition, perfumes vary in strength according to the weather and the time of day. Generally, the best time to enjoy rose fragrances is in the cool of the morning, and a newly opened blossom will be more fragrant than an old, fading one.

while refreshing, is light — a fresh, apple-like smell. Besides, in their pursuit of brighter colors and standardized flower forms, modern breeders have been willing to accept and promote roses that have no perfume at all.

Some modern roses, such as the hybrid teas 'Chrysler Imperial' and 'Double Delight'™ or the floribunda 'Margaret Merrill'™, are outstandingly fragrant. It is worth noting, though, that perfume makers, the people who harvest roses to extract their fragrances, use only antique, once-blooming types. Certainly for the richest and most sophisticated perfumes, the gardener should look to the older classes such as the damasks, gallicas, and Bourbons. Those old-timers have a complexity and individuality of fragrance that is unequaled among modern roses. Old books record instances of connoisseurs in the last century identifying individual cultivars while blindfolded, naming each rose as it was held to their noses by the perfume alone. That is a feat no living expert can duplicate with modern roses.

Actually, one contemporary breed does come close to equaling the bouquets of the antique classes, but this group of roses — the English roses — is not exactly modern. British nurseryman David Austin breeds this type by crossing antiques with modern everbloomers (*see pp.110–112*). His original goal was to create a breed of roses that would combine the best qualities of both eras, and his introductions do have anachronistically fine perfumes. Set one of them below a bedroom window or by the entrance to the garden, and you will guarantee a summer of romance.

Chapter Three

A GALLERY OF EASY ROSES

*You know the kind of roses you need; you can see what you want
in your mind's eye. But connecting these images with the name of an actual rose may
seem daunting. It shouldn't be. In the following pages, you will find profiles and portraits
of more than 150 easy roses, with all the details you need to make the right choices.*

There are roses for every kind of climate, roses for every region, shrubs of every size from dwarf to giant, and flowers of every color and description. Whether your garden is informal or formal, large or small, there are roses in this gallery to suit your style and your needs.

If you haven't already settled on the classes that are best for your garden, then you should begin by browsing the introductions that this chapter provides. The profiles are grouped by class, and each grouping begins with a general description of the strengths and regional adaptations of that class. In part, the roses are grouped this way because it highlights the differences between the classes and helps you to select the ones best suited to your needs and your taste. In addition, though, this arrangement ensures that once you settle on a particular class, you will

have at your fingertips not one but a whole palette of suitable easy roses.

For example, if you read the introduction to the hybrid rugosa roses and determine that they are the best fit for your cold, exposed garden in South Dakota, then you have immediately at hand not one easy rose but eleven, all hybrid rugosas, that will perform well for you. Or, if in leafing through the gallery, you are struck by the antique charm of the tea rose 'Duchesse de Brabant' you may decide that the old-fashioned charm of its lush pink blossoms is just what you want to wrap around the terrace of your south Georgia home. Maybe you'd like a compatible yellow rose to plant there too; among the eight tea roses grouped together you'll find one of that hue as well: 'Isabella Sprunt'.

Each profile of an individual rose begins with a photographic portrait, for how a rose looks is, of course, the gardener's first concern. A rose must please your eye. Alongside the photograph is the official cultivar name, the name under which the rose has been registered with the American Rose Society. This name is listed first because it is the name under which you are most likely to find the rose advertised in catalogs and at garden centers. Some roses, however, especially the ones that have been longest in our gardens, have accumulated one or two or even several alternate names. The hybrid rugosa rose 'Frau Dagmar Hartopp', for instance, may also be found under the names 'Frau Dagmar Hastrup' and 'Fru Dagmar Hastrup'. Likewise, the species rose *Rosa spinosissima* is also sold as R. *pimpinellifolia*. To protect the shopper from the confusion that such multiple names might cause, all of a rose's unregistered aliases are included in its profile, under the heading "Other Names."

The description of each rose begins with a concise summary of the practical considerations that are most important to making an intelligent choice. What sort of shrub does the rose make? Is it too tall for the flower border, or a sprawling shrub best reserved for use as ground cover? Does the rose bloom just once a year or does it rebloom? And are the flowers fragrant? All of the roses included in this gallery are vigorous, healthy shrubs, but is this particular one especially disease resistant? That information may be crucial if you garden in a hot and humid climate, or if you intend to plant the rose in a less than ideal site, someplace in which the rose is likely to experience greater than average stress.

The blossom is the heart of the rose's beauty, but an outstanding cultivar may offer colorful hips as well, or perhaps a glossy, handsome foliage. You'll find these features noted under "Other Interest." Usually when gardeners select a plant, they have a particular application in mind. They may want rosebushes that will fill their vases with elegant and lasting cut flowers, or maybe they want rosebushes that will make a tough but colorful hedge. Information about each rose's particular strengths has been included under the heading "Special Uses." Included there, too, are notes about whether this rose tolerates difficult conditions, such as poor soil or partial shade.

These clustered yellow blossoms have the languid elegance of a southern belle, and in fact the Yellow Lady Banks Rose is best adapted to the warmer regions of the Southeast and Southwest. Profiled on page 127, Yellow Lady Banks is a species rose, one of a class that still preserves the wild rose's vigor and natural good health.

A rose is not a good rose for you if it cannot tolerate your climate, and under "Hardiness" you will find information about the geographical range in which each rose thrives. Tolerance to winter cold is what defines rose hardiness in Canadian gardens, so only one Canadian hardiness zone is listed for each rose, the most northerly zone in which that cultivar flourishes. Because the United States extends much further south, a rose's hardiness there is defined not only by its tolerance for winter cold but also for summer heat. Accordingly, the U.S. hardiness for each rose is expressed as a range, from the coldest USDA zone to the warmest in which that rose flourishes.

Next comes information about the rose's pedigree. This entry begins with the name of the breeder or the nursery firm that created the rose, and follows with the year in which it was introduced onto the market. Appended to this is the parentage — the names of the roses that were crossed to produce the profile's subject — when that is known.

This data may seem trivial, but, actually, it can be very useful in helping you assemble your own palette of roses. Like painters or fashion designers, each rose breeder has an individual style, and if you like one of his creations, chances are you will like others. If you find Dr. Griffith Buck's modern shrub rose 'Carefree Beauty'™ to your taste, then you should definitely take a look at his grandiflora rose, 'Earth Song'.

Likewise the parentage of the rose can be very informative. If, for example, you find that the modern 'Constance Spry' is spectacular in your garden, you probably should investigate its parents, the gallica rose 'Belle Isis' and the floribunda rose 'Dainty Maid'. Looks run in families and so does the ability to thrive in your garden.

One other aspect of a rose's pedigree may be important, and that is the date of its introduction. This is the year in which the rose first appeared in gardens and nursery catalogs. If you shopped for

period furniture to suit the style of your Victorian house, surely you'll want to plant the garden with roses of the period, too.

The rose profiles also include a longer, more detailed description of the strengths and beauties of each rose, and information about any special uses to which that cultivar may lend itself. If the blossom of a rose darkens in color or fades as it ages, you'll find that noted. If the blossoms are unusually large or small for a rose of that class, this will be mentioned. Comments from regional consultants are also included.

Shopping for roses can be a frustrating business, for even when you know what you want, you may not know where to buy it. What use is it to select the perfect rosebush for your garden if you then cannot find a source for it? That is why you will find a guide to nursery sources for each rose at the end of its profile. Check the letter and number codes under this heading and compare them to the listings in Appendix B (*pp*.210–213). This makes it easy for you to identify a source for any rose in this chapter that interests you.

For some gardeners, the Gallery of Easy Roses offers all the roses they will ever need. Most, however, will want to explore further. For them, the following pages are a guide and an invitation.

Most famous of Dr. Griffith Buck's "prairie roses," 'Carefree Beauty'™ is a remarkable shrub, one that combines a homesteader's toughness with flowers of luxurious, perfumed delicacy. Disease resistant, cold hardy, and a visual treat, this modern shrub proves that roses can be easy.

ALBA ROSES

"Time-tested" takes on a special meaning when applied to the roses of this class. Rose historians believe it was the ancient Romans who planted alba roses in the gardens of Europe, and these roses enjoyed their period of greatest popularity in the late 18th century. What caused them to lose favor after that was their modesty: the albas produce relatively small blossoms (typically 2-3½ in [5-9cm] across) in soft shades of cream, white, or light pink, and they bloom just once each year, flowering only in late spring or early summer. These quiet beauties could not compete with the bolder, reblooming roses that began to make a name for themselves by the early 19th century.

Modern gardeners, however, are rediscovering the solid virtues of the albas. Hardy as oak trees, they overwinter without protection as far north as USDA zone 4 (Canadian zone 3). In fact, the albas need some winter cold if they are to flourish, and they do not thrive in the warmer regions of the Southwest and Southeast where winters are virtually frost free.

In addition to their cold tolerance, the alba roses also exhibit a remarkable resistance to diseases and pests. In a study at the Minnesota Landscape Arboretum, the albas demonstrated no susceptibility to blackspot or powdery mildew, or to the more serious insect pests. These are truly carefree roses; most form naturally mounded, graceful shrubs that need little pruning. But their greatest attraction is an intangible. The perfume of an alba rose in full bloom is perhaps the sweetest of any rose, and one whiff will leave the gardener with a new definition of fragrance.

ALBA ROSES

'Alba Maxima'

Habit: Upright, treelike shrub, 6–8 ft (1.8–2.4m) tall

Bloom: Profuse, late spring to early summer

Fragrance: Strong

Disease Resistance: Excellent

Other Interest: Ornamental hips

Special Uses: Specimen, landscape; tolerates poor soils, partial shade

Hardiness: USDA zones 4–8; Canadian zone 3

Pedigree: Ancient origin; cultivated before 1867

Other Names: 'Maxima', *Rosa alba maxima*, Jacobite Rose

The blossoms of this rose are relatively small — 2½–3 in (6.3–7.5cm) in diameter — but full, packed with as many as 200 petals, and they carry a truly heady perfume. Like all albas, this cultivar is once-blooming, but it provides color later in the season with a crop of attractive hips.

A favorite subject of the Renaissance painters, this rose gained notoriety as the symbol of Britain's exiled Stuart kings. At one time, a partiality for 'Alba Maxima' was tantamount to treason. Today this long-cultivated rose remains popular not only for its beauty but also for its hardiness and ability to thrive under difficult growing conditions, including partial shade.

Sources: USA — HI, R4; Canada — CaP2

'Félicité Parmentier'

Habit: Upright, compact shrub 4 ft (1.2m) tall

Bloom: Spring to early summer

Fragrance: Strong

Disease Resistance: Good

Other Interest: Gray-green foliage

Special Uses: Border specimen, hedge; tolerates poor soils, partial shade

Hardiness: USDA zones 4–8; Canadian zone 3

Pedigree: Cultivated since 1834

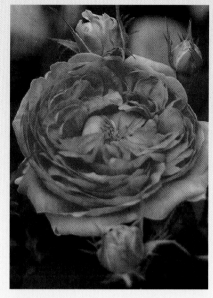

'Königin von Dänemarck'

Habit: Open, spreading shrub, 5 ft (1.5m) tall and wide

Bloom: Spring to early summer

Fragrance: Strong

Disease Resistance: Outstanding

Special Uses: Hedge; tolerates poor soils, shade

Hardiness: USDA zones 4–8; Canadian zone 3

Pedigree: Cultivated since 1826

Other Names: 'Belle Courtisanne', 'Queen of Denmark'

As a group, the alba roses are large shrubs, and their vigorous growth can overwhelm a small garden. 'Félicité Parmentier' is an exception, a more mannerly shrub that doesn't jostle its neighbors. Its blossoms are one of the sweetest pleasures of early summer. Borne in clusters, they are a soft pink in color, saucer-shaped, and "quartered" — the petals are clustered so as to form four distinct quadrants within the circular flower — and the center of each is a green "eye," rather like the button at the center of an overstuffed sofa cushion. When not in bloom, this shrub provides a visually restful mass of attractive gray-green foliage.

Sources: USA — G3, R1, R3; Canada — CaC1, CaH1, CaP2

The most brightly colored of the alba roses, the flowers of 'Königin von Dänemarck' open a brilliant pink but then gradually fade, ending up nearly white. With this distinctive coloration, these flowers also offer an unusually elegant form. They are neatly quartered, with as many as three, four, or five divisions among the petals and a button-eye center. In addition, they are outstandingly fragrant. Though somewhat coarse, the blue-green leaves are the ideal color to set off the warmth of the flowers.

Sometimes planted as a hedge, this rose can become leggy if not restrained by an annual shortening of the canes after it finishes blooming in early summer.

Sources: USA — F2, H3, R7; Canada — CaC1, CaP1, CaP2

BOURBON ROSES

Among the many ugly legacies of European imperialism there is at least one that is supremely beautiful, and that is the Bourbon class of roses. The Bourbons all spring from a bush found in a hedge enclosing a planter's field on a French colony in the Indian Ocean, the Île de Bourbon. Like many colonials, this rose represented a blending of invader and local, for it seems to have been a natural cross of a European garden rose with an Asian one.

At any rate, this rose, and the many "Bourbon roses" bred from it, combine the best qualities of East and West. Like their European parent, the Bourbons are cold hardy through USDA zone 6 (and Canadian zone 6) and some overwinter successfully in USDA zone 4; like their Asian ancestor, they rebloom. Bourbons do not produce flowers as continuously as hybrid teas; instead, they bear the bulk of their flowers in a heavy surge in late spring and early summer, though they do continue to flower sporadically through the summer and into fall. This makes them an excellent choice for the gardener who wants to combine a longer blooming season with old-fashioned richness and perfume.

The Bourbons are the epitome of Victorian lushness. The blossoms are large, even huge, often making an almost perfect globe of crepe petals. Their perfumes are intense, and the shrubs tend to be vigorous.

Because of their Asian roots, the Bourbons perform well in the South as well as the North, and they are not fazed by the combination of summer heat and humidity that make the Mid-Atlantic states and the upper Southeast a trial for other kinds of roses. In the Deep South (USDA zones 9 and 10), however, they are likely to need regular spraying with fungicides.

BOURBON ROSES

'Boule de Neige'

Habit: Upright shrub, 5 ft (1.5m) tall and 3 ft (.9m) wide

Bloom: Long midseason bloom with occasional recurrence

Fragrance: Strong

Disease Resistance: Good

Special Uses: Pillar, fence

Hardiness: USDA zones 6–9; Canadian zone 6

Pedigree: Lacharme, 1867; 'Blanche Lafitte' × 'Sappho'

When the double white flowers of 'Boule de Neige' (ball of snow) are fully open, the outer petals roll back at the tips, which does give the blossoms a rounded, snowball-like look. Borne in clusters, the flowers are cream-colored rather than snow white and have a strong damask rose fragrance.

This is one of the Bourbons that performs particularly well in the Southeast — though in such a climate, midsummer may bring some blackspot. A vigorous shrub, it produces long, arching canes that can be tied down along a fence or wreathed around a pillar. 'Boule de Neige' also shows to good advantage flexing its muscles freely at the back of a border or bed.

Sources: USA — HI, R5, S2; Canada — CaH2, CaP2

BOURBON ROSES

'Gipsy Boy'

Habit: Vigorous shrub, 6 ft (1.8m) tall, 8 ft (2.4m) wide

Bloom: Early summer

Fragrance: Light

Disease Resistance: Good

Hardiness: USDA zones 4–8; Canadian zone 5

Pedigree: Lambert, 1909

Other Names: 'Zigeunerknabe'

BOURBON ROSES

'Madame Isaac Pereire'

Habit: Upright, bushy shrub, 5–6 ft (1.5–1.8m) tall

Bloom: Recurrent

Fragrance: Intense

Disease Resistance: May be susceptible to blackspot and powdery mildew; infection rarely proves serious

Special Uses: Specimen, climber

Hardiness: USDA zones 6-9; Canadian zone 6

Pedigree: Garçon, 1881

There is some argument as to whether this rose belongs among the Bourbons. Although the breeder, Peter Lambert of Germany, classed 'Gipsy Boy' as a Bourbon, he never revealed its parentage, so the truth will never be known. But two things are certain: this is one of the easiest roses to grow, and when it's in full bloom — the long, arching canes bowing under the weight of the small crimson-purple blossoms — it is spectacular.

The foliage of 'Gipsy Boy' is healthy but somewhat coarse, and the canes are prickly. This is not a rose to include in the flower bed or a formal setting, but it is an excellent choice for use as a landscape shrub or to plant along the edge of a meadow. It is also exceptionally hardy for a Bourbon, overwintering without protection in USDA zone 4.

Sources: USA — A1, V1; Canada — CaH2, CaP2

The cabbage-shaped, deep raspberry-purple blossoms of 'Madame Isaac Pereire' are held by connoisseurs to have the richest, most delicious fragrance of any rose. What's more, they are just as visually satisfying. Large, fully double, and quartered, these blooms may measure 5 in (13cm) across, and they have all the ruffled luxuriance of a Victorian crinoline petticoat.

Unfortunately, this rose's foliage is not entirely free of fungal diseases, but any infection rarely proves serious. And when 'Madame Isaac Pereire' blooms, all else will be forgotten. Its vigorous, upright habit makes it a good candidate to train along a fence.

Sources: USA — C2, G1, S1; Canada — CaH2, CaP1, CaP2

BOURBON ROSES

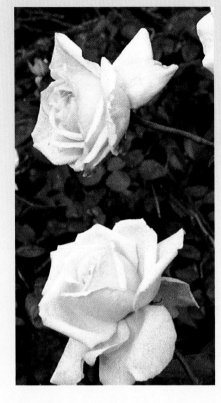

'Souvenir de la Malmaison'

Habit: Compact shrub, 3–4 ft (0.9–1.2m) tall

Bloom: Abundantly recurrent

Fragrance: Medium to strong

Special Uses: Border, container

Hardiness: USDA zones 6–9; Canadian zone 6

Pedigree: Beluze, 1843; 'Mme. Desprez' × tea rose

Other Names: 'Queen of Beauty' and 'Fragrance'

Though hardy to USDA zone 6 and a good performer in the North, this rose loves a warm climate. 'Souvenir de la Malmaison' is one of the few Bourbons that turns up in old country gardens in the Southeast, and it reaches its greatest perfection in the dry warmth of the Southwest. Those who have seen it at its best speak of it as the quintessential old rose. The creamy blush pink blossoms are large, flat, and quartered; the petals naturally form a cross, and the perfume they exhale is deliciously spicy. It's distinctive among the Bourbons, as it rarely grows to more than 3 ft (.9m) tall. 'Souvenir de la Malmaison' can be planted in small gardens or even raised in a container.

Sources: USA — A1, H3, R5; Canada — CaH1, CaH2, CaP2

Introducing

CENTIFOLIA ROSES

A class of genuine antiques, these are the roses that starred in the paintings of the Dutch old masters. Certainly these are roses of substance. *Centifolia* means "hundred petaled," and the centifolia rose blossoms are, as a rule, full, with petals tightly packed. In size, they range from little pompons 1 in (2.5cm) across to big blossoms 4 in (10.2cm) in diameter — a 3 in (7.6cm) blossom is about average for centifolias. "Cabbage roses" is an old common name for these roses, and this prosaic label refers to the way the petals envelop each other like the leaves in a head of cabbage. Don't be fooled by the unromantic name, though. If antique charm is your aim, centifolias are the roses for you.

From a practical standpoint, these roses are also well suited to the needs of modern gardeners. Centifolias tend to be exceptionally cold hardy and resistant to pests and diseases. As shrubs, they are usually loose and open in form, though they are often compact and may not grow beyond a height and spread of 3 ft (.9m). They bloom just once each year, typically in early summer, filling the garden with perfume in their season.

In general the centifolias are roses for the northern half of the United States, and they are excellent candidates for Canadian gardens.

CENTIFOLIA ROSES

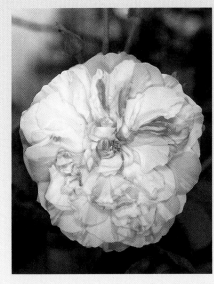

'Centifolia Variegata'

Habit: Vigorous, spreading shrub, 6 ft (1.8m) tall and wide

Bloom: Early summer

Fragrance: Strong

Disease Resistance: Good

Special Uses: Pillar; tolerates heat and humidity

Hardiness: USDA zones 4–8, Canadian zone 5

Pedigree: Unknown

Other Names: 'Village Maid', 'Cottage Maid'

CENTIFOLIA ROSES

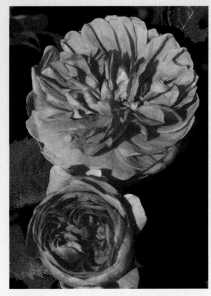

'Rose des Peintres'

Habit: Vigorous, upright shrub, 5–6 ft (1.5–1.8m) tall

Bloom: Profuse early-summer bloom

Fragrance: Strong

Disease Resistance: Good

Special Uses: Pillar; tolerates poorer soils

Hardiness: USDA zones 4–7; Canadian zone 5

Pedigree: Unknown; cultivated prior to 1838

Other Names: 'Centifolia Major'

Regional consultant Peter Haring of the American Rose Society recommends this as the only centifolia that has successfully made the transition with him from New York to Louisiana. Though hardy to USDA zone 4, 'Centifolia Variegata' is able to tolerate the heat and humidity of a southeastern summer.

Like most centifolias, 'Centifolia Variegata' has a rather open, rangy habit. It is best used as a pillar rose or trained along a horizontal fence or low wall. The large, richly fragrant blooms open creamy white with pink stripes, then fade to white with lilac stripes.

Sources: USA — H1, R7

Another shrub that takes well to being trained on a pillar or fence, 'Rose des Peintres' bears very double (200 petals), fragrant, bright pink blooms, often with button-eye centers. As is true of so many of the older roses, the blossoms of 'Rose des Peintres' have a memorable perfume. The name, which translates as "rose of the painters," refers to the fact that portraits of this flower frequently appeared in 18th-century Dutch paintings, particularly those of Jan van Huysum.

Though somewhat more sensitive to cold than 'Centifolia Variegata', this rose is also a safe bet for cold northern gardens and should overwinter successfully in USDA zone 4.

Sources: USA — H1, L1, R1; Canada — CaP2

Introducing

CHINA ROSES

As the name suggests, the ancestors of these roses came mostly from China. Arriving in Europe in the days of the sailing ships, the original China roses excited great interest among the gardeners of that era because they were the first regularly reblooming roses western gardeners had seen. China roses became the focus for rose breeders, as they tried to cross these cold-sensitive imports with the more cold-hardy European garden roses to create a race that would combine the best features of each. Over the years, the China roses played a part in creating all the different classes of modern everblooming roses.

For sheer practicality, though, the original China roses and their China hybrid offspring have never been surpassed. These roses do not thrive where winters are cold — most Canadian gardeners can admire them only in photographs. China roses have proven wonderfully well adapted to the southeastern United States, however, for they tolerate both humid heat and drought. Often a China rose will be found blooming happily in an abandoned garden or beside a gravesite where it has received no care for half a century or more. China roses also perform well in the Southwest and the Mid-Atlantic states.

The individual blossoms of the China roses are not, as a rule, spectacular. They may measure no more than 2 in (5.1cm) across, though 3 in (7.6cm) is the average, and some China roses reach a diameter of 4 in (10.2cm). When in full bloom, however, the Chinas mount a display in which the quantity of flowers more than compensates for any individual shortcomings. The reliability of their rebloom makes them stars of the late summer and fall garden.

CHINA ROSES

'Archduke Charles'

Habit: Erect shrub, 3–5 ft (0.9–1.5m) tall

Bloom: Reblooming, spring through fall

Fragrance: Moderate

Disease Resistance: Good

Special Uses: Hedge, specimen

Hardiness: USDA zones 7–9; Canadian zone 8

Pedigree: Laffay, prior to 1837

The fascination of this China rose lies in its changeable flower color: the full flowers open with crimson outer petals and white or pale pink centers that darken gradually to a solid, rich crimson. The rate of this color change depends on the intensity of the sun, with the petals darkening faster in strong sunlight. As buds open one after another on 'Archduke Charles', the same bush may sport flowers in a selection of different colors.

Sources: USA — A1, C2, R5

'Ducher'

Habit: Compact shrub, 3–5 ft (0.9–1.5m) tall

Bloom: Recurrent, spring through fall

Fragrance: Good

Disease Resistance: Good

Special Uses: Container

Hardiness: USDA zones 7–9; Canadian zone 8

Pedigree: Ducher, in 1869

'Louis Philippe'

Habit: Compact shrub, 3–5 ft (0.9–1.5m) tall

Bloom: Recurrent, spring through fall

Fragrance: Slight

Disease Resistance: Good

Special Uses: Drought tolerant

Hardiness: USDA zones 7–9; Canadian zone 8

Pedigree: Guérin, in 1834

Other Names: 'Louis Philippe d'Angiers'

'Ducher' is generally conceded to be the only white rose of this class. In fact, the blossoms are more of an ivory or cream color than pure white. Traces of pink stain the outer petals of the round flower buds, which open into small, fragrant double blooms that are fuller and more elegant than those of most China roses. 'Ducher' reblooms regularly throughout the summer, and because it is smaller than most members of its class, it works well as a container plant. The new foliage is purplish red, maturing to a fresh apple green all season.

Sources: USA — AI, C2, G2

This China rose has long since proven its adaptability. Though French by birth, it arrived in Texas the first year it was on the market and has survived more than 150 years of that state's weather extremes. Indeed, 'Louis Philippe' is one of the roses commonly found around abandoned homesteads in the Deep South.

The cupped double flowers are dark crimson with blush pink centers, and the petals are occasionally streaked with purple. Unusually reliable in the recurrence of its bloom, 'Louis Philippe' commonly flowers from spring to early winter, and even in warm spells during the cold months.

Sources: USA — AI, C2, G2

'Mutabilis'

Habit: Shrub, 4–6 ft (1.2–1.8m) tall

Bloom: Recurrent, spring through fall

Disease Resistance: Good

Other Interest: Flower color deepens with age, bronze new growth

Special Uses: Specimen; can be trained against a wall

Hardiness: USDA zones 7–9; Canadian zone 8

Pedigree: China; introduced to the West prior to 1894

'Old Blush'

Habit: Upright shrub, 3–6 ft (0.9–1.8m) tall

Bloom: Reblooms from spring to winter

Fragrance: Slight

Disease Resistance: Excellent pest and disease resistance

Other Interest: Attractive hips

Special Uses: Specimen, hedge; drought tolerant

Hardiness: USDA zones 5–9; Canadian zone 6

Pedigree: China; introduced to the West by 1752

Other Names: 'Old China Monthly', 'Common Blush China', 'Old Pink Daily', among others

M utabilis' is aptly named, for its pointed orange buds open into single rounds of clear yellow petals that gradually change to shades of orange, pink, and finally crimson. Flowers of all these colors will adorn a single plant at the same time, and the sight of the fluttering, five-petaled flowers perched on the bush has earned this cultivar the common name "butterfly rose." Even the foliage is exceptional, as the new growth is bronze in hue.

Sources: USA — A1, C2, H1

O ne of the oldest southern garden roses, this cultivar remains a favorite. The generosity of its bloom is partly responsible for this: 'Old Blush' is continuously in flower through all but the very coldest months. This rose is virtually indestructible and is commonly found lingering at abandoned homesites long after every other evidence of habitation is gone. Once established, it can withstand many weeks without irrigation or rain.

Borne in clusters, the medium-size lilac-pink flowers are slightly fragrant. If not deadheaded (snipped off as they wither), the flowers will produce large orange hips.

Sources: USA — C2, G1, G2; Canada — CaP2

Introducing

DAMASK ROSES

Fragrance is the outstanding characteristic of these roses. This quality is gratifying for the gardener, but it has also made the flowers an important commercial crop; they are the source of attar of roses, the basis of many perfumes and cosmetics. If the fragrance of damask roses is intense, however, their colors are typically delicate, ranging in hue from creamy whites through soft pinks, with just an occasional red. The size of the damask roses is also modest. The blossoms may measure no more than 1¾ in (3.4cm) across in the cultivars with the smallest blossoms, though 2½ to 3 in (6.4 to 7.6cm) is the average.

Legend has it that returning Crusaders brought home the first of this class of roses from the Syrian city of Damascus. Whatever the truth of that, the damask roses perform particularly well in the drier climates of the western United States. They are reliably hardy through USDA zone 5, and into zone 4, and make thorny, rangy shrubs that look most at home in informal settings. For example, the damask roses fit easily into the sunny edge of a woodland, where their tolerance for poorer soils and for partial shade allows them to flourish.

DAMASK ROSES

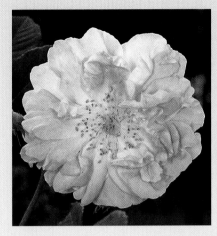

'Celsiana'

Habit: Upright, vigorous shrub, 4–5 ft (1.2–1.5m) tall

Bloom: One long early-summer bloom

Fragrance: Intense

Disease Resistance: Generally good, but can be prone to powdery mildew

Special Uses: Pillar, trellis, informal landscape

Hardiness: USDA zones 4–9, to zone 8 in Southeast; Canadian zone 5

Pedigree: Unknown; cultivated prior to 1750

This antique was supposed to be Dutch in origin and to have been introduced into France (then the rose capital of the world) in the mid-18th century by a Parisian nurseryman, Monsieur Cels. Whatever its background, this damask is an unusually elegant rose that bears semidouble, light pink flowers with silky, ruffled petals, pretty golden stamens, and a wonderful damask fragrance. The contrast of the flowers with the cool, gray-green foliage is particularly pleasing. Like most of the damasks, this rose makes a tall shrub with arching canes. One of the damasks that performs well in the upper part of the Southeast, 'Celsiana' needs encouragement — good soil and a sunny, airy spot — if it is to remain healthy through the summer there.

Sources: USA — AI, GI, R4; Canada — CaH2, CaP2

'Madame Hardy'

Habit: Upright, vigorous shrub, 6 ft (1.8m) tall

Bloom: Early summer

Fragrance: Good

Disease Resistance: Good

Special Uses: Specimen, pillar, fence; tolerates partial shade

Hardiness: USDA zones 4–9; Canadian zone 5

Pedigree: Hardy, 1832

'Rose de Rescht'

Habit: Mounded, vigorous shrub, 3 ft (.9m) tall

Bloom: Prolonged spring bloom, recurrent

Fragrance: Strong

Disease Resistance: Good

Special Uses: Small garden, container; tolerates shade

Hardiness: USDA zone 5; Canadian zone 4b

Pedigree: Ancient origin, possibly Persian; collected in the 1940s

Other Names: 'DeRescht'

In a particularly mild southern California winter, regional consultant Clair Martin warns, this rose may not experience enough chilling to produce any flowers the next spring. But, he adds, 'Madame Hardy' is worth waiting for.

This popular damask bears clusters of large, very double, fragrant white blooms, each with a green eye at its center. Aside from its flowering, this rose is remarkable for its adaptability. It grows well in the Southeast, has withstood temperatures of –32°F (–35.5°C) at the Minnesota Landscape Arboretum, and is one of the shrubs you'll find flourishing in abandonment in the ghost towns of the California gold country.

Sources: USA — C2, GI, R4; Canada — CaHI, CaH2, CaP2

Unlike its once-blooming relatives, this damask not only bears a large flush of flowers in late spring or early summer but also repeats with another surge of intensely perfumed flowers in fall. Opening fuchsia-crimson, the blossoms fade as they age to a soft lilac. The reblooming habit, combined with the compact size of the shrub and the old-fashioned charm of the flowers, makes 'Rose de Rescht' an unusual and useful rose. It's easy to tuck into tight corners to lend some old-rose charm to a small garden, and it furnishes a distinctive and appealing planting for a container, too.

Sources: USA — CI, R5, W2; Canada — CaHI, CaH2, CaP2

Introducing

FLORIBUNDA ROSES

"Cluster-flowered" is the official designation for this group of roses, and so they are. Floribundas bear vivid flowers in natural bouquets. Even as individual blossoms, these flowers can be impressive, ranging up to 5 in (12.7cm) in diameter in the largest cultivars. More commonly, though, they range from 3 to 4½ in (7.62–11.4cm) across, and there are some small-blossomed floribundas whose flowers measure no more than 1½–2½ in (3.8–5.1cm). Even the smaller-flowered floribundas are showstoppers when in full bloom, and these roses are superb for planting in massed bedding displays. Floribundas also make outstanding landscape shrubs and fit easily into the background of a flower border or bed.

Floribundas arose from crosses between polyantha roses *(see pp.123–125)* and hybrid teas *(see pp.92–98).* Although they have the hybrid teas' everblooming habit, they bear their flowers on neater, more rounded shrubs, and they also tend to be more cold tolerant. Midwest regional consultant Kathy Zuzek has found no hybrid teas that overwinter without protection at the Minnesota Landscape Arboretum (USDA zone 4), but a number of floribundas, such as 'Nearly Wild' *(see p.76)* will.

In general, floribundas perform well across the United States and southern Canada from USDA zone 5 (Canadian zone 6) south to zone 9. They prefer the dry climate of the West, however, and are a better choice for the Southwest than the Southeast. Some varieties are hardy to Canadian zone 5 where winter snow cover is permanent.

FLORIBUNDA ROSES

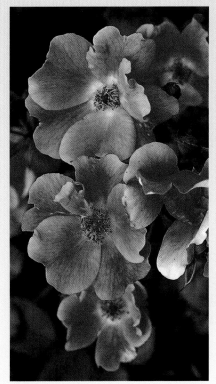

'Betty Prior'

Habit: Upright, bushy shrub, 3–4 ft (0.9–1.2m) tall

Bloom: Prolific bloomer, recurrent

Fragrance: Moderate

Disease Resistance: Good

Special Uses: Landscape, specimen

Hardiness: USDA zones 5–9; Canadian zone 6

Pedigree: D. Prior & Son, 1938; 'Kirsten Poulsen' × seedling

One of the first floribunda hybrids, 'Betty Prior' has maintained its popularity with its abundant clusters of fragrant, bright pink flowers. Single rounds of five petals, these blooms look like large dogwood blossoms, and they show off well against the glossy foliage. The simplicity of the flowers helps this rose to blend easily with perennials and annuals in a mixed border. 'Betty Prior' also works well as a foundation planting or hedge. Because this rose is disease resistant, the foliage typically remains unmarred by fungal infections. A heavy and reliable rebloomer, 'Betty Prior' is also outstandingly cold hardy for a floribunda.

Sources: USA — AI, CI, OI; Canada — CaH2, CaMI

FLORIBUNDA ROSES

'Escapade'®

Habit: Upright, spreading shrub, 2½–3 ft (.8–.9m) tall

Bloom: Prolific bloomer, recurrent

Fragrance: Slight

Disease Resistance: Good

Special Uses: Low hedge, landscape, specimen

Hardiness: USDA zones 5–9; Canadian zone 6

Pedigree: R. Harkness & Co., 1967; 'Pink Parfait' × 'Baby Faurax'

FLORIBUNDA ROSES

'Europeana'

Habit: Vigorous, rounded shrub, 3 ft (.9m) tall, 2 ft (.6m) wide

Bloom: Recurrent

Fragrance: Slight

Disease Resistance: Moderate

Other Interest: Glossy, bronze-green foliage

Hardiness: USDA zones 5–9; Canadian zone 6

Pedigree: deRuiter, 1963; 'Ruth Leuwerik' × 'Rosemary Rose'

The simple pink flowers of this rose, each with a white eye at its center, bear a familial resemblance to those of 'Betty Prior' but are fuller, with more petals, and they have a definite perfume. 'Escapade'® is also a reliable and generous rebloomer and a good source of cut flowers. Vigorous, hardy, and healthy, it has clean, glossy, light green foliage and a graceful spreading profile. This rose can serve as a landscape shrub, a foundation planting, or a low hedge, and it blends easily into a mixed border of flowers and other shrubs. It also makes excellent material for a flowering hedge.

Sources: USA — H1, V1; Canada — CaP1, CaP2

If red roses — true reds — are what you prefer, this is the floribunda for you. The flowers of 'Europeana' are large (up to 3 in [7.6cm] in diameter), full, and a clear crimson in color — just the thing to cut and give to someone special. Best of all, these blossoms are borne in natural bouquets, large clusters garnished with glossy, bronze-green foliage.

'Europeana' is as close to truly everblooming as you will find in a rose. If planted en masse in formal beds, as it often is, this shrub can be overwhelming when in full bloom. A more sophisticated effect can be achieved by setting plants out singly as a foundation planting, an accent in a flower border, or a container plant. If bold statements are your style, plant an informal hedge of 'Europeana'.

This rose is not immune to fungal diseases, so be sure to plant it in an open, sunny spot, and leave space around it for the air to circulate and blow away disease spores.

Sources: USA — C1, E1, W1; Canada — CaH2, CaP2

'French Lace'

Habit: Upright, bushy shrub, 4 ft (1.2m) tall

Bloom: Recurrent

Disease Resistance: Good

Special Uses: Specimen

Hardiness: USDA zones 7–9; Canadian zone 7

Pedigree: Warriner, 1980; 'Dr. A. J. Verhage' × 'Bridal Pink'

'Gene Boerner'

Habit: Upright, bushy shrub, slender habit, 4–5 ft (1.2–1.5m) tall

Bloom: Recurrent

Disease Resistance: Excellent

Special Uses: Hedge, specimen

Hardiness: USDA zones 5–9, good in Southeast; Canadian zone 6

Pedigree: E. S. Boerner, 1969; 'Ginger' × ('Ma Perkins' × 'Garnette Supreme')

This is a somewhat tender rose and is not reliably winter hardy north of USDA zone 7. In the milder climates of the Mid-Atlantic coast and the upper Southeast, however, 'French Lace' is a star. It is one of the half dozen roses that regional consultant Clair Martin of the Huntington Botanical Gardens in San Marino, California, recommends most highly for the Southwest.

Certainly, the flowers are spectacular. Double, pale apricot to creamy white, they have the elegant form of a classic hybrid tea. But the floribunda shows through in the flowers' abundance, for they appear in generous clusters of up to 12 blooms.

Sources: USA — BI, CI, OI; Canada — CaH2, CaP2

A classic among floribundas, 'Gene Boerner' bears large, medium pink flowers with the look of a hybrid tea, but they are denser, with 35 petals per bloom; this gives the blossoms a voluptuous beauty when fully open. This rose has an unusually tall and slender profile for a floribunda, making it an excellent choice for a narrow border space or a small backyard. It is also exceptionally tolerant of heat and humidity; Bill Welch *(see pp.23–25)* says that 'Gene Boerner' is utterly reliable even in central Texas, a region where intensely hot and humid summers are hard on floribundas.

Sources: USA — BI, DI, OI; Canada — CaPI, CaP2

'Iceberg'

Habit: Upright, bushy shrub, 4 ft (1.2m) tall

Bloom: Excellent recurrent bloom

Fragrance: Strong

Disease Resistance: Good disease resistance, but somewhat susceptible to blackspot

Other Interest: Virtually thorn-free

Special Uses: Hedge, standard (tree), specimen; moderately shade tolerant

Hardiness: USDA zones 5–9; Canadian zone 6

Pedigree: Kordes, 1958; 'Robin Hood' × 'Virgo'

Other Names: 'Schneewitchen', 'Fée de Neiges'

'Independence'

Habit: Midsize shrub, 3 ft (.9m) tall

Bloom: Intermittent rebloom

Fragrance: Moderate

Disease Resistance: Good

Other Interest: Purplish new growth

Hardiness: USDA zones 5–9; Canadian zone 6

Pedigree: Kordes, 1951; 'Baby Chateau' × 'Crimson Glory'

One of the most cold tolerant of the floribundas, this rose also performs well in the South, though a slight susceptibility to blackspot makes it less than an ideal choice for the Southeast. In the drier Southwest, however, regional consultant Clair Martin of the Huntington Botanical Gardens in San Marino, California, says that 'Iceberg' is one of the half dozen roses he recommends most highly as both easy and rewarding. Wherever you garden, the abundance and beauty of its blooms are likely to make 'Iceberg' irresistible. The double (30 petals), 3 in (7.6cm) flowers are pure white, very fragrant, and held in clusters above the semiglossy, light green foliage. 'Iceberg' makes an excellent plant for a winter-hardy hedge that will continue to bloom from late spring to fall — and into the winter in the South.

Sources: USA — BI, CI, OI; Canada — CaHI, CaRI

The brilliant orange-red blossoms of 'Independence' make a dramatic contrast to the bronze-purple color of the new growth, and the 4½ in (11cm) fragrant double flowers continue to show up well against the dark, glossy green of the mature leaves. Although the flowering may be more intermittent than that of other floribundas, this rose mounts a fine display when it does bloom, bearing its large and shapely blossoms in bunches of as many as 10 per cluster. The provenance of this rose is significant. It was bred by the German nurseryman Wilhelm Kordes, a master rosarian whose name is synonymous with hardy and healthy shrubs.

Sources: USA — VI

'Ma Perkins'

Habit: Upright shrub, 3 ft (.9m) tall

Bloom: Recurrent

Fragrance: Slight

Disease Resistance: Good

Special Uses: Specimen

Hardiness: USDA zones 5–9; Canadian zone 6

Pedigree: Boerner, 1952; 'Red Radiance' × 'Fashion'

'Margaret Merrill'®

Habit: Upright, vigorous, bushy shrub, 3½–4½ ft (1.1–1.4m) tall

Bloom: Exceptionally recurrent

Fragrance: Exceptional

Disease Resistance: Excellent

Special Uses: Specimen, hedge

Hardiness: USDA zones 5–9; Canadian zone 6

Pedigree: Harkness, 1978; 'Rudolph Timm' × 'Dedication' × 'Pascali'®

A vigorous, compact bush, this rose is as exciting now as it was when it first appeared on the market almost half a century ago. Its flowers are unusual for a floribunda: shell pink flushed with apricot and cream, they are deeply cupped, more like those of an old-time Bourbon rose in form than a typical floribunda. The blossoms are also fragrant, a virtue that is lacking in many other floribunda roses.

The foliage of this rose is a deep, glossy green, and the shrub itself, though vigorous, is compact. 'Ma Perkins' makes a useful accent for a border, an excellent container plant, and a handsome flowering hedge.

Sources: USA — R6

Considered by some to be the perfect floribunda, 'Margaret Merrill'® has large, fragrant, blush white double flowers (28 petals), which begin as hybrid tea–type buds and open very wide, singly and in clusters. These blossoms, which measure 4 in (10cm) across, are unusually large for a floribunda and powerfully fragrant, with a perfume that has been compared to citrus and spice. Although this rose shows some susceptibility to blackspot, it performs well even in a humid climate and is especially valuable as a source of cut flowers.

Sources: USA — C1, C2, O1; Canada — CaH2, CaP2

'Nearly Wild'

Habit: Compact, bushy shrub, 3–4 ft (0.9–1.2m) tall

Bloom: Recurrent

Fragrance: Moderate

Disease Resistance: Some susceptibility to blackspot

Special Uses: Border accent, container

Hardiness: USDA zones 4–9; Canadian zone 5

Pedigree: Brownell, 1941; 'Dr. W. Van Fleet' × 'Leuchstern'

'Sun Flare'

Habit: Low, compact shrub, 3 ft (.9m) tall

Bloom: Recurrent

Fragrance: Light

Disease Resistance: Slight susceptibility to blackspot, exceptional resistance to mildew

Other Interest: Glossy, deep green foliage

Hardiness: USDA zones 5–9; Canadian zone 6

Pedigree: William Warriner, 1981; 'Sunsprite' × seedling

A Rhode Island couple, Josephine and Walter Brownell, were pioneers in the quest for easy roses. Early in this century, at their nursery in Little Compton, they began intentionally breeding for cold-hardy, disease-resistant roses. 'Nearly Wild,' one of their later creations, is also one of their most successful. Like many of the Brownell roses, this one counts the hardy memorial rose, *Rosa wichuraiana,* among its ancestors, and it has inherited that rose's toughness. Yet 'Nearly Wild' makes a neat, bushy shrub. Its five-petaled flowers have the simplicity of a species rose, as the name suggests, but they are fully 2 in (5cm) across and borne in clusters of 15 to 25 throughout the season.

One of a very few floribunda roses that overwinter successfully without special protection at the Minnesota Landscape Arboretum, 'Nearly Wild' has shown a slight susceptibility to blackspot in the arboretum's tests. Its compact size makes this rose a good choice for a small garden, and it fits easily into a flower border or container planting.

Sources: USA — AI, CI, H3; Canada — CaCI, CaHI, CaH2

One of this rose's parents, 'Sunsprite', was a famous and popular rose. 'Sunflare' shares its parent's healthy, vigorous constitution, and the offspring's flowers are even more handsome. In fact, among the thousands of roses at the Huntington Botanical Gardens in San Marino, California, regional consultant Clair Martin says this is one of the half dozen cultivars he recommends most highly as an easy and rewarding rose.

Its buds have the pointed, scrolled form of the hybrid teas, and they open into broad, luminous yellow, double blossoms with a distinct scent of licorice. Borne in clusters of up to a dozen, the blossoms appear consistently throughout the season.

Sources: USA — BI, JI, RI; Canada — CaH2, CaPI

Introducing

GALLICA ROSES

The origin of these roses is lost in prehistory, but they seem to have inhabited northern European gardens for millennia. During the Middle Ages, they were fixtures of monastery gardens, where they were cultivated chiefly for their powerful perfume. The blossoms of some gallica roses even keep their fragrance when dried, and that made gallica petals a favorite ingredient of soaps and salves in an age when hygiene was poor and bad smells the rule.

Surely, though, the monks also favored gallica roses because they are so easy to grow. Blooming just once a year, in early summer, gallicas are extraordinarily cold hardy shrubs that could be relied on to overwinter without harm in a northern European winter; in North America, they are hardy to USDA zone 4 (Canadian zone 5). Because they require winter chilling, however, gallicas perform poorly in the warmer regions of the Southeast and Southwest.

The blossoms of the gallica rose are neat, densely packed rosettes that average 2½ to 3½ in (6.4 to 8.9cm) across, and the bushes themselves are compact, usually forming dense shrubs no more than 3½ ft (1.1m) tall. The gallicas' compact size helped them fit into the confined spaces of a cloister garden and makes them perfect for confined modern plots.

As a rule, gallica roses are disease and pest resistant, and they adapt easily to a variety of soils, appreciating good soils but also growing well in poorish, dry ones. They also tolerate a moderate degree of shade, though the blossoms lose the intensity of their hues in such situations.

GALLICA ROSES

'Belle de Crécy'

Habit: Upright, rounded shrub, 3–4½ ft (0.9–1.4m) tall

Bloom: Long, single season of bloom

Fragrance: Strong

Disease Resistance: Good

Other Interest: Bristly but virtually thornless canes, blue-green foliage

Special Uses: Specimen

Hardiness: USDA zones 4–8; Canadian zone 5

Pedigree: Roeser, prior to 1829

This is one of the most popular gallica roses, and deservedly so. The blossoms of 'Belle de Crécy' are large, flattened rosettes with a potent perfume; they open pink but soon deepen in hue to a mauve-violet with a green button center. This gives 'Belle de Crécy' a special interest: at any given time, a single shrub may bear blooms in shades of pink, mauve, and deep violet. In addition, the backs of the petals (what rosarians call the reverse) are a distinctly paler pink than the fronts, which gives these flowers an added delicacy.

A vigorous, midsize shrub, this rose makes good material for an informal hedge but also can hold its own as a specimen planting.

Sources: USA — AI, GI, WI; Canada — CaCI, CaHI, CaP2

GALLICA ROSES

'Belle Isis'

Habit: Compact, rounded shrub, 3 ft (.9m) tall

Bloom: One early-summer blossoming

Fragrance: Moderate

Disease Resistance: Good

Other Interest: Bristly but thornless canes, gray-green foliage

Special Uses: Border, specimen

Hardiness: USDA zones 4–8; Canadian zone 5

Pedigree: Parmentier, 1845

GALLICA ROSES

'Camaieux'

Habit: Upright, rounded shrub, 3–4 ft (0.9–1.2m) tall

Bloom: One early-summer blossoming

Fragrance: Strong

Disease Resistance: Good, but susceptible to mildew in warm, humid climates

Other Interest: Ornamental hips, few thorns

Special Uses: Specimen, border accent

Hardiness: USDA zones 4–8; Canadian zone 5

Pedigree: Vibert, c. 1830

This compact shrub bears loose little saucers of petals with a strong fragrance but a delicate coloration. In contrast to most other gallicas, whose flowers tend toward intense pinks and purplish reds, 'Belle Isis' has pale cream flowers that seem brushed with coral pink and even a hint of lemon yellow.

This shrub's tidy profile makes it a good choice for smaller gardens, and it fits into a perennial border without overwhelming its neighbors. At the Minnesota Landscape Arboretum, 'Belle Isis' has proven both reliably winter hardy and virtually disease free.

Sources: USA — G3, H1, V1; Canada — CaC1, CaP2

In the early 19th century, there was a fashion for striped and spotted roses, and the French nurseryman J. P. Vibert was something of a specialist in that sort of flower. 'Camaieux' is one of his most interesting creations, a rose with the exquisite appeal of cloisonné. Every petal in the strongly fragrant, double blooms of 'Camaieux' seems deliberately placed to create a perfect, flattened round. The blossoms open blush white with even, deep pink stripes, then fade to white striped with mauve-purple. This striking coloring and the shrub's neat, compact habit make this an unusual specimen worthy of a place of prominence in the garden.

Sources: USA — G3, R2, R4; Canada — CaC1, CaH2, CaP2

'Cardinal de Richelieu'

Habit: Upright, compact shrub, 3–4 ft (0.9–1.2m) tall

Bloom: One early-summer blossoming

Fragrance: Strong

Disease Resistance: Good, slight susceptibility to blackspot

Special Uses: Specimen, cut flower

Hardiness: USDA zones 4–8; Canadian zone 5

Pedigree: Laffay, 1840

'Hippolyte'

Habit: Arching shrub, 6 ft (1.8m) tall, 4 ft (1.2m) wide

Bloom: One early-summer blossoming

Fragrance: Moderate

Disease Resistance: Good

Other Interest: Almost thornless

Special Uses: Pillar, fence

Hardiness: USDA zones 4–8; Canadian zone 5

Pedigree: Origin unknown, possibly early 19th century

Other Names: 'Souvenir de Kean'

Some rosarians argue that the "Cardinal" is not pure gallica. They see a trace of China in the smooth, shiny foliage. Certainly, though, this rose is pure gallica in its flowers. There is a dark purple hue among gallicas that is found in no other roses, and the blossoms of 'Cardinal de Richelieu' are the finest examples of this coloration. They make a strong and unusual contrast in a garden bed or as cut flowers, and the individual blossoms show nicely against the shrub's dark green leaves. Small wonder that this tough, medium-size shrub is one of the most commonly planted of all gallica roses. This rose has survived several winters without any injury at the Central Experimental Farm, Ottawa, in northern Canadian zone 5.

Sources: USA — A1, H4, R5; Canada — CaC1, CaH2, CaP2

This rose's small, neat, wine purple flowers have an exquisite, antique precision; they look almost like zinnias but smell far too sweet. The blossom color is most intense when 'Hippolyte' is grown in a semishaded spot. Unlike most gallicas, 'Hippolyte' produces long, flexible canes that can be trained horizontally along a fence or wound up around a post. Left untrained, this shrub is not a good choice for a formal design, but it is a star in a cottage-type planting where the arching canes can spill outward with all their natural grace.

The namesake of this rose is the Amazon Queen Hippolyta, and it is similarly sturdy as well as beautiful. It's a survivor — one of those roses that collectors find flourishing in abandoned gardens.

Sources: USA — M2, R4; Canada — CaH2, CaP2

Introducing

GRANDIFLORA ROSES

A miscellaneous class of roses, the grandifloras were created by crossing hybrid tea roses with floribundas. The results have been uneven, but the best of the grandifloras bear their flowers in clusters like their floribunda parents, whereas the individual blossoms preserve the elegant form of a hybrid tea. Grandifloras are also more consistent in their blossom size than are the floribundas, for their flowers measure within a range of 3–4½ in (7.6–11.4cm) in diameter.

As shrubs, the size and vigor of the grandifloras have varied widely from cultivar to cultivar — those included here are time-tested favorites that have shown themselves to be outstanding, reliable garden shrubs. In general, they flourish wherever hybrid teas do, which means that grandifloras are best reserved for the Southwest, Northwest, Mid-Atlantic states, and those parts of the Rocky Mountain West, the Midwest, and the Northeast where winter temperatures do not drop below –10°F (–23° C) — USDA zone 6 and southward. In Canada they thrive only in the southeast and the coastal regions of the maritime provinces and British Columbia.

Grandifloras are likely to prove disease prone in the Southeast's combination of heat and humidity, though they should remain healthier at the higher altitudes of the upper South.

GRANDIFLORA ROSES

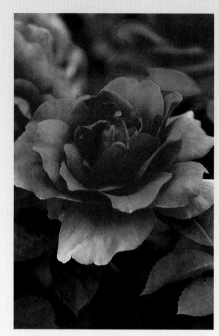

'Earth Song'

Habit: Upright, bushy shrub, 4–5 ft (1.2–1.5m) tall

Bloom: Abundant, recurrent bloom

Fragrance: Moderate

Disease Resistance: Good

Special Uses: Hedge

Hardiness: USDA zones 5–9; Canadian zone 6

Pedigree: Buck, 1975; 'Music Maker' × 'Prairie Star'

The late Dr. Griffith Buck bred roses specifically for disease resistance and cold hardiness, and in 'Earth Song' he achieved a remarkable success. Although regional consultant Donna Fuss in Hartford, Connecticut, describes grandifloras as one of the least reliable classes of roses in her area, she makes an exception for 'Earth Song', which is one of her most outstanding performers. 'Earth Song' has overwintered successfully for almost a decade at the Minnesota Landscape Arboretum, where winter temperatures regularly drop to –30°F (–34°C). Often the cold there has killed back its canes, but because grandifloras flower best on new growth, 'Earth Song' bounces back from such natural pruning to flower satisfactorily by early the following summer.

Its blossoms open into classic high-centered hybrid tea buds, then spread their petals into large 4–4½ in (10–11.5cm) cups of rich red. The foliage is handsome, too: dark and glossy.

Sources: USA — H4, K1, R5

'Love'

Habit: Upright, sparsely branched shrub, 3–4 ft (0.9–1.2m) tall

Bloom: Recurrent, long flowering season

Fragrance: Very slight

Disease Resistance: Good

Special Uses: Specimen, excellent cut flower

Hardiness: USDA zones 5–9; Canadian zone 6

Pedigree: Warriner, 1980; seedling × 'Redgold'

'Pearlie Mae'

Habit: Compact shrub, 3 ft (.9m) tall

Bloom: Recurrent

Fragrance: Moderate

Disease Resistance: Good

Special Uses: Specimen, border accent, cut flower

Hardiness: USDA zones 5–9; Canadian zone 6

Pedigree: Buck, 1981; 'Music Maker' × ('Queen Elizabeth'® × 'Country Music')

This is one of just two grandiflora roses that regional consultant Donna Fuss in Hartford, Connecticut, recommends for planting in her part of New England. Her garden, however, lies at the northern edge of this rose's range.

Actually, 'Love' is a grandiflora that could easily pass for a hybrid tea. It is a compact shrub that bears high-centered buds resembling those of a hybrid tea. These buds open into bright red blooms with a flamboyant difference: the back of each petal is silvery pink, giving the blossoms of 'Love' a hand-painted look.

Sources: USA — H5, J1, O1; Canada — CaH1, CaH2

Another one of Griffith Buck's hardy, prairie-bred roses, this shrub was named for the singer Pearl Bailey, and appropriately so, for 'Pearlie Mae' is a fine performer and a real trouper. Of vigorous growth and with a tendency to sprawl, this bushy grandiflora bears deep pink buds in clusters of one to eight that open to 4 in (10cm) blossoms of golden yellow tinged with salmon. The leathery green foliage is dark olive green and persistently healthy, making this a fine choice for a specimen shrub or accent shrub in a flower border. 'Pearlie Mae' is also an outstanding source of cut flowers.

Sources: USA — H1, H4, K1, R5; Canada — CaP2

GRANDIFLORA ROSES

'Queen Elizabeth'®

Habit: Upright, vigorous shrub, 5–7 ft (1.5–2.1m) tall

Bloom: Abundant, recurrent bloom

Fragrance: Moderate

Disease Resistance: Excellent

Special Uses: Border, excellent cut flower

Hardiness: USDA zones 5–9; Canadian zone 6

Pedigree: Lammerts, 1954; 'Charlotte Armstrong' × 'Floradora'

This was the founding rose of its class, the very first grandiflora, and it remains one of the best. 'Queen Elizabeth'® sets a high standard for any kind of rose, with its disease resistance, hardiness, and abundant, almost continuous bloom. Its large, double, medium pink flowers appear singly or in small clusters and range in form from high-centered to cupped. Because all the flowers in a cluster commonly open at once, this shrub is also a convenient source of cut flowers: a single bush of 'Queen Elizabeth'® can fill a vase. A tall, narrow shrub, 'Queen Elizabeth'® should be set at the back of a border so that it won't block the view.

Sources: USA — BI, DI, EI; Canada — CaH2, CaP2

HYBRID MUSK ROSES

Old-rose fanciers in the North use the hybrid musks to extend the flowering season of their gardens, because although the hybrid musks have the hardiness and everblooming habit of modern roses, their modest, softly shaded blossoms are closer in style to those of centuries past, and their musk perfume has a delicate antique flavor.

In fact, this class is a latecomer that dates only to the turn of this century. It originated with a cross of a repeat-blooming but cold-sensitive Noisette rose *(see pp.120–122)* with a hybrid of the tough and hardy Chinese species *Rosa multiflora.* The offspring inherited the Noisette's smaller recurrent flowers, but it has the adaptability of a multiflora.

Indeed, few classes of roses are as adaptable, for the hybrid musks flourish in the Southeast and Southwest yet also overwinter successfully as far north as USDA zone 4 (Canadian zone 5). The hybrid musks are not spectacular plants (the blossoms range in size from ¾ to 3 in [1.9 to 7.6cm]), but they are dependable and useful in every region included in this book. Because their stems are long and flexible, they may be trained along a fence or pruned back from time to time to form a lanky shrub.

'Ballerina'

Habit: Compact, arching shrub, 4–5 ft (1.2–1.5m) tall and wide

Bloom: Recurrent bloom

Fragrance: Slight

Disease Resistance: Good

Other Interest: Few thorns, ornamental hips

Special Uses: Hedge, climber; tolerates partial shade

Hardiness: USDA zones 4–9; Canadian zone 5

Pedigree: Bentall, 1937

'Cornelia'

Habit: Vigorous, arching shrub, 6–8 ft (1.8–2.4m) tall, taller if trained as a climber

Bloom: Recurrent

Fragrance: Moderate

Disease Resistance: Good

Special Uses: Specimen, climber; tolerates alkaline soils, partial shade

Hardiness: USDA zones 5–9; Canadian zone 6

Pedigree: Pemberton, 1925

A good rose for mild climates, 'Ballerina' also flourishes in the North. At the northern edge of its range, winter cold may kill it back almost to the ground, but typically it will send up new shoots to provide a good show of flowers the following summer.

'Ballerina' bears abundant, large trusses of small, pink, single flowers, each with a white eye and bright yellow stamens. It can be grown in a mixed border or as a hedge, allowed to cascade over a wall, or even trained as a climber, producing clouds of blossoms all season, followed by small, bright orange hips in the fall.

Sources: USA — AI, BI, R4; Canada — CaHI, CaH2, CaP2

Northern winters (at least through USDA zone 5) will not bother this rose, nor will southern summers. The long, arching canes of 'Cornelia' spread gracefully to make a large, attractive shrub, or they can be tied in while still young and trained along a fence or over an arch. If restrained by an annual pruning after the end of the first flush of blossoms, this rose will make a mound 5 ft (1.5m) high and wide. As a climber, its canes may reach several feet more. In June, 'Cornelia' covers itself with clusters of small, very double and fragrant, apricot-pink flowers with gold stamens. The bloom continues well into fall.

Sources: USA — AI, C2, R2; Canadian — CaH2, CaP2

'Danaë'

Habit: Vigorous, arching shrub, 5 ft (1.5m) tall and wide, taller if trained as a climber

Bloom: Recurrent, good fall flowering

Fragrance: Strong

Other Interest: Ornamental hips; dark, shiny foliage

Special Uses: Pillar, fence, informal hedge; tolerates partial shade

Hardiness: USDA zones 5–9; Canadian zone 6

Pedigree: Pemberton, 1913; 'Trier' × 'Gloire de Chedane-Guinoiseau'

'Lavender Lassie'

Habit: Vigorous, very upright shrub, 5–6 ft (1.5–1.8m) tall, 8–10 ft (2.4–3.0m) if trained as a climber

Bloom: Abundantly recurrent

Fragrance: Strong

Special Uses: Hedge, specimen, climber; tolerates partial shade

Hardiness: USDA zones 5–9; Canadian zone 6

Pedigree: Kordes, 1960

Its dark, shiny foliage provides an elegant setting for the little egg-yolk yellow flower buds of 'Danaë'. These open into clusters of creamy, 2 in (5cm), semidouble flowers with delicately ruffled petals. Their strong scent is described as a combination of fruit and musk. This rose makes a wonderful show in the fall, with its combination of repeat bloom and orange-red hips.

Though hardy in the North and in southern Canada, this rose is an outstanding performer in warmer climates. It does especially well in the Southeast, where its canes may reach a length of 12 ft (3.6m). In the South, it is also shade tolerant, flourishing with only a couple of hours of full sun daily.

Sources: USA — A1, C2, H1; Canada — CaH2, CaP2

While not exactly lavender, the semidouble, strongly scented flowers of this hybrid musk do have definite overtones of blue mixed in with the pink, and the large clusters in which they appear make them even more striking.

Few roses bloom as well as this one in a semishaded spot. With occasional pruning, 'Lavender Lassie' can be maintained as a large shrub or as an informal hedge, but its canes can also be left to grow unchecked and trained vertically up a wall or trellis.

Sources: USA — A1, H1, J2; Canada — CaH2, CaP2

Introducing

HYBRID PERPETUAL ROSES

Throughout the second half of the 19th century, hybrid perpetuals reigned supreme in North American rose gardens, and they remained the rose of choice until they were knocked off their pedestal by those glamorous newcomers, the hybrid teas.

Unfortunately, the hybrid perpetuals share the hybrid teas' essential flaw: in their pursuit of large, glamorous blossoms and repeat bloom, the breeders of the hybrid perpetuals too often ignored the quality of their creations as garden shrubs. Still, among the 3,000-odd types of hybrid perpetual roses released onto the market in the last century, some are not only beautiful when in bloom but also make healthy, hardy, shapely shrubs.

None, however, is truly "perpetual" blooming, as the name would have you believe. Actually, hybrid perpetual roses bloom heavily in the spring and again in the fall, with just a trickle of flowers during the intervening months. As a rule, the flowers are large, ranging from 3 to 5 in (7.6–12.7cm) in diameter, with a few cultivars bearing giant blossoms 6–7 in (15.2–17.8cm) across. The hybrid perpetual blossoms are also full and fragrant, and at their best these flowers are among the most spectacular of any roses. Their color ranges from white to pink, rose, carmine, and scarlet; there are no true yellows or oranges in this class.

Cold hardy to USDA zone 5 (Canadian zone 6), hybrid perpetuals will usually overwinter even in USDA zone 4, though there the canes are likely to be killed back to the snow line. They grow well as far south as USDA zone 8; however, they are prone to fungal diseases where the summers are very hot.

HYBRID PERPETUAL ROSES

'Baronne Prévost'

Habit: Upright shrub, 4 ft (1.2m) tall, 3 ft (.9m) wide

Bloom: Heavy late-spring to early-summer flowering with occasional repeat

Fragrance: Strong

Disease Resistance: Moderate

Special Uses: Container

Hardiness: USDA zones 4–8; Canadian zone 5

Pedigree: Desprez, 1842

Though sometimes troubled by blackspot and mildew, 'Baronne Prévost' is possibly the most disease resistant of the hybrid perpetuals. For this reason, it is one of the few that flourish in the humid Southeast. Because this rose is also notably cold tolerant, it is a good choice for areas such as the lower Northeast and Mid-Atlantic states, where a hard winter may be followed by a summer of heat and humidity, and for southern Ontario.

Its blossoms are luxurious: broad, flattened, pink rosettes with a button eye at the center. While not quite as big as those of 'Paul Neyron', the blossoms of 'Baronne Prévost' are borne more prolifically. This old-time aristocrat flowers heavily in late spring or early summer, then sporadically throughout the summer, with a heavier repeat in autumn. This is a tough shrub, one that works well in a mixed border of flowers and shrubs.

Sources: USA — A1, G3, H3, R1, R4, S2, V1; Canada — CaH2, CaP2

'Mabel Morrison'

Habit: Upright, vigorous shrub, 4–5 ft (1.2–1.5m) tall

Bloom: Good mid-season bloom with fall repeat bloom

Fragrance: Moderate

Disease Resistance: Good

Special Uses: Border accent, cut flower; tolerates a range of soils

Hardiness: USDA zones 5–8; Canadian zone 6

Pedigree: Broughton, 1878; sport of 'Baroness Rothschild'

'Paul Neyron'

Habit: Vigorous, upright shrub, 4–6 ft (1.2–1.8m) tall

Bloom: Recurrent

Fragrance: Moderate

Disease Resistance: Somewhat susceptible to powdery mildew

Special Uses: Specimen, border accent, hedge; tolerates poor soils

Hardiness: USDA zones 5–8; Canadian zone 6

Pedigree: Levet, 1869; 'Victor Verdier' × 'Anna de Diesbach'

The hybrid perpetuals tend to be tall and ungainly shrubs, but this relatively compact cultivar with its healthy, handsome foliage is a happy exception. 'Mabel Morrison' is not a common rose, but it is one that deserves to be better known. Its large cupped blossoms are extraordinary; they look almost like outsize water lilies. Opening a pale blush pink, the flowers then fade to a pure white throughout most of the season, though fall may turn them a deeper tinge of pink. Pleasantly perfumed, these blossoms make wonderful cut flowers. 'Mabel Morrison' also makes a good addition to a mixed border of flowers and shrubs, especially since it flourishes in a variety of soils.

Sources: USA — R1, R4, R5; Canada — CaP2

'Paul Neyron' is a giant among roses: it bears what may be the largest flowers of any rose in cultivation. The fragrant, rich pink, tousled blooms may measure 7 in (18cm) across, and they are exhibited proudly atop strong, upright canes. Even the leaves of this rose, which are large, glossy green, and bold, are remarkable.

This vigorous shrub needs room in which to flex its muscles. 'Paul Neyron' makes a strong statement at the back of a mixed border of flowers and shrubs and works well as a flowering hedge.

Sources: USA — A1, G1, R5; Canada — CaH1, CaH2, CaP2

Introducing

HYBRID RUGOSA ROSES

If any roses ever deserved the label "easy," surely it is the rugosas. Indeed, in the northern half of the United States, these roses set the standard against which all others are measured.

The ancestor of this class is a central Asian species, *Rosa rugosa*. This is a rose that can withstand Siberian winters and temperatures as low as −50° F (−45°C). In addition to its tolerance for cold, this shrub is also extraordinarily tolerant of salt and dry soil and has escaped from cultivation to colonize beaches throughout New England.

The best rugosa hybrids have inherited not only their wild ancestor's hardiness but also its glossy, furrowed foliage. This is almost completely immune to fungal diseases, and because rugosas are notably pest resistant, they are perfect for those who hate to spray.

Rugosas bloom throughout the summer, bearing clove-scented midsize flowers that commonly run 2½–3½ in (6.4–8.9cm) across, though a few may spread to 4 in (10.2cm). This display is followed by a fall show of enormous, tomato red hips that contrast boldly with the yellow, reddish, or purplish foliage.

These dense, suckering, thorny shrubs make excellent hedges and are ideal landscape shrubs for windy and exposed sites. The compact cultivars integrate easily into a flower border and when massed serve as a handsome ground cover.

Carefree and reliable throughout Canada and in the Northeast, Midwest, Rocky Mountain West, and Northwest regions of the United States, hybrid rugosas are less satisfactory in the Southwest and Southeast, where they thrive only at higher altitudes or in less humid coastal regions.

HYBRID RUGOSA ROSES

'Fimbriata'

Habit: Upright shrub, 4 ft (1.2m) tall and wide

Bloom: Recurrent

Fragrance: Strong

Disease Resistance: Outstanding

Other Interest: Wrinkled, light green foliage

Special Uses: Specimen, hedge, woodland planting; tolerates wide range of soils, partial shade

Hardiness: USDA zones 2–8; Canadian zone 2b

Pedigree: Morlet, 1891; *R. rugosa* × 'Mme. Alfred Carriere'

Other Names: 'Dianthiflora', 'Phoebe's Frilled Pink'

The blossoms of this shrub do not look like those of the typical rugosa; in fact, they do not look like roses at all, but instead resemble pale pink carnations. But 'Fimbriata' is a typical rugosa in its toughness, for this shrub tolerates not only extreme cold but also poor soils and light shade. It isn't just disease resistant; it's virtually disease free.

The spicily perfumed blossoms, clean foliage, and dense, relatively compact growth make 'Fimbriata' an excellent accent in a perennial border. Its hardiness and adaptability make this shrub a good choice for the northern gardener with a challenging site.

Sources: USA — R1, R4; Canada — CaC1, CaH1, CaP2

'Frau Dagmar Hartopp'

Habit: Upright, vigorous, spreading shrub, 3–4 ft (0.9–1.2m) tall and wide

Bloom: Recurrent

Fragrance: Moderate

Disease Resistance: Outstanding

Other Interest: Ornamental hips, colorful autumn foliage

Special Uses: Low hedge, border accent

Hardiness: USDA zones 2–8; Canadian zone 2b

Pedigree: Hastrup, 1914

Other Names: 'Frau Dagmar Hastrup', 'Fru Dagmar Hastrup'

This compact rugosa is an ideal candidate for a smaller garden. Its clove-scented, light pink, single flowers open to reveal knots of golden stamens at their centers, and they recur throughout the summer. Indeed, this rose is seldom out of bloom through the warm-weather months and usually is heavily laden with flowers. In fall, the flowers give way to large, tomato red hips as the leaves turn orange or yellow. To ensure a good crop of hips and the best autumn display, plant another rugosa rose such as the species type *Rosa rugosa alba* or *R. rugosa rubra* nearby, as cross-pollination increases the fruit production of 'Frau Dagmar Hartopp'.

Sources: USA — AI, CI, R4; Canada — CaCI, CaHI,CaMI, CaP2

'Hansa'

Habit: Upright, vigorous, vase-shaped shrub, 7 ft (2.1m) tall and wide

Bloom: Recurrent, long flowering season

Fragrance: Strong

Disease Resistance: Outstanding

Other Interest: Ornamental hips; wrinkled, glossy green foliage

Special Uses: Hedge

Hardiness: USDA zones 2–8; Canadian zone 2b

Pedigree: Schaum and Van Tol, 1905

Hansa' is a large, vigorous rugosa with very thorny canes. It creates an effective barrier hedge, but you may find it too attractive to relegate to the edges of the garden, for this rose also makes a fine specimen in the herb garden. 'Hansa' is particularly compatible with herbs because, unlike most roses, it thrives in the dry, sandy soils that most herbs prefer. Yet 'Hansa' doesn't object to a richer soil, and it flourishes well in the perennial border. Its large, double, reddish purple flowers have a strong, spicy scent, bloom freely through the season, and in fall are followed by large, orange-red hips. The foliage is typically wrinkled and glossy green.

Sources: USA — C2, R4, R7; Canada — CaCI, CaHI, CaP2

'Henry Hudson'

Habit: Low, bushy shrub, 3 ft (.9m) tall, 4 ft (1.2m) wide

Bloom: Recurrent

Fragrance: Moderate

Disease Resistance: Outstanding

Special Uses: Hedge

Hardiness: USDA zones 2–8; Canadian zone 2b

Pedigree: Svejda, 1976; 'Schneezwerg' seedling

'Jens Munk'

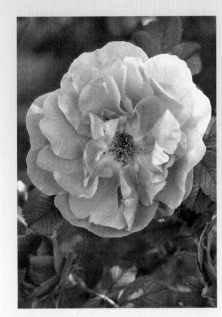

Habit: Dense, bushy shrub, 5 ft (1.5m) tall and wide

Bloom: Recurrent

Fragrance: Strong

Disease Resistance: Outstanding

Special Uses: Landscape, hedge

Hardiness: USDA zones 2–8; Canadian zone 2b

Pedigree: Svejda, 1974; 'Schneezwerg' × 'Frau Dagmar Hartopp'

One of the many fine roses introduced by Agriculture Canada, 'Henry Hudson' can be counted on for hardiness and color. Its flowers are large, semidouble, and white with a tuft of golden stamens at the center throughout most of the summer, though fall's cooler weather may stain them with a touch of pink. The fragrance of the flowers is classic rugosa: a spicy clove perfume. The foliage is also typical of the class — small to midsize and deeply furrowed.

This dense, low-growing shrub is a perfect choice for a long-blooming hedge that requires no trimming, but it also holds its own quite successfully as a specimen shrub. Like all the Agriculture Canada introductions, 'Henry Hudson' roots readily from cuttings and grows well on its own roots.

Sources: USA — CI, KI, R4; Canada — CaCI, CaH2

Another hybrid from Agriculture Canada, 'Jens Munk' has the same toughness and recurrent bloom as 'Henry Hudson', but with large, double blooms of a clear medium pink. Gilding the center of each rose is a knot of threadlike golden stamens. As an additional attraction, 'Jens Munk' offers a strong, spicy perfume. The foliage is medium green and clean. This rose is quick to establish itself after transplanting, soon forming a substantial, well-rounded shrub even in a challenging site. Its only flaws are a susceptibility to stem girdler (see p.204) and a paucity of hips. Despite these drawbacks, 'Jens Munk' makes a fine specimen plant as well as a tall and sturdy hedge.

Sources: USA — AI, OI, R4; Canada — CaCI, CaPI

'Linda Campbell'

Habit: Upright, bushy shrub, 3–5 ft (0.9–1.5m) tall

Bloom: Abundantly recurrent

Disease Resistance: Excellent

Special Uses: Hedge

Hardiness: USDA zones 4–8; Canadian zone 5

Pedigree: Moore, 1990; 'Anytime' × 'Rugosa Magnifica'

Other Names: 'Tall Poppy'

'Max Graf'

Habit: Vigorous, low-growing shrub, 2 ft (.6m) tall, 10 ft (3m) wide

Bloom: One midsummer flowering

Fragrance: Light

Disease Resistance: Excellent

Special Uses: Ground cover, planting on banks

Hardiness: USDA zones 2–8; Canadian zone 2

Pedigree: Bowditch, 1919; (probably *Rosa rugosa* × *R. wichuraiana*)

This compact shrub was created by crossing a hybrid rugosa with a miniature rose; fortunately, 'Linda Campbell' inherited its rugosa parent's disease resistance and cold hardiness. Unlike most red rugosa roses, whose flowers generally tend toward mauve or purplish, 'Linda Campbell' has pure red blossoms. Borne in large, impressive sprays throughout the summer and into the fall, these flowers are cupped and double; their only defect is a lack of fragrance. The foliage is dark green and semiglossy, and the shrub is bushy and upright. This is a first-rate rose for a hedge or for use as a landscape shrub, foundation planting, or specimen shrub.

Sources: USA — CI, KI, R4; Canada — CaHI, CaH2

Although the single pink flowers of 'Max Graf' are somewhat modest-looking, they are borne in large clusters rather late in the season, when most other roses are past the peak of their first flush of blooms. 'Max Graf' has been widely used as a low-maintenance ground cover along highways and in urban areas, where it thrives in the most miserable growing conditions. Given the more friendly conditions found in the average garden, the large, dark green, slightly glossy leaves provide an elegant backdrop for other plantings or the shrub's own blossoms.

Sources: USA — AI, RI, R4; Canada — CaCI, CaH2, CaP2

'Rotes Meer'

Habit: Vigorous, low-growing shrub, 3 ft (.9m) tall and wide

Bloom: Abundant, recurrent

Fragrance: Moderate

Disease Resistance: Excellent

Other Interest: Ornamental hips

Special Uses: Border, low hedge

Hardiness: USDA zones 3–8; Canadian zone 4

Pedigree: Baum, 1984

Other Names: 'Purple Pavement'

'Snow Owl'

Habit: Vigorous, low-growing shrub, 3–4 ft (0.9–1.2m) tall and wide

Bloom: Recurrent

Fragrance: Moderate

Disease Resistance: Outstanding

Other Interest: Ornamental hips

Special Uses: Low hedge, border

Hardiness: USDA zones 3–8; Canadian zone 3

Pedigree: Uhl, 1989

Other Names: 'Schnee Eule', 'White Pavement'

Whether as 'Rotes Meer' or 'Purple Pavement', this new rugosa is winning an increasing following. It refutes a long-standing criticism of the rugosa hybrids that however hardy they might be, they are simply too large to fit into smaller gardens or even the more intimate areas of larger landscapes. 'Rotes Meer', however, makes a dense, neat dome just 3 ft (.9m) high and wide and is compact enough for even a postage-stamp garden. It serves equally well as a border accent, a compact landscape shrub, or material for a low hedge. The foliage is clean and crisp, and the fragrant, double, deep violet-crimson flowers with contrasting golden stamens are borne more or less continuously throughout the summer and into the fall. Indeed, its autumn display may be its most remarkable, for new flowers continue to open even as the red hips fatten and ripen.

Sources: USA — CI, R4, R7; Canada — CaH2, CaP2

Snow Owl' is the fragrant, white-flowered sibling of 'Rotes Meer'. It has the same compact growth, and it is well covered with foliage, dense and spreading. It produces flat, 3 in (7.5cm), semidouble (10–15 petals) blooms freely throughout the season. In autumn, the blossoms give way to attractive orange-scarlet hips.

Both 'Snow Owl' and 'Rotes Meer' belong to a series of roses called the "pavement roses," which were developed for roadside plantings. To succeed in such a situation, these roses had to demonstrate a tolerance for both heat and intense cold, as well as for drought, poor soils, and salt spray. These characteristics make the pavement roses outstanding choices not only for planting along a sidewalk or driveway but also for seaside gardens and for the demanding climate of the Upper Midwest and southern prairies and high-altitude regions of the Rocky Mountain West.

Sources: USA — JI, RI, R4; Canada — CaH2

HYBRID RUGOSA ROSES

'Thérèse Bugnet'

Habit: Vigorous, upright shrub, 6–7 ft (1.8–2.1m) tall, 5 ft (1.5m) wide

Bloom: Recurrent

Fragrance: Moderate

Other Interest: Rich fall leaf color

Special Uses: Specimen, hedge; tolerates partial shade

Hardiness: USDA zones 2–8; Canadian zone 2b

Pedigree: Bugnet and P. H. Wright, 1950; (*Rosa acicularis* × *R. rugosa kamtschatica*) × (*R. amblyotis* × *R. rugosa plena*) × 'Betty Bland'

This Canadian rose has the hardiness one expects of a rose that thrives practically up into the Canadian North. But 'Thérèse Bugnet' offers much more than just persistence. It bears clusters of pointed, deep pink buds in spring that open into bouquets of large, ruffled, double flowers of bright lilac-pink. After a prolonged first flush of flowers, this rose reblooms at a more modest pace, but reliably, until the end of the growing season. Its crop of hips is sparse, but 'Thérèse Bugnet' offers as consolation a fine fall foliage show, as its blue-green foliage turns a rich red. Regional consultant Trevor Cole says this is a good choice for gardeners in the upper Great Plains states and Canada. It is incredibly hardy, flowers for weeks, and is friendly as a cut flower because the upper part of the stems is almost thornless.

Sources: USA — A1, C2, G1; Canada — CaC1, CaH1, CaP2

HYBRID TEA ROSES

Ironically, the hybrid teas' excessive popularity is their main defect. Because they are routinely planted in situations where they cannot succeed, they have developed a reputation for unreliability.

A fairer assessment would be to categorize the hybrid tea roses as the thoroughbreds of the garden: they can put on a breathtaking performance, but only on their own turf. Hybrid tea roses should be planted only where winter temperatures do not drop below −10°F (−23°C), in USDA zone 6 (Canadian zone 6) and southward, and they should not be planted in regions where summers combine heat and humidity.

Basically, these are roses for the southwestern United States, the less humid parts of the Mid-Atlantic region, the milder sections of the Rocky Mountain West, the Midwest, the Northeast, the Pacific Northwest, and coastal British Columbia. But a few hybrid teas grow and bloom well even in the upper Southeast — though these are not the ones you will customarily find at the local garden center.

The principal virtue of the hybrid teas is the perfection of their long-stemmed, high-centered blossoms. Averaging 4–5 in (10.2–12.7cm) in diameter, these may in exceptional cases run as small as 3½ in (8.9cm) or as large as 5½ in (14cm). They are the classic florist roses, and with good reason. As shrubs, the hybrid teas tend to be twiggy and somewhat ungainly, so ingenuity is required to work them into the garden.

'Alec's Red'®

Habit: Vigorous, upright shrub, 4 ft (1.2m), may reach 7 ft (2.1m) in warm climates

Bloom: Recurrent

Fragrance: Heavy

Disease Resistance: Good

Other Interest: Medium green foliage

Special Uses: Specimen, espalier; tolerant of poorer soils

Hardiness: USDA zones 6–9; Canadian zone 6

Pedigree: Alexander M. Cocker, 1970; 'Fragrant Cloud' × 'Dame de Coeur'

O ne of the common criticisms of hybrid tea roses is that their flowers lack fragrance. 'Alec's Red'® proves that this isn't necessarily true. Its heavily scented flowers are crimson to cherry in color and very large, up to 6 in (15cm) across, and full (45 petals). Stockier than most hybrid teas, this rose can, with some attention to pruning, make a fine border specimen, especially in cool climates where the growth tends to be more compact. In warmer regions, its upright, vigorous growth makes it best suited to training against a wall or up a fence or pillar.

Sources: USA — G2, R1, R3; Canada — CaC1, CaP1, CaP2

'Chrysler Imperial'

Habit: Upright, compact shrub, 4–6 ft (1.2–1.8m) tall

Bloom: Recurrent

Fragrance: Strong

Disease Resistance: Good, but prone to mildew in cool, wet climates

Special Uses: Cut flower

Hardiness: USDA zones 6–9; Canadian zone 6

Pedigree: Dr. W. E. Lammerts, 1952; 'Charlotte Armstrong' × 'Mirandy'

T his rose created a sensation in 1952, and more than four decades later, it remains one of the best of its class. Its 4½–5 in (11.5–12.8cm) blossoms are double and deep red, with a velvety sheen and a strong citrus scent. Superb in a mixed border, 'Chrysler Imperial' also excels as a source of cut flowers.

This rose is best suited to regions with temperate winters and warm, dry summers, though regional consultant David Earl Bott notes that it is a favorite in Utah too. Where summers are cool, not only is 'Chrysler Imperial' prone to mildew, but the blossoms can take on an unattractive purplish tone.

Sources: USA — A1, B1, C1; Canada — CaH2, CaP1

'Double Delight'™

Habit: Upright, bushy, spreading shrub, 3½–4 ft (0.9–1.2m) tall

Bloom: Recurrent

Fragrance: Spicy

Disease Resistance: Prone to mildew in cool, wet climates

Other Interest: Red-tinted new foliage

Special Uses: Border accent, long-lasting cut flower

Hardiness: USDA zones 6–9; Canadian zone 6

Pedigree: Swim and Ellis, 1977; 'Granada' × 'Garden Party'®

Other Names: 'ANDeli'

'Folklore'®

Habit: Tall, vigorous, upright shrub, 6–8 ft (1.8–2.4m) tall

Bloom: Recurrent bloom extending into late fall

Fragrance: Strong

Disease Resistance: Good

Other Interest: Glossy green foliage

Special Uses: Hedge

Hardiness: USDA zones 6–9; Canadian zone 6

Pedigree: Kordes, 1977; 'Fragrant Cloud' × seedling

This is a chameleon hybrid tea: its buds open creamy white with a strawberry edge, but then its petals gradually darken to all red. The flowers have a spicy scent and reappear throughout the season. They make long-lasting cut flowers.

Because its flowers are so striking — gaudy, some would say — this is not the easiest rose to integrate into a garden design, but 'Double Delight'™ does make an eye-catching accent in the landscape, and it is one of the best-performing hybrid tea roses in the Southeast.

Sources: USA — BI, CI, OI; Canada — CaH2, CaP2

Breeding vigor and toughness into its roses without sacrificing beauty has long been a specialty of the German nursery Wilhelm Kordes Söhne, and 'Folklore'® is a fine example of this art. Its tall, semiclimbing habit makes 'Folklore'® an excellent choice for a tall hedge or barrier, and its tendency to bloom later than most hybrid teas (with good repeat in the fall) extends the rose season. The blossoms are large, double, and very fragrant, and the pale undersides lend a dramatic note of contrast to the orange-pink of the petals.

Sources: USA — CI, EI, OI; Canada — CaH2, CaRI

'Helen Traubel'

Habit: Vigorous shrub, 3–4 ft (0.9–1.2m) tall

Bloom: Recurrent

Fragrance: Moderate

Disease Resistance: Good

Special Uses: Hedge

Hardiness: USDA zones 6–9; Canadian zone 6

Pedigree: Herbert Swim, 1951; 'Charlotte Armstrong' × 'Glowing Sunset'

'Mister Lincoln'®

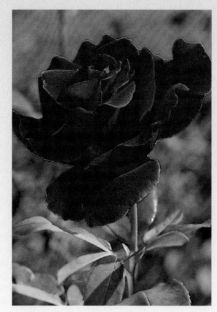

Habit: Upright, vigorous shrub, 4½–5½ ft (1.4–1.8m) tall

Bloom: Recurrent, good all-season bloom

Fragrance: Strong

Disease Resistance: Good

Special Uses: Cut flower

Hardiness: USDA zones 5–9; Canadian zone 6

Pedigree: Herbert Swim and O. L. Weeks, 1964; 'Chrysler Imperial' × 'Charles Mallerin'

This is an unusually adaptable rose for a hybrid tea, and although it originated in California, it grows well in cool as well as hot climates. 'Helen Traubel' sports huge (5–6 in [12.7–15.2cm]), double, pink and apricot flowers on a tall, vigorous plant with leathery, matte green foliage. The only defect is that the flowers tend to have "weak necks" — that is, the stems are slender, so the blossoms nod rather than stand stiffly erect. This habit is graceful in the landscape, but it makes 'Helen Traubel' flowers poor material for cutting and arranging. Nevertheless, this is one of the half dozen rose cultivars that regional consultant Clair Martin of the Huntington Botanical Gardens in San Marino, California, recommends most highly to southwestern gardeners in search of easy and rewarding roses.

Sources: USA — H5, R1, R6

For many rose lovers, 'Mister Lincoln'® defines the long-stemmed red rose, and for more than 30 years this cultivar has remained a favorite. An unusually consistent bloomer, this dark red hybrid tea provides a long season of large (5–6 in [12.7–15.2cm]), double flowers with a strong perfume. Supposed to be somewhat prone to mildew in cool climates and shady spots, 'Mister Lincoln'® is one of the hybrid teas that perform well in the Southeast. Regional consultant David Earl Bott also recommends it as an excellent choice for the Rocky Mountain states.

Sources: USA — B1, B3, C1; Canada — CaH2, CaP1

'Olympiad'™

Habit: Upright, compact shrub, 4–5 ft (1.2–1.5m) tall

Bloom: Recurrent, good all-season bloom

Fragrance: Slight

Disease Resistance: Good

Other Interest: Very thorny stems, olive green foliage

Special Uses: Hedge, excellent cut flower

Hardiness: USDA zones 5–9; Canadian zone 6

Pedigree: Sam McGredy, 1982; 'Red Planet' × 'Pharaoh'

Other Names: 'Olympia', 'Olympiade'

'Pascali'®

Habit: Upright shrub, 5 ft (1.5m) tall, 2½ ft (.8m) wide

Bloom: Recurrent

Fragrance: Light

Disease Resistance: Excellent

Special Uses: Cut flower, mixed border

Hardiness: USDA zones 6–9; Canadian zone 6

Pedigree: Lens, 1963; 'Queen Elizabeth'® × 'White Butterfly'

Other Names: 'Blanche Pasca', 'Lenip'

The official flower of the 1984 Los Angeles Olympic Games, this rose is as impressive a performer as any of the athletes at those games, for it thrives in such disparate climates as southern California and coastal New England. This cultivar's brilliant medium red, double flowers have an especially velvety texture. If you protect yourself from its thorns, you will find 'Olympiad'™ to be an excellent source of long-lasting cut flowers. Its thorniness, however, makes it an unusually secure barrier when planted as a hedge.

Sources: USA — B1, D1, O1; Canada — CaH2, CaP2

Many gardeners consider this to be the very finest white rose, and, in fact, 'Pascali'® was voted the world's favorite rose of any color in 1991. Certainly, 'Pascali'® makes an outstanding contribution to a mixed border of shrubs and flowers and is an excellent source of long-lasting cut flowers. Its green-tinged buds are of the classic hybrid tea type, and they open in a display of lightly fragrant, pure white blossoms that persists more or less continuously throughout the growing season.

The disease and pest resistance of 'Pascali'® is outstanding for a hybrid tea, but like nearly all of its class, this rose is somewhat susceptible to blackspot; plant it in an airy spot with full sun.

Sources: USA — C1, E1, R6, W1; Canada — CaH2, CaP2

HYBRID TEA ROSES

'Peace'

Habit: Upright, vigorous shrub, 4–5 ft (1.2–1.5m) tall

Bloom: Recurrent, abundant all-season bloom

Fragrance: Slight

Disease Resistance: Good

Hardiness: USDA zones 5–9; Canadian zone 6

Pedigree: Meilland, 1945; ('George Dickson' × 'Souv. de Claudius Pernet') × ('Joanna Hill' × 'Charles P. Kilham') × 'Margaret McGredy'

Other Names: 'Madame Antoine Meilland', 'Gloria Dei', 'Gioia'

HYBRID TEA ROSES

'Radiance'

Habit: Upright shrub, 4–6 ft (1.2–1.8m) tall

Bloom: Recurrent

Fragrance: Strong

Disease Resistance: Good

Other Interest: Large orange hips

Special Uses: Landscape specimen; once established, tolerates poor soil, drought

Hardiness: USDA zones 6–9; Canadian zone 6

Pedigree: Hook and Henderson, 1908; 'Enchanter' × 'Cardinal'

Other Names: 'Pink Radiance'

The story of this rose is pure melodrama. It was bred in France in the last years before World War II, and escaped as unnamed cuttings in the last American diplomatic bag to leave the country before the Nazi conquest. Recognized as a winner, the rose was propagated by an American nursery and released in 1945. Because it returned with the peace to a liberated France, that was the name the rose was given. Later, the 'Peace' rose decorated all the tables at the organizational meeting of the United Nations.

Amazingly, this flower has lived up to all the promotional bally-hoo. Its flowers are lush, large and double, pale yellow edged with rose-pink. Vigorous, healthy, and hardy throughout most of the range of the hybrid teas, 'Peace' has demonstrated some susceptibility to blackspot in the Southeast.

Sources: USA — BI, CI, OI; Canada — CaH2, CaP2

For those hybrid tea admirers who are searching for hardier roses within this class, often the older, less inbred cultivars are the best choices. 'Radiance' is a case in point. Dating back to the turn of the century, you will find this rose flourishing in abandoned or neglected gardens and old cemetery plantings, even in the Southeast. Once it has its roots established well, it tolerates both poor and dry soils, and it will still furnish a generous crop of large, double, soft pink flowers. These have an old-fashioned look that make 'Radiance' a good choice for people restoring older gardens. A well-formed shrub, this rose also offers an old-fashioned damask rose perfume.

Sources: USA — AI, VI

'Schwarze Madonna'®

Habit: Midsize shrub, 3–4 ft (0.9–1.2m) tall

Bloom: Recurrent

Disease Resistance: Exceptional

Special Uses: Cut flower, specimen

Hardiness: USDA zones 6–9; Canadian zone 6

Pedigree: Kordes, 1992

Other Names: 'Barry Fearn'

'Touch of Class'™

Habit: Upright, vigorous shrub, 4–5 ft (1.2–1.5m) tall

Bloom: Recurrent, excellent all-season bloom

Fragrance: Slight

Disease Resistance: Good

Other Interest: Dark green, semiglossy foliage

Special Uses: Cut flower

Hardiness: USDA zones 5–9; Canadian zone 6

Pedigree: Kriloff, 1984; 'Micaëla' × ('Queen Elizabeth'® × 'Romantica')

Other Names: 'Maréchal le Clerc'

The first aspect of this rose on which every new owner remarks is the intense dark red of the blossoms, which make a striking addition to any planting. Gradually, though, the gardener comes to appreciate that 'Schwarze Madonna'® has another, more practical virtue: it is extraordinarily disease resistant. Actually, this rose is remarkably carefree and exceptionally adaptable for a hybrid tea, flourishing in the North and South, East and West. It comes with the highest recommendation of Northeast regional consultant Donna Fuss, the rosarian at Hartford, Connecticut's Elizabeth Park Rose Garden, who admits that her region's combination of winter cold and summer heat and humidity can be challenging for hybrid tea roses.

Sources: USA — G2, R1; Canada — CaH2, CaP1

This rose is a favorite among rosarians, who win ribbons at rose shows with its perfectly formed, high-centered blossoms. But though it is a star performer, it is not a prima donna. In fact, 'Touch of Class'™ makes a good garden plant and comes with a strong recommendation from regional consultant David Earl Bott as an outstanding rose for the Rocky Mountain West and from regional consultant Clair Martin as one of the best for southwestern gardens. It flowers consistently throughout the season, bearing large, double, medium pink blooms shaded with coral and cream. Only in fragrance is it somewhat lacking: 'Touch of Class'™ offers only a slight perfume.

Sources: USA — B1, D1, O1; Canada — CaH2, CaP1

Introducing

MINIATURE ROSES

When the first miniature roses appeared early in the 18th century, they were prized as curiosities. In recent years, however, miniature roses have been playing an increasingly important role in the garden, enabling roses to appear in all sorts of new applications.

The term miniature is relative; shrubs of this class range in height from a few inches to 18 in (45cm), while climbing miniatures may extend their canes several feet. The perfectly formed blossoms, which are commonly of the hybrid tea type, range in size from ½ to 2 in (1.3–5.0cm) across.

For the owners of small gardens, these dwarf roses have obvious advantages. But the miniatures also make a handsome edging for a larger bed, and they fit neatly into a window box or hanging basket. They fit the scale of a rock garden, and the climbing types work well as ground covers.

Despite the delicacy of their appearance, the miniatures can be quite hardy. Tolerance for cold varies from cultivar to cultivar, but in general the miniature roses overwinter without protection through USDA zone 5 and Canadian zone 6. Even in colder regions, these low-profile shrubs often survive the winter without damage if buried under an insulating blanket of snow or covered with evergreen boughs. Their ability to nestle into the still spot at the foot of a wall, where they will escape dehydrating winds, makes miniatures a good choice for the desert Southwest.

MINIATURE ROSES

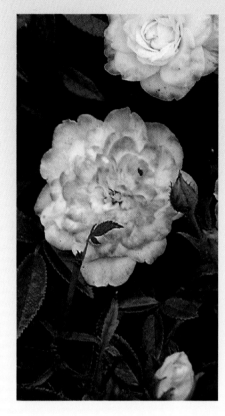

'Cinderella'

Habit: Upright, vigorous shrub, 8–10 in (20–25cm) tall

Bloom: Recurrent

Fragrance: Strong

Disease Resistance: Good

Other Interest: Thornless

Special Uses: Border, rock garden, container

Hardiness: USDA zones 5–9; Canadian zone 6

Pedigree: de Vink, 1953; 'Cécile Brünner' × 'Tom Thumb'

A truly miniature rose, 'Cinderella' grows on a scale small enough to fit into the crevices of a rock garden and is at home in a hanging basket or window box. The full, double blossoms are officially described as white, but in fact they have a rosy blush to them when they open and then pale as they age. Like the other popular classes of everbloomers, the miniature roses are often lacking in fragrance, but 'Cinderella' is an exception, for its blossoms have a robust, spicy perfume.

This rose's diminutive stature should not discourage the owners of large properties from including it in their plantings. Used as an edging or set in the front of a flower border, 'Cinderella' has no trouble holding its own.

Sources: USA — B2, C2, N1; Canada — CaH1, CaK1

'Gourmet Popcorn'

Habit: Upright, rounded shrub, 18–24 in (45–60cm) tall

Bloom: Recurrent

Fragrance: Moderate

Disease Resistance: Good

Special Uses: Landscape, border, container

Hardiness: USDA zones 4–9; Canadian zone 5

Pedigree: Desmero, 1986; sport of 'Popcorn'

'Green Ice'

Habit: Vigorous, lax shrub, 8 in (20cm) tall, 16 in (40cm) wide

Bloom: Recurrent

Fragrance: Light

Disease Resistance: Good

Special Uses: Climber, container

Hardiness: USDA zones 5–9; Canadian zone 6

Pedigree: Moore, 1971; (*Rosa wichuraiana* × 'Jet Trail') × 'Floradora'

The flowers of 'Gourmet Popcorn' are semidouble and pure white with golden centers — just like kernels of buttered popcorn, in fact — and they are borne in large clusters throughout much of the growing season. This is an excellent compact border or landscape shrub with very disease-resistant dark green foliage. It is also exceptionally cold hardy, and Midwest consultant Kathy Zuzek reports that gardeners in Excelsior, Minnesota, overwinter 'Gourmet Popcorn' without any artificial protection; the rose's small stature allows it to hide beneath the natural insulation of a blanket of snow. Yet it also performs well in Louisiana, according to Southeast consultant Peter Haring.

Sources: USA — B1, C1, G1; Canada — CaHI

Green flowers provide an arresting accent for the flower garden, especially when they are as shapely as the blossoms of 'Green Ice'. Its pointed buds open into high-centered, fully double, white blooms that mimic in miniature the classic form of the hybrid tea. Though they open icy white, they gradually darken to a pleasing soft green. The foliage is attractive, too: delicate and glossy.

This shrub's lax habit of growth lends itself to training along a low wall or fence, but it also shows to good advantage when displayed in a hanging basket. 'Green Ice' fits easily into a rock garden and makes an unusual edging plant. For a bolder statement, mass several plants together.

Sources: USA — B2, C2, N1; Canada — CaHI

'Jean Kenneally'™

Habit: Upright shrub, 24–30 in (60–75cm) tall, 12 in (30cm) wide

Bloom: Recurrent

Fragrance: Moderate

Disease Resistance: Good

Special Uses: Border, container

Hardiness: USDA zones 5–9; Canadian zone 6

Pedigree: Bennett, 1984; 'Futura' × 'Party Girl'

'Jeanne Lajoie'

Habit: Vigorous, long-caned shrub, 5–8 ft (1.5–2.4m) tall

Bloom: Profuse, recurrent

Fragrance: Moderate

Disease Resistance: Good

Special Uses: Climber, hedge, specimen, container

Hardiness: USDA zones 5–9; Canadian zone 5b

Pedigree: Sima, 1975; ('Casa Blanca' × 'Independence') × 'Midget'

This miniature comes highly recommended by regional consultant David Earl Bott of Utah as a healthy, reliable rose for the Rocky Mountain West. 'Jean Kenneally'™ bears hybrid tea–shaped, double, apricot blooms, singly and in clusters, repeatedly throughout the summer and into the fall. These flowers are lightly scented and make excellent cut flowers.

Tall and robust for a miniature, 'Jean Kenneally'™ adapts well to a container, but it can also serve as a compact shrub in the landscape at large. It makes an exceptionally beautiful low flowering hedge, and several plants can be massed together to give it a stronger presence in a mixed planting of shrubs and flowers. Like most miniatures, 'Jean Kenneally'™ also works well as an edging.

Sources: USA — B2, J2, N1; Canada — CaHI

Considered by many to be the best climbing miniature rose, 'Jeanne Lajoie' has earned an outstanding review from regional consultant David Earl Bott of Utah. Aside from its vigor and good health, this rose is remarkable for the sheer number of its flowers; though individually small, as a group they cover the bush at the peak of its bloom. 'Jeanne Lajoie' keeps reblooming, too, throughout the growing season. The blossoms are markedly fragrant, a quality that is too often lacking among miniatures.

This rose can be cultivated as a beautiful, long-blooming low hedge or trained up a trellis or fence as a climber. If allowed to sprawl, it makes a most attractive ground cover.

Sources: USA — B2, J2, N1; Canada — CaHI

'Kristin'™

Habit: Bushy shrub, 24–30 in (60–75cm) tall

Bloom: Recurrent

Fragrance: Slight

Special Uses: Cut flower, border, container

Hardiness: USDA zones 5–9; Canadian zone 5b

Pedigree: Benardella, 1992

Other Names: 'Kristen', 'Pirouette'

'Minnie Pearl'™

Habit: Upright shrub, 10–14 in (25–35cm) tall

Bloom: Recurrent

Fragrance: Slight

Disease Resistance: Good

Special Uses: Border, container, edging, cut flower

Hardiness: USDA zones 5–9; Canadian zone 6

Pedigree: Saville, 1982; ('Little Darling' × 'Tiki') × 'Party Girl'

This is another miniature rose that has received commendations from growers in both North and South; it is a favorite of regional consultants Donna Fuss in central Connecticut and Peter Haring in Louisiana. The carmine-tipped white blossoms are long-lasting and borne one to a stem, making this an excellent source of very refined cut flowers.

Like many others of the more recent introductions, this miniature rose is a more robust shrub than the midgets of years past. In fact, 'Kristin'™ is the equal of many polyantha roses in size, and like them it should be regarded as a compact landscape shrub. It also makes an exceptional accent for a flower border, as 'Kristin'™ won't tower over its neighbors.

Sources: USA — B2, J2, M3, N1; Canada — CaH1

This versatile miniature can serve as an outstanding border or edging shrub, and its small but perfectly formed blossoms make striking cut flowers. It comes with the endorsement of regional consultant David Earl Bott of Utah as a hardy and rewarding rose.

Comfortable in a container or a window box, this rose, like the other miniatures, is perfectly suited to the needs of gardeners with small properties. 'Minnie Pearl'™ is also an excellent rose for older gardeners who find conventional roses too much of a strain on their backs: by planting this particularly compact miniature into a pot and setting it up on a waist-high wall or other support, they can take the stooping out of their rose cultivation.

Sources: USA — B2, J2, N1

'Nozomi'

Habit: Prostrate shrub, 2 ft (.6m) tall, 6 ft (1.8m) wide

Bloom: One prolonged annual flowering

Fragrance: Slight

Other Interest: Plum-colored new foliage, maturing to a dark, glossy green

Special Uses: Container, climber, border

Hardiness: USDA zones 5–9; Canadian zone 6

Pedigree: Onodera, 1968; 'Fairy Princess' × 'Sweet Fairy'

'Red Cascade'

Habit: Vigorous, prostrate shrub, 12–18 ft (3.6–5.5m) canes

Bloom: Profuse, recurrent, long blooming season

Fragrance: Slight

Disease Resistance: Good

Special Uses: Climber, container, weeping shrub; tolerates poor soils, partial shade

Hardiness: USDA zones 6–9; Canadian zone 6

Pedigree: Moore, 1976; (*Rosa wichuraiana* × 'Floradora') × 'Magic Dragon'

Although its foliage and flowers are diminutive, this rose's canes are long, so it is classed as a climbing miniature. The flowers, which are borne in abundant clusters throughout most of the summer, are single, pearly pink, and star-shaped.

A spreading habit makes 'Nozomi' appropriate for display in a hanging basket, cascading over a wall, or climbing a trellis or other support. It can also be allowed to weave itself through perennials in a mixed border, and when grafted as a standard, it makes a superb tree rose. Though hardy enough for northern gardens, 'Nozomi' also flourishes in the Southeast.

Sources: USA — A1, H3, R4; Canada — CaH2, CaP2

To class a 15 ft (4.5m) rose as a miniature seems ridiculous, but 'Red Cascade' is diminutive in everything but the length of its canes. The leaves are small, leathery, and dark green, and the flowers, which measure just an inch (2.5cm) across, are a dark, rich red. This rose is outstandingly vigorous: fast-growing and in bloom virtually all season, it thrives even in less than ideal circumstances. It's equally effective as a cascading shrub or climbing a pillar or fence. Regional consultant Peter Haring, who gardens in Louisiana, recommends this rose as a ground cover, a suggestion that northern gardeners can try too.

Sources: USA — A1, B2; Canada — CaH1

Introducing

MODERN SHRUB ROSES

This is a class of roses defined by what they aren't: roses that are too large to be miniatures, are short to be climbers, and don't belong to any of the other rose classes end up in this one. To generalize about this miscellaneous class would be foolish, since among these shrubs of diverse parentage there are examples of almost every imaginable kind of rose. That, however, is the great attraction of the shrub roses: in this botanical grab bag, you are sure to find something suited to your garden.

Here, too, is where you will find the experiments of imaginative rose breeders. Many of the best of Griffith Buck's "prairie roses" are classified as modern shrub roses, as are the ultrahardy roses bred by Agriculture Canada and the exciting new English roses being bred by the brilliant British nurseryman David Austin.

For the gardener's convenience, these shrubs have been grouped according to provenance, so all of David Austin's English Roses are presented together. As always, there are family resemblances, and chances are if you like one David Austin, Dr. Griffith Buck, or Agriculture Canada rose, you will want to look at others.

MODERN SHRUB ROSES

'Alchymist'

Habit: Upright shrub, 6 ft (1.8m) tall

Bloom: Profuse flowering in early summer with little or no recurrence

Fragrance: Medium

Disease Resistance: Excellent, though some susceptibility to blackspot

Other Interest: Glossy, bronze-green foliage, red-tinted new growth

Hardiness: USDA zones 5–9; Canadian zone 6

Pedigree: Kordes, 1956; 'Golden Glow' × *Rosa eglanteria* hybrid

The breeder of this rose didn't start with lead, but he did produce true gold, something the old-time alchemists could only dream of. Tall and rangy, 'Alchymist' may be grown as a shrub or a fountain of arching canes, or it can be tied in as a climber to shinny up a pillar. The flowers, as the name suggests, have golden overtones, but the yellow is mixed with apricot to give the blossoms a luscious warmth. The flowers are quartered — the petals arranged in a cruciform — which gives them an old-fashioned look, and the shrub behaves like an antique, flowering heavily in early summer but very little or not at all subsequently. Like all the Kordes shrubs, this one is notably cold hardy.

Sources: USA — A1, C1, R1, R7, S2; Canada — CaH2, CaP2

'Basye's Blueberry'

Habit: Erect shrub, 6–8 ft (1.8–2.4m) tall

Bloom: Recurrent

Fragrance: Moderate

Disease Resistance: Good

Other Interest: Thornless, good fall leaf color

Special Uses: Landscape, specimen, hedge

Hardiness: USDA zones 5–9; Canadian zone 6

Pedigree: Robert Basye, 1982

'Flower Carpet Pink'™

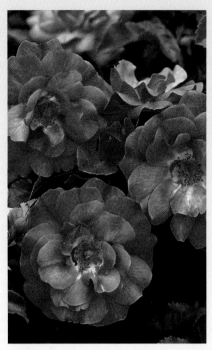

Habit: Low, spreading shrub, 2½ ft (.8m) tall, 3 ft (.9m) wide

Bloom: Recurrent, long flowering season

Fragrance: Moderate

Disease Resistance: Good

Other Interest: Outstanding fall leaf color

Special Uses: Hedge, ground cover, border accent, container, hanging basket

Hardiness: USDA zones 4–10; Canadian zone 4

Pedigree: Noack, 1989; 'Immensee'® × 'Amanda'

Other Names: 'Blooming Carpet', 'Emera', 'NOAtraum'

If you're tired of pruning thorny branches, this modern shrub rose is for you. Its rounded leaves, thornless stems, and reddish fall color give it the look of a blueberry bush. The difference lies in the flowers: 'Basye's Blueberry' bears large, fragrant, pink, semidouble flowers with bright yellow stamens repeatedly throughout the growing season.

Though it is hardy well into the North, 'Basye's Blueberry' was bred in central Texas by the late Dr. Robert Basye of Texas A&M University, and it flourishes in that region's heavy clay, alkaline soils. An outstanding shrub for the Southeast, it should prove a good choice for the Southwest and Rocky Mountain West, too.

Sources: USA — AI

When this rose was introduced onto the market, it was trumpeted as "the environmental rose," a shrub that flourished without the protection of sprays. In fact, it is a hardy, reliable rose where the weather is cool. In the Southeast, however, it is not immune to blackspot and mildew, and it grows best with some protection from the afternoon sun.

Where it likes the climate, 'Flower Carpet Pink'™ is a terrific shrub to use as a low hedge or ground cover or to combine with perennials in a mixed border. It bears 1½ in (3.8cm) wide, deep pink, semidouble blooms in clusters of 15–25 flowers well into the fall. These late flowers show up vividly against this rose's autumn foliage of red and bronze.

Sources: USA — CI, KI, R4

'Golden Wings'

Habit: Upright, vigorous shrub, 5–6 ft (1.5–1.8m) tall

Bloom: Early, recurrent bloom

Fragrance: Slight

Disease Resistance: Good

Special Uses: Landscape, climber

Hardiness: USDA zones 3–8; Canadian zone 3

Pedigree: Shepherd, 1956; 'Soeur Thérèse' × (*Rosa spinosissima altaica* × 'Ormiston Roy')

'Assiniboine'

Agriculture Canada Rose

Habit: Upright shrub, 4 ft (1.2m) tall, 3 ft (.9m) wide

Bloom: Abundant midseason bloom, intermittent repeat

Fragrance: Slight

Disease Resistance: Outstanding

Other Interest: Glossy foliage

Special Uses: Landscape; tolerates summer drought and heat, as well as cold

Hardiness: USDA zones 3–7; Canadian zone 3b

Pedigree: Marshall, 1962; 'Donald Prior' × *Rosa arkansana*

Golden Wings' has long been considered a valuable landscape shrub because of its hardiness, disease resistance, and recurrent bloom. One of the first roses to bloom in spring, it attracts the foraging honeybees with its 2½–3 in (6.5–7.5cm), pale yellow, five-petaled disks. These flowers are highly fragrant, and the knots of saffron-colored stamens at their centers give them a special interest. The light green foliage is notably disease resistant but may prove susceptible to blackspot in humid climates.

Attractive as a large, upright shrub, 'Golden Wings' can also be trained to climb a wall or run along a split-rail fence.

Sources: USA — C1, G3, R4; Canada — CaH1, CaP1

This is a rose for northern gardeners, especially Canadians of the prairie provinces, who can claim this introduction from the Morden Research Station in Manitoba as one of their own. 'Assiniboine' doesn't need to appeal to patriotism, however, for gardeners south of the border will be just as appreciative of this hardy, healthy, reliable shrub that survives intense cold unprotected. Its only fault (if it can be called one) is that the rebloom is intermittent; this shrub blooms in surges rather than continuously. While not as showy as the blossoms of the typical hybrid tea, the flowers are definitely worth waiting for. They are large, semidouble, and wine red.

Sources: Canada — CaH2

'Champlain'

Agriculture Canada Rose

Habit: Compact shrub, 3 ft (.9m) tall and wide

Bloom: Reliably recurrent

Fragrance: Light

Disease Resistance: Resistant to mildew and blackspot

Other Interest: Attractive, fine-textured foliage, exceptional resistance to insect pests

Special Uses: Hedge, mixed border, specimen; exceptionally cold tolerant

Hardiness: USDA zones 3–7; Canadian zone 3

Pedigree: Svejda, 1982; (*Rosa kordesii* × seedling) × ('Red Dawn' × 'Suzanne')

'Morden Blush'

Agriculture Canada Rose

Habit: Upright, compact shrub, 3–4 ft (0.9–1.2m) tall

Bloom: Abundant, recurrent

Disease Resistance: Good

Special Uses: Hedge, landscape, specimen, border accent; tolerates summer drought and heat, as well as cold

Hardiness: USDA zones 3–7; Canadian zone 2b

Pedigree: Colicutt and Marshall, 1988; ('Prairie Princess' × 'Morden Amorette') × ('Prairie Princess' × ['White Bouquet' × {*Rosa arkansana* × 'Assiniboine'}])

Canadian consultant Trevor Cole favors this shrub above all others of the Canadian explorer series, and it's easy to see why. 'Champlain' is not only extraordinarily hardy, it's also a remarkably generous shrub, producing clusters of rich, velvety red blossoms nearly continuously from early summer until the first hard frost of fall. Each of these blossoms is a doubled cup of petals with a tuft of golden stamens at the center. This rose would be a winner even if it weren't so disease resistant and tough. Its only fault, if this is indeed a fault, is that this shrub is slow to make new growth, and is not an outstandingly vigorous grower.

A bit freer in its flowering than some of the other Morden roses, this shrub bears sprays of 2–3 in (5–7.5cm), flattened, double flowers throughout the summer. Despite its name, the flower color is more like the *recovery* from a blush: the blossoms of 'Morden Blush' open a light peach-pink, then fade to ivory. The foliage is matte green and generally healthy, though in humid eastern summers it may show some susceptibility to blackspot. This shrub's low, compact growth, hardiness, and recurrent bloom have earned it a place in smaller gardens and in cold climates, but it's also popular in larger, warmer gardens as well.

Sources: USA — CI, HI, KI, MI, OI, RI, R4, R7; Canada — CaCI, CaH2, CaP2

Sources: USA — HI, JI, R4; Canada — CaHI, CaH2, CaP2

'Morden Ruby'

Agriculture Canada Rose

Habit: Dense shrub, 3½ ft (1.1m) tall, 5 ft (1.5m) wide

Bloom: Abundant, recurrent

Fragrance: Slight

Disease Resistance: Good

Special Uses: Hedge, landscape; tolerates summer drought and heat, as well as cold

Hardiness: USDA zones 2–7; Canadian zone 2

Pedigree: Marshall, 1977; 'Fire King' × ('J. W. Fargo' × 'Assiniboine')

This shrub outdoes itself in early summer with a heavy crop of flowers, then settles in to bloom at a more moderate rate through the rest of the summer and into the fall. The blossoms, which are borne in clusters of 5–10, are large (3 in [7.5cm] in diameter on average), very double, and, as the name suggests, ruby red. Their fragrance is only slight.

'Morden Ruby' makes an imposing shrub with a spreading habit even in adverse climates. In Minnesota Landscape Arboretum trials, it reached a height of 3½ ft (1m) and a width of 5 ft (1.5m). All in all, this is an outstanding shrub for a landscape specimen or a flowering hedge in a cold, exposed site.

Sources: USA — KI, MI, R4; Canada — CaCI, CaH2

'Carefree Beauty'™

Dr. Griffith Buck Rose

Habit: Upright, spreading shrub, 5 ft (1.5m) tall, 3 ft (.9m) wide

Bloom: Recurrent

Fragrance: Moderate

Disease Resistance: Excellent

Special Uses: Hedge, landscape; tolerates summer drought and heat, as well as cold

Hardiness: USDA zones 4–8; Canadian zone 4

Pedigree: Buck, 1977; seedling × 'Prairie Princess'

This is the best known of the hardy "prairie roses" that Griffith Buck bred at Iowa State University. His goal was to combine cold tolerance with disease resistance and abundant flowering. 'Carefree Beauty'™ is an outstanding success in all three areas. Regional consultant Donna Fuss of Elizabeth Park Rose Garden in Hartford, Connecticut, recommends it to gardeners because, as she says, it "looks like what most people think a rose should look like" and yet is disease resistant and winter hardy even in New England. This rose bears large (4½ in [11.5cm]), fragrant, semidouble, light rose flowers in clusters on vigorous canes, and blooms into the fall to bear an attractive crop of hips.

Sources: USA — CI, MI, R4, R7; Canada — CaH2, CaP2

'Country Dancer'

Dr. Griffith Buck Rose

Habit: Upright, vigorous shrub, 3 ft (.9m) tall and wide

Bloom: Recurrent

Fragrance: Moderate

Disease Resistance: Good disease and pest resistance

Special Uses: Hedge, mixed border, specimen, cut flower; tolerates summer drought and heat, as well as cold

Hardiness: USDA zones 3–8; Canadian zone 3

Pedigree: Buck, 1973; 'Prairie Princess' × 'Johannes Boettner'

'Golden Unicorn'

Dr. Griffith Buck Rose

Habit: Vigorous, upright shrub, 3–4 ft (0.9–1.2m) tall and wide

Bloom: Abundant, recurrent flowering

Fragrance: Moderate

Disease Resistance: Good

Special Uses: Landscape shrub

Hardiness: USDA zone 3 (southern half)–zone 7; Canadian zone 3

Pedigree: Buck, 1984; 'Paloma Blanca' × ('Carefree Beauty'™ × 'Antike')

If your space for roses is limited and you want a single rose that will function as a practical, attractive landscape shrub and provide cut flowers for the house, 'Country Dancer' is the cultivar for you. Its fragrant, deep rose, semidouble flowers bloom all summer on a healthy shrub with glossy dark green leaves. The individual blossoms have an elegance and visual impact that makes them effective contributors to a floral arrangement, and as cut flowers they are unusually long-lasting. What's more, this rose's compact size makes it ideal for smaller spaces.

Sources: USA — CI, H4, MI, R4, R7; Canada — CaH2

Dr. Griffith Buck's vision for the rose was a populist one: he sought to create a strain of shrubs that would flourish with minimal care in the climatic extremes of this continent's heartland. It's ironic that today his rose should be known mainly to connoisseurs. That is changing, however, as a new generation of nurserymen reintroduces them to the general public. It still takes some hunting to locate 'Golden Unicorn', but hopefully that is changing.

It should, for this rose is a wonderfully hardy shrub that bears large, fragrant, shallow-cupped blossoms of yellow edged with orange-red. This shrub's disease resistance and abundant, recurrent bloom make it a terrific landscape rose for northern gardens, and it is a special favorite of northeastern consultant Donna Fuss, the rosarian at Elizabeth Park Rose Garden in Hartford, Connecticut.

Sources: USA — H4

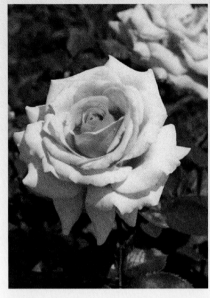

'Hawkeye Belle'

Dr. Griffith Buck Rose

Habit: Vigorous, erect shrub, 4 ft (1.2m) tall and wide

Bloom: Recurrent

Fragrance: Powerful

Disease Resistance: Good

Special Uses: Specimen, hedge; tolerates summer drought and heat, as well as cold

Hardiness: USDA zones 4–8; Canadian zone 5

Pedigree: Buck, 1975; ('Queen Elizabeth'® × 'Pizzicato') × 'Prairie Princess'

'Abraham Darby'™

English Rose

Habit: Upright, vigorous shrub, 5–6 ft (1.5–1.8m) tall, 10 ft (3m) if trained as a climber

Bloom: Recurrent

Fragrance: Strong

Disease Resistance: Very resistant to powdery mildew, somewhat susceptible to blackspot and rose rust

Special Uses: Large shrub, climber

Hardiness: USDA zones 5–9; Canadian zone 6

Pedigree: Austin, 1985; 'Yellow Cushion' × 'Aloha'

This rose descends in part from the great grandiflora rose 'Queen Elizabeth'® (the original rose of that class). Through a series of crosses involving his own 'Prairie Princess', Griffith Buck created something that, like the grandifloras, bears roses of the hybrid tea type but is considerably hardier. His new rose, 'Hawkeye Belle', is a healthy landscape shrub that bears flowers like those of a hybrid tea. The long pink buds open to large (4½ in [11.5cm]), double, white flowers with an azalea pink flush. These blossoms are strongly fragrant and borne abundantly over a long season. The shrub itself is relatively compact, a 4 ft (1.2m) mound of foliage and flowers.

Sources: USA — H4, R4; Canada — CaH1, CaH2

One parent of 'Abraham Darby'™ is the climbing hybrid tea 'Aloha', so although this rose may be maintained as a large shrub, with a little training it will also perform well as a climber. Its large, double, cupped, apricot-pink flowers suffused with yellow will cover a trellis or wall and perfume your garden.

Like most English roses, 'Abraham Darby'™ combines an old-fashioned look and fragrance with the everblooming habit of a modern rose. It's a good choice for temperate parts of the Northeast and Midwest, and a superb one in the Mid-Atlantic states, Pacific Northwest, and Southwest. Indeed, regional consultant Jim Adams at the National Arboretum in Washington, D.C., and regional consultant Clair Martin at the Huntington Botanical Gardens in San Marino, California, recommend English roses in general as among the most handsome and trouble-free roses for their regions of the country.

Sources: USA — G1, R4, R5, W1, W2; Canada — CaH2, CaP2

'Constance Spry'®

English Rose

Habit: Upright, vigorous shrub, 7 ft (2.1m) tall and wide, 10 ft (3m) if trained as a climber

Bloom: Long early-summer to midsummer flowering, not recurrent

Fragrance: Powerful myrrh scent

Disease Resistance: Good

Special Uses: Informal shrub, climber; tolerant of partial shade

Hardiness: USDA zones 4–9; Canadian zone 4

Pedigree: Austin, 1961; 'Belle Isis' × 'Dainty Maid'

'Fair Bianca'®

English Rose

Habit: Upright, compact shrub, 2½–3 ft (.8–.9m) tall and wide

Bloom: Recurrent

Fragrance: Strong

Disease Resistance: Good

Special Uses: Small specimen, cut flower

Hardiness: USDA zones 5–9; Canadian zone 6

Pedigree: Austin, 1982; parentage includes 'Belle Isis'

The first of David Austin's English Roses, 'Constance Spry'® was only a partial realization of the nurseryman's dream. His goal (which he has since achieved) was to combine the classic form and beauty of the old garden roses with the everblooming habit of contemporary ones, but 'Constance Spry'® blooms just once a season. Even so, this rose has been a great success, winning enduring popularity among a generation of gardeners with its large, cupped, double flowers. Ranging in color from pale to medium pink, these blossoms have the elegant form of an old rose — and the sweet fragrance, too.

Had the flowers been less appealing, 'Constance Spry'® would certainly have won a following with its carefree, reliable nature. This rose just grows well. Its long canes can be contained through pruning, and it can be grown as a large-flowered specimen shrub. If allowed to stretch, it makes an outstanding, vigorous climber.

Sources: USA — P1, R5, W1; Canada — CaC1, CaH2, CaP2

The English roses tend to be more expansive in our sunnier North American climates than in their native Britain, so fitting them into a small garden can be difficult. 'Fair Bianca'®, however, offers a good solution to that problem. Even at the Huntington Botanial Gardens in San Marino, California, where many of the English roses perform more like climbers than shrubs, 'Fair Bianca'® remains a compact, reblooming shrub. Its heirloom-type flowers are fully double and cupped, with small green eyes at the center. The perfume is powerful and reminiscent of anise.

Sources: USA — H1, O1, R5, W1, W2; Canada — CaH1, CaH2, CaP2

'Graham Thomas'™

English Rose

Habit: Upright, narrow shrub, 5–7 ft (1.5–2.1m) tall

Bloom: Recurrence varies with climate, good late-season flowering

Fragrance: Rich

Disease Resistance: Good

Special Uses: Large shrub, climber

Hardiness: USDA zones 6–9; Canadian zone 6

Pedigree: Austin, 1983; seedling × ('Charles Austin® × 'Iceberg' seedling)

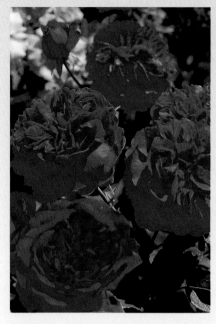

'L. D. Braithwaite'®

English Rose

Habit: Upright, spreading shrub, 4 ft (1.2m) tall, 5 ft (1.5m) wide

Bloom: Good recurrence

Fragrance: Light

Disease Resistance: Good

Other Interest: Bronze new growth

Special Uses: Border shrub; tolerates partial shade

Hardiness: USDA zones 5–9; Canadian zone 6

Pedigree: Austin, 1988; 'Mary Rose'® × 'The Squire'®

Named for the great British plantsman and rose historian, 'Graham Thomas'™ was the first truly yellow English rose, and many gardeners today consider it the finest yellow rose of all. Its double, cupped, 4 in (10cm) flowers are a luminous deep gold, and they have a warm tea rose fragrance. To create his English roses, nurseryman David Austin crosses old, once-blooming roses with modern everbloomers, and the frequency with which his roses rebloom varies from cultivar to cultivar. 'Graham Thomas'™ falls somewhere in the middle: it bears a large flush of flowers in late spring or early summer and then reblooms somewhat irregularly. A large and lanky shrub at the northern edge of its range, it makes a wonderful climber in warmer climates.

Sources: USA — HI, PI, R4, WI, W2; Canada — CaHI, CaH2, CaPI, CaP2

This vigorous, open shrub looks best at the back of a border, where its somewhat sparse foliage will not appear as a defect and its clusters of large, fully double, fire-engine red flowers can preside over the surrounding blossoms. 'L. D. Braithwaite'® blooms consistently throughout the season, but in the heat of midsummer the color may fade to cerise-pink.

An unusually dependable rose, 'L. D. Braithwaite'® blooms well even in situations where it receives as few as five hours of direct sunlight a day.

Sources: USA — HI, OI, RI, WI; Canada — CaCI, CaPI, CaP2

'Tamora'

English Rose

Habit: Upright, compact shrub, 2–3 ft (.6–.9m) tall

Bloom: Excellent recurrence

Fragrance: Strong myrrh scent

Disease Resistance: Good

Other Interest: Dark green, wrinkled foliage

Special Uses: Border, container

Hardiness: USDA zones 5–9; Canadian zone 6

Pedigree: Austin, 1983; 'Chaucer'® × 'Conrad Ferdinand Meyer'

'Frühlings-morgen'

Kordesii Rose

Habit: Upright, arching shrub, 5–6 ft (1.5–1.8m) tall, 4–5 ft (1.2–1.5m) wide

Bloom: Profuse early flowering, no rebloom

Fragrance: Strong

Other Interest: Ornamental hips

Special Uses: Specimen, hedge; tolerates poor soils, light shade

Hardiness: USDA zones 5–8; Canadian zone 6

Pedigree: Kordes, 1942; ('E. G. Hill' × 'Cathrine Kordes') × *Rosa spinosissima*

Other Names: 'Spring Morning'

As America's leading expert on English roses, regional consultant Clair Martin of the Huntington Botanical Gardens in San Marino, California, has grown more than 100 of these innovative shrubs. 'Tamora' is at the top of his list of recommendations of easy-to-grow, outstanding performers.

This rose produces fragrant, fully double rosettes in shades of apricot with pink-orange shadings on a slow-growing, compact shrub that flourishes as a container plant or in the front of a border. Since 'Tamora' performs best in warmer climates and thrives in dry conditions, it is especially at home in the Southwest.

Sources: USA — HI, KI, R5; Canada — CaH2, CaP2

The Kordes nursery, Germany's leading producer of roses, has kept as its goal through several generations of family ownership to produce roses adapted to northern Europe's often harsh climate. Yet 'Frühlingsmorgen', despite a robust nature, has a deceptively delicate appearance. The name means "spring morning," and in fact this rose is one of the first to bloom in the spring. With its simple charm, it is reminiscent of a species type, and like the wild roses, it does not rebloom. (There may be a few additional flowers later on in the year, but the gardener should not count on this.) The large, single flowers have rose pink to cherry pink petals with primrose yellow centers surrounding bright maroon stamens. This rose makes a fine informal flowering hedge, but it also works well as a specimen shrub.

Sources: USA — G3, HI, R7; Canada — CaH2

'Illusion'

Kordesii Rose

Habit: 8–10 ft (2.4–3.0m) canes in warmer climates; spreading shrub, 4 ft (1.2m) tall, 6½ ft (2m) wide in colder climates

Bloom: Recurrent

Fragrance: Moderate

Disease Resistance: Outstanding

Other Interest: Leathery, glossy green foliage

Special Uses: Specimen, climber

Hardiness: USDA zones 4–8; Canadian zone 5b

Pedigree: Kordes, 1961; *Rosa wichuraiana* × *R. rugosa*

'Rosenstadt Zweibrücken'®

Kordesii Rose

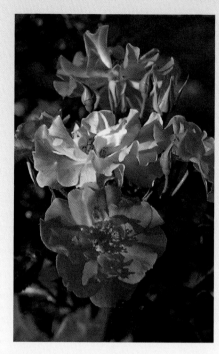

Habit: Upright, compact shrub, 3 ft (.9m) tall and wide

Bloom: Abundant, recurrent flowering

Fragrance: Slight

Disease Resistance: Good

Special Uses: Border, container

Hardiness: USDA zones 5–8; Canadian zone 6

Pedigree: Kordes, 1989

Another good shrub for the north country, 'Illusion' bears bunches of medium-size, lightly fragrant, double, red flowers in early summer. After reblooming moderately in midsummer, it starts flowering heavily again at summer's end and into the fall. Nurseryman Wilhelm Kordes bred this from two exceptionally hardy and disease-resistant species, and according to regional consultant Donna Fuss, this shrub is an exceptional performer at Elizabeth Park Rose Garden in Hartford, Connecticut. In the warmer part of its range, 'Illusion' develops long, flexible canes that can be trained along a fence or up a trellis.

Sources: USA — H2, V1; Canada — CaP2

Why the Kordes nursery of Sparrieshoop, Germany, has not won greater recognition in North America remains something of a mystery. For four generations this family has been breeding prize-winning roses that have been favorites among European gardeners. Perhaps the problem lay in the fact that until recently, gardeners on this side of the Atlantic did not especially value hardiness and self-sufficiency in roses, the two outstanding characteristics of the Kordes roses. As North American gardeners come to their senses, however, one hopes the Kordesii roses such as 'Rosenstadt Zweibrücken'® will begin to enjoy the recognition and sales here that they deserve.

As roses go, 'Rosenstadt Zweibrücken'® is a particularly easy one to like. Many of the Kordesii shrubs are sprawling plants, but this cultivar is compact, almost a dwarf, and perfectly suited to smaller gardens or for inclusion in a mixed border. 'Rosenstadt Zweibrücken'® bears almost single coral-red blooms with yellow centers punctuated by brilliant red stamens.

Sources: USA — K1, R4, R7; Canada — CaH2

'Bonica'®

Meidiland™ Rose

Habit: Spreading, arching, vigorous shrub, 3–5 ft (0.9–1.5m) tall

Bloom: Recurrent, long blooming season

Fragrance: Slight

Disease Resistance: Excellent

Special Uses: Landscape, hedge, specimen

Hardiness: USDA zones 4–9; Canadian zone 5

Pedigree: Meilland, 1982; (*Rosa sempervirens* × 'Mlle. Marthe Carron') × 'Picasso'

Other Names: 'Bonica 82', 'Démon', 'MEIdomonac'

'Carefree Delight'™

Meidiland™ Rose

Habit: Upright, arching shrub, 5 ft (1.5m) tall, 4 ft (1.2m) wide

Bloom: Recurrent, long flowering season

Fragrance: Slight

Disease Resistance: Excellent

Special Uses: Landscape, specimen

Hardiness: USDA zones 4–9; Canadian zone 5b

Pedigree: Meilland, 1994; ('Eyepaint'® × 'Nirvana'®) × 'Smarty'®

Other Names: 'Bingo Meidiland'

This is the rose that, more than any other, persuaded gardeners to look again at roses for use as landscape shrubs. In 1987, 'Bonica'® became the first shrub rose ever to be named an All-America Rose Selection. That is an honor awarded to just a couple of new roses each year, after a selection process based on evaluation in certified gardens all over the United States.

Vigorous and outstandingly healthy, 'Bonica'® makes a fine accent in a mixed border, is a low-maintenance hedging plant, and works well with other shrubs in a foundation planting. Its 1–2 in (2.5–5.0cm) diameter, medium pink, double flowers with lighter edges are produced in clusters in midsummer, with excellent repeat bloom.

Sources: USA — B1, B3, C1; Canada — CaC1, CaH2

Carefree Delight™ lives up to its name in its resistance to the most troublesome diseases: mildew, blackspot, and rose rust. The clusters of single, 3½ in (9cm) wide, carmine-pink flowers, each with a creamy white center, show up strikingly against the dark green foliage, and they appear and reappear throughout the growing season.

Like the rest of the Meidiland™ roses, bred in France by the Meilland family nursery, 'Carefree Delight'™ requires no more maintenance than an azalea or a lilac: just an early-spring feeding with a slow-release fertilizer and a light shaping with the pruning shears a month or so later. For a carefree flowering shrub or hedge, this plant has few equals among roses, or indeed among any other kind of garden shrub.

Sources: USA — C1, D1, O1

'Carefree Wonder'™

Meidiland™ Rose

Habit: Erect shrub, 4–5 ft (1.2–1.5m) tall

Bloom: Recurrent

Fragrance: Slight

Disease Resistance: Excellent

Special Uses: Hedge, landscape

Hardiness: USDA zones 4–9; Canadian zone 5b

Pedigree: Meilland, 1990; ('Prairie Princess' × 'Nirvana'®) × ('Eyepaint'® × 'Rustica'®)

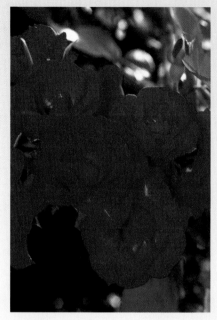

'La Sevillana'®

Meidiland™ Rose

Habit: Bushy, vigorous shrub, 3 ft (.9m) tall and wide

Bloom: Profuse summer and fall bloom

Fragrance: Slight

Disease Resistance: Good

Other Interest: Bronze-green foliage

Special Uses: Ground cover, landscape

Hardiness: USDA zones 6–9 ; Canadian zone 6

Pedigree: Meilland, 1978; (['MEIbrim' × 'Jolie Madame'®] × ['Zambra'® × 'Zambra'®]) × (['Tropicana' × 'Tropicana'] × ['Poppy Flash' × 'Rusticana'])

Bred from one of Dr. Griffith Buck's roses ('Prairie Princess'), 'Carefree Wonder'™ has that parent's hardiness and disease resistance, combined with a truly spectacular display of flowers. In mid-season large, medium pink, double blooms begin to open in sprays of one to four, each with a lighter pink reverse and a white eye. In cool weather, the petals develop a deep pink etching. In 1991, this became the second shrub rose ever to win an All-America Rose Selection award, and it is superb as a low-maintenance landscape shrub or an informal, unclipped hedge.

Sources: USA — C1, O1, R4; Canada — CaH2, CaP2

This rose comes highly recommended by regional consultant Clair Martin of the Huntington Botanical Gardens in San Marino, California. "It's never out of bloom!" Certainly, with the vermilion, semidouble flowers that it bears in large clusters in early summer to midsummer, 'La Sevillana'® makes a bold statement massed as a ground cover or landscape shrub. In autumn, it blooms all over again, making this a great rose rather than merely a good one. It can add a flamboyant splash of color to a summer border and more than holds its own in a foundation planting or as a low hedge. The foliage is attractive, too: a dark bronze-green.

Sources: USA — T1

'Scarlet Meidiland'™

Meidiland™ Rose

Habit: Vigorous, spreading shrub, 3 ft (.9m) tall by 6 ft (1.8m) wide

Bloom: Recurrent

Fragrance: None

Disease Resistance: Good

Other Interest: Persistent red hips

Special Uses: Landscape shrub, tolerates light shade

Hardiness: USDA zones 4-9; Canadian zone 2b

Pedigree: Meilland,1985; 'MEItiraca' × 'Clair Matin'®

'White Meidiland'™

Meidiland™ Rose

Habit: Low, spreading shrub, 2–2½ ft (.6–.8m) tall, 6 ft (1.8m) wide

Bloom: Recurrent

Fragrance: Slight

Disease Resistance: Excellent

Other Interest: Dark green foliage

Special Uses: Landscape, ground cover

Hardiness: USDA zones 4–9; Canadian zone 4b

Pedigree: Meilland, 1986; 'Temple Bells' × 'MEIgurami'

Small, cherry pink, semidouble flowers in large clusters cover this plant in midseason, and the shrub reblooms reliably into fall. That's when 'Scarlet Meidiland'™ develops its second source of color: in fall, the shrub bears bright red hips, and these persist well into winter. Bred for hardiness and disease resistance, 'Scarlet Meidiland'™ also tolerates light shade. The vigorous, trailing growth of the canes makes this a good choice for a tall ground cover or for planting in areas that receive little maintenance. All in all, this rose is a star, even by comparison with its remarkable relatives, the Meidiland™ roses. Donna Fuss, Northeast consultant, has grown it in Hartford, Connecticut's Elizabeth Park, and she describes the rose as, simply, "wonderful."

Sources: USA — B3, H2, R5; Canada — CaH2

White Meidiland'™ bears the largest flowers of the Meidiland™ series, and the blossoms are unusually full, with more than 40 petals each. As the name indicates, the flowers are white — pure white — and they make a striking contrast to the dark green, glossy foliage. Unfortunately, the blossoms don't fall away naturally as they wither, so the bush can look distinctly shabby at the end of a heavy flush of bloom unless you take the time to deadhead it.

This low, spreading shrub can make a spectacular display when several plants are massed together to spill over the edge of a retaining wall or cascade down a slope. Yet 'White Meidiland'™ serves equally well as a specimen plant, if placed where each sumptuous flower can be admired in detail.

Sources: USA — GI, HI, R5; Canada — CaH2

Introducing

MOSS ROSES

No other roses can equal the nostalgia of moss roses. These are the roses that decorate antique valentines and your great-grandmother's china. You will recognize these roses instantly by the mosslike growth that encrusts the buds and the bases of the flowers. This growth of course is not really moss but rather a bristling of sticky glands that exude a pine-scented resin. The whiskering is soft and light in some of the moss roses, though in others it is quite dense and sometimes hard and prickly.

With flowers that, as a rule, are sweetly scented and which average 2½–3½ in (6.4–8.9cm) in diameter, the moss roses are not only distinctive but charming. Their air of old-fashioned elegance makes them an ideal choice for a cottage garden and a good complement for a Victorian house.

Aside from the novelty of the mossing, this class of roses has a number of practical advantages. They are cold-hardy shrubs that in favorable conditions will endure for decades and, though like most antique roses the mosses bloom just once a year, their flowers usually have a powerful perfume.

Outstandingly cold hardy, they overwinter successfully in USDA zone 4 and the southern part of Canadian zone 4, yet they also thrive down into USDA zone 8 in arid regions.

MOSS ROSES

'Common Moss'

Habit: Open shrub, 5 ft (1.5m) tall and wide

Bloom: One annual flowering in late spring to early summer

Fragrance: Exceptionally strong

Other Interest: Mossing on buds and flowers, attractive foliage

Hardiness: USDA zones 4–8; Canadian zone 4

Pedigree: Dutch; cultivated by 1696

Other Names: 'Communis', 'Old Pink Moss', *Rosa centifolia muscosa*

Commonly considered to be the first rose of this class, 'Common Moss' remains one of the best. The distinctive buds are appealing, overgrown with the mossy glands that give these roses their name, and when brushed they smell pleasantly of balsam. When the flowers open in late spring or early summer, they unfurl into clear pink, 3 in (7.5cm) bowls with button-eye centers. Their fragrance is strong and rich, a classic old-rose perfume. Their stems are arching and prickly, and the foliage of 'Common Moss' is dark green and roughly toothed along the edges.

Sources: USA — H4, V1; Canada — CaP2

'Deuil de Paul Fontaine'

Habit: Compact shrub, 3 ft (.9m) tall and wide

Bloom: Flowers in late spring to early summer, again in late summer to fall

Fragrance: Strong

Disease Resistance: Prone to powdery mildew

Other Interest: Reddish mossing on buds

Special Uses: Border accent, specimen

Hardiness: USDA zones 4–8; Canadian zone 5

Pedigree: Fontaine, 1873

'Salet'

Habit: Upright, arching shrub, 4–5 ft (1.2–1.5m) tall

Bloom: Recurrent

Fragrance: Strong

Disease Resistance: Good

Special Uses: Specimen

Hardiness: USDA zones 4–8; Canadian zone 5

Pedigree: Lacharme, 1854

This rose's susceptibility to powdery mildew makes it less than an ideal candidate for an easy rose, but its many virtues outweigh this fault. Nevertheless, it should be planted in a warm, dry spot to help keep its foliage healthy.

'Deuil de Paul Fontaine' blossoms are among the darkest and most dramatic of the moss roses; the petals are a velvety crimson-purple with paler undersides. Even the mossing on the buds and the base of the flower is a dark red. Both the flowers and the moss are highly fragrant, and unlike most of the roses in this class, 'Deuil de Paul Fontaine' reblooms in late summer and fall.

Sources: USA — R4, R5; Canada — CaP2

The most reliably recurrent of the moss roses, 'Salet' bears a large flush of its big, fragrant, rose pink saucers of petals in late spring or early summer, and then it reblooms intermittently into the fall. These flowers have the strong, sweet fragrance characteristic of this class. The mossing on the buds and bases of the flowers is light. The foliage is bright green and coarse.

Its size makes it well suited to use as a specimen shrub. Like all the moss roses, 'Salet' has a special nostalgic charm that fits perfectly with a cottage-garden planting. It also looks perfectly at home in an herb garden.

Sources: USA — AI, GI, R4; Canada — CaP2

NOISETTE ROSES

This is a class of garden roses native to the United States, for the first Noisettes sprang from a seedling raised by John Champneys, a South Carolina rice planter, sometime around the year 1811. Known as 'Champneys' Pink Cluster', this rose was seized upon by a neighbor, Philippe Noisette, who sent it to his brother Louis, a nurseryman in France. And so the progeny of John Champneys' rose appeared under French names and were classed as Noisette roses.

Even in exile, however, the Noisettes remained roses of the American South. They flourish in the Southeast and Southwest as far south as USDA zone 10 but are too cold sensitive to over-winter reliably north of USDA zone 7, and are a better bet in zone 8. As a rule, the Noisettes are less resistant to blackspot and mildew than the tea and China roses, and they should be reserved for open, sunny spots with good air circulation.

Vigorous and long limbed, the Noisettes make fine climbers or sprawling shrubs. Their fragrant flowers tend to be small — 1½–2½ in (3.8–6.4cm) in diameter — but are borne in clusters in late spring and intermittently on into fall.

NOISETTE ROSES

'Céline Forestier'

Habit: Upright, vigorous shrub, 8–10 ft (2.4–3.0m) tall

Bloom: Recurrent

Fragrance: Highly perfumed

Disease Resistance: Good

Other Interest: Few thorns

Special Uses: Pillar

Hardiness: USDA zones 8–10; Canadian zone 6

Pedigree: Leroy, 1858

This is southeastern consultant Peter Haring's favorite Noisette, and when it comes into full bloom in late spring, 'Céline Forestier' does put on a remarkable show. The large, fully double flowers have green buttons at the centers and are quartered — the circle of petals seemingly divided into quadrants. The color is a lemon-cream, and the potent perfume is one of fruit and spice. What's more, if you miss the spring blossoming, you can look forward to subsequent flushes in summer, fall, and, in warm climates, winter. Somewhat tender, 'Céline Forestier' can be slow to establish itself after planting, but it generally thrives when trained up a south- or west-facing wall or pillar.

Sources: USA — A1, G3, R1; Canada — CaP2

'Jaune Desprez'

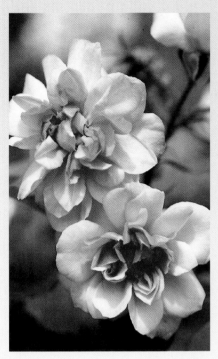

Habit: Upright, vigorous shrub, 12–18 ft (3.6–5.5m) tall

Bloom: Recurrent

Fragrance: Strong

Special Uses: Climber

Hardiness: USDA zones 8–10; Canadian zone 6

Pedigree: Desprez, 1830; 'Blush Noisette' × 'Parks' Yellow Tea-Scented China'

'Lamarque'

Habit: Vigorous, upright shrub, 10–18 ft (3.0–5.5m) tall

Bloom: Excellent recurrence

Fragrance: Strong

Disease Resistance: Good

Special Uses: Climber

Hardiness: USDA zones 8–10; Canadian zone 6

Pedigree: Marechal, 1830; 'Blush Noisette' × 'Parks' Yellow Tea-Scented China'

True yellows were rare among garden roses of the last century, because almost none of the species native to Europe bears flowers of that color. So the appearance of this yellow-flowered Noisette created something of a stir in gardening circles in 1830. The flat, semidouble flowers are not a pure yellow, but instead a lovely soft apricot with slight rose shadings. Because they are very sweetly scented, try growing this rose on an arch where you can stand under it and let the perfume surround you.

Sources: USA — A1, G3, R2; Canada — CaH2

Though its parentage is identical to that of 'Jaune Desprez', 'Lamarque' produces large, fragrant double blossoms. Borne in clusters, they are white with just a touch of pale yellow at their centers. This rose is known for blooming well into the fall and for quickly covering any support it is offered. It is also notably long-lived: one specimen recently discovered in San Antonio, Texas, has been reliably dated to the year 1890.

One of the best climbing roses for growing in the Southeast, 'Lamarque' provides almost year-round color where winters are mild. Despite its antique origins, this is definitely a rose with contemporary virtues.

Sources: USA — A1, C2, G2

'Natchitoches Noisette'

Habit: Compact shrub, 3–5 ft (0.9–1.5m) tall

Bloom: Recurrent

Fragrance: Moderate

Disease Resistance: Good

Special Uses: Border, specimen

Hardiness: USDA zones 8–10; Canadian zone 6

Pedigree: Unknown; shrub found in Natchitoches, Louisiana

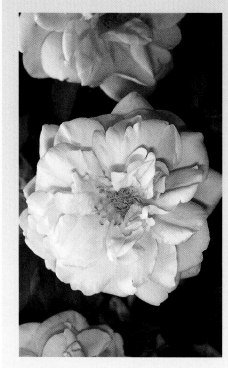

'Rêve d'Or'

Habit: Vigorous, upright shrub, 10–18 ft (3.0–5.5m) tall

Bloom: Recurrent, good repeat bloom

Fragrance: Moderate

Disease Resistance: Outstanding

Special Uses: Pillar

Hardiness: USDA zones 8–10; Canadian zone 6

Pedigree: Ducher, 1869; seedling of 'Mme. Schultz'

Other names: 'Golden Chain'

The original identity of this found old rose is a mystery. Although definitely an old-timer, it was unknown until Bill Welch *(see p.23)* discovered it growing on an old gravesite in Natchitoches, Louisiana. The rose's parentage is unknown, but its medium-size, cupped, light pink flowers borne in clusters are typical of Noisettes, and so is its tendency to bloom throughout the year. Accordingly, this foundling has been fairly securely labeled.

Whatever its origins, 'Natchitoches Noisette' is an outstanding shrub with a neat, compact habit of growth, a light but pleasant fragrance, and exceptionally disease-resistant foliage.

Sources: USA — AI, VI

Dream of gold" is the translation of this French rose's name, and it aptly evokes the flowers' soft, romantic look. Borne in clusters of three to five blooms, the perfumed globes are peach-gold when 'Rêve d'Or' begins blooming in the spring and buff yellow throughout the rest of the year. Unfortunately, like a dream, this rose can quickly vanish, for it doesn't rebloom as reliably and regularly as other Noisettes.

The sprawling canes are ideal for training up a warm wall or over a trellis or arbor. But do not trust the catalog descriptions that tout 'Rêve d'Or' as nearly thornless; according to those who have grown it, this is not true. So if you let this rose wreathe a gate or walkway, set it so that there will be sufficient clearance for the safe passage of passersby.

Sources: USA — AI, G3, SI; Canada — CaP2

Introducing

POLYANTHA ROSES

Sometime around the middle of the 19th century, a French nurseryman rescued a rosebush discarded from a local public park. The discarded bush was a curiosity — a Chinese import — and from it the nurseryman bred a group of seedlings. These proved to be tough and vigorous but also compact, typically ranging in height and spread from 1 to 4 ft (0.3–1.2m).

The polyanthas, as this strain came to be known, also turned out to be generous rebloomers that bear repeated flushes of small (1–2 in [2.5–5.1cm]) clustered flowers throughout the summer and fall. The flower colors are delicate — creams, pinks, and golds — and the foliage is notably disease resistant. This characteristic, combined with their tolerance for alkaline soils and intense sun, has made the polyanthas superb roses for the Southeast and Southwest. They flourish through USDA zone 9 and into zone 10; many are quite cold hardy and flourish into southern New England, southern Canada, and the milder regions of the Rocky Mountain West. Polyanthas also perform well in the Mid-Atlantic region.

Perfect for containers, polyanthas are an obvious choice for any situation in which a compact plant is desired. Their dense, mounded shape also makes them a natural for formal gardens.

POLYANTHA ROSES

'Cécile Brünner'

Habit: Compact shrub, 3–4 ft (0.9–1.2m) tall and wide

Bloom: Recurrent, profuse, long-season bloom

Fragrance: Slight

Disease Resistance: Good

Other Interest: Exquisite coral pink buds; tolerant of poor soils, partial shade

Special Uses: Container, specimen; tolerates poor soil and partial shade

Hardiness: USDA zones 5–9; Canadian zone 6

Pedigree: Pernet-Ducher, 1881; said to be a cross between a double multiflora rose and the tea rose 'Souvenir d'un Ami'

The small, exquisite, coral pink buds of 'Cécile Brünner' have made it the quintessential boutonniere flower. Growing in clusters, the flowers open into something like a hybrid tea blossom just 1–2 in (2.5–5.1cm) in diameter. The fragrance is light but distinctively spicy, and the stems are smooth and brownish purple. The thorns are few but sharp and hooked, to grab the careless. The foliage is a smooth dark green.

You'll recognize this rose as soon as its buds start to open. These are the pink roses you've seen on old-fashioned valentines, and a spray of 'Cécile Brünner' "sweetheart roses" is still the ultimate romantic gesture. In addition to the original compact form of the shrub, there is also a climbing form, which in mild climates can reach a height of 20 ft (6m). Both thrive in the Southeast and Southwest and flourish even in poor soils and partial shade.

Sources: USA — AI, CI, WI; Canada — CaH2, CaP2

'La Marne'

Habit: Erect shrub, 4–6 ft (1.2–1.8m) tall

Bloom: Excellent recurrence

Fragrance: Slight

Disease Resistance: Exceptional

Other Interest: Almost thornless

Special Uses: Landscape, hedge

Hardiness: USDA zones 7–9; Canadian zone 8

Pedigree: Barbier, 1915; 'Mme. Norbert Levavasseur' × 'Comtesse du Cayla'

'Marie Pavié'

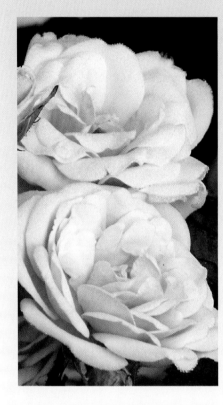

Habit: Bushy, very compact shrub, 1½–4 ft (0.5–1.2m) tall

Bloom: Recurrent

Fragrance: Moderate

Disease Resistance: Good

Other Interest: Thornless

Special Uses: Container, hedge, specimen, landscape

Hardiness: USDA zones 5–9; Canadian zone 6

Pedigree: Allégatière, 1888

Sporting almost thornless canes with dark, shiny leaves, 'La Marne' makes an easy-care landscape shrub or hedge plant. It produces loose clusters of cupped, semidouble, blush pink flowers repeatedly through the season, and the blossoms show up well against the dark green, shiny foliage. Not only is the foliage handsome, but it is also healthy. In fact, its extraordinary resistance to fungal diseases makes 'La Marne' an excellent rose for the hot and humid Southeast. It is vulnerable to cold, however, and isn't reliably winter hardy north of the southern part of USDA zone 7. Large for a polyantha, 'La Marne' is too expansive for most containers.

Sources: USA — AI

With pink buds that open into clusters of fragrant, creamy white, semidouble flowers (each only 2 in [5.1cm] wide), 'Marie Pavié' is both dainty and charming when in bloom — and it's generally in bloom from late spring right through to fall. This rose is also versatile: With some pruning, it makes an excellent container plant. Left to grow unchecked, a row of them can create a handsome low hedge. And because it is free of both thorns and diseases, this is an excellent rose to plant in the kitchen garden. One of the hardier polyanthas, 'Marie Pavié' overwinters reliably through USDA zone 6.

Sources: USA — AI, C2, G3; Canada — CaH2

POLYANTHA ROSES

'Perle d'Or'

Habit: Vigorous, open shrub, 4 ft (1.2m) tall

Bloom: Recurrent, long flowering season

Fragrance: Strong

Special Uses: Landscape, specimen

Hardiness: USDA zones 5–9; Canadian zone 6

Pedigree: Rambaux, 1884; 'Madame Falcot' × Polyantha

Other Names: 'Yellow Cécile Brünner'

POLYANTHA ROSES

'The Fairy'

Habit: Low, compact, spreading shrub, 2–3 ft (.6–.9m) tall

Bloom: Outstandingly recurrent, late to bloom but continuing well into fall

Fragrance: Slight

Disease Resistance: Good

Other Interest: Small, glossy green leaves

Special Uses: Landscape, border accent, mass planting; tolerates poor soils, some shade

Hardiness: USDA zones 4–9; Canadian zone 5

Pedigree: Bentall, 1932; possibly 'Paul Crampel' × 'Lady Gay'

The alternate name for this rose, 'Yellow Cécile Brünner', underlines the pronounced resemblance of this rose to its polyantha relative. But whereas the flowers of 'Cécile Brünner' are pink, those of 'Perle d'Or' are, as the name suggests, touched with gold. This rose's tiny, pointed buds are a warm apricot; they take on a buff tone as they open, then gradually age to a golden pink. The fully opened blossoms spread into little pompons with a pronounced perfume; they keep their color better if the rose is set where it receives some afternoon shade.

The size of this shrub varies with the climate. In most gardens, it will reach a height and spread of about 4 ft (1.2m), but at the northern edge of its range it will be smaller, and in the Deep South it is liable to prove considerably more expansive.

Sources: USA — AI, C2, R2; Canada — CaH2, CaP2

A delicate-looking but tough little plant, 'The Fairy' is the only rose of this class recommended for northern gardens by regional consultant Kathy Zuzek at the Minnesota Landscape Arboretum. This cultivar begins flowering late in the season, but after the first blossoms open, it remains in bloom more or less continuously until cold weather arrives in in late fall, long after most other roses have passed their peak. Its low, arching habit adapts well to the front of a border, or plant in large groups for a grand effect. 'The Fairy' is often sold as a standard, or tree rose.

Sources: USA — AI, C2, OI; Canada — CaCI, CaHI, CaH2

Introducing

PORTLAND ROSES

This is a small class of roses that probably never included more than 100 cultivars, even in its 19th-century heyday. Currently, there are fewer than a dozen Portland roses still available. These survivors, however, enjoy a loyal following because they combine rugged hardiness with old-fashioned charm.

Although the first Portland rose seems to have come from Italy, this class of roses is at home in the North, usually overwintering successfully in USDA zone 5 (Canadian zone 6). The Portlands were greatly admired in the early 19th century because they are not only hardy but also reblooming. After producing a heavy crop of flowers in early summer, they flower again occasionally throughout the summer and into the fall.

Though the Portland rose blossoms are large — 3–4 in (7.6–10.2cm) in diameter — and usually very fragrant, for the most part this class has been replaced by showier, freer-flowing roses. There is an appealing simplicity to the Portland blossoms, however, and as shrubs these roses have a durability that continues to make them good choices for the modern low-maintenance garden. Well adapted to the Northeast, Midwest, Rocky Mountain West, and milder regions of Canada, these roses suffer where summers are hot and humid.

PORTLAND ROSES

'Comte de Chambord'

Habit: Upright, compact shrub, 3–4 ft (0.9–1.2m) tall

Bloom: Abundant, recurrent bloom

Fragrance: Strong

Disease Resistance: Good

Special Uses: Border accent, specimen

Hardiness: USDA zones 5–8; Canadian zone 6

Pedigree: Moreau-Robert, 1860; 'Baronne Prévost' × Portland rose

This popular Portland rose bears very full blossoms with as many as 200 petals. Large, fragrant, and quartered, with button-eye centers, the flowers of this rose open in shades of pink, mauve, and violet. 'Comte de Chambord' reblooms unusually freely for a Portland rose, and in good soil and full sun it may remain in flower almost continuously. This, together with its compact size, makes it an excellent candidate for smaller gardens. 'Comte de Chambord' has an old-world charm that makes it ideal for a cottage garden. It also lends a special air of elegance to a perennial border.

Sources: USA — G3, R4, R5; Canada — CaH1, CaH2, CaP2

Introducing

SPECIES ROSES

Members of this class are wild roses — but wild roses of a special kind. Species roses originate with plants or cuttings that are collected from the wild, but typically they come from exceptionally vigorous and handsome specimens. This means that the "wild" or species roses you find in a catalog are not typical of what you would find if you set out for a walk in the country, wildflower guide in hand.

The special strength of the species roses is their wildness. These are roses that have had to take care of themselves. One famous California nurseryman, Francis Lester, described the species roses as "Nature's unspoiled children," explaining that these bushes "are accustomed to neglect." If you choose species roses adapted to your climate and soil, they will take care of themselves in your garden, too.

Appreciating species roses requires a shift in perspective: you must set aside the preconception that says that beautiful roses must look like the ones you see at the florist. Species roses commonly bear simple, so-called single flowers, with just five petals, and these blossoms most often measure no more than 1 or 2 in (2.5–5.1cm) in diameter. Most often, they bloom just once a season. What's more, they tend to make expansive shrubs, which means they are best reserved for informal plantings. Within such a setting, though, they offer not only unrivaled hardiness but also a subtle, understated beauty matched by few man-made hybrids.

SPECIES ROSES

Rosa banksiae lutea (Yellow Lady Banks Rose)

Habit: Sprawling climber, 20–30 ft (6–9m)

Bloom: Early spring

Fragrance: Light

Disease Resistance: Exceptional

Special Uses: Fence, wall; tolerates full sun or partial shade, salt spray

Hardiness: USDA zones 8–9, best in Southeast and Southwest; Canadian zone 8

Pedigree: Native to southern China; introduced to England in 1824

Other Names: 'Banksia', *R. banksiae* 'Lutea'

Blooming in early to late spring, depending on the climate, this rambler produces sprays of clear yellow, double flowers, each 1 in (2.5cm) across. Although this rose is not hardy where winter temperatures drop below 10°F (–12°C), its disease resistance, thornless canes, and free-flowering habit make it popular in milder climates. In USDA zones 9 and 10, the foliage on the gracefully arching stems remains evergreen. In colder regions, this rose makes an excellent container plant if moved to a sheltered area in winter.

There is also a white form of this species, *Rosa banksiae banksiae* (sometimes listed as *R. banksiae alba-plena*), whose blossoms offer a stronger, violet-scented perfume.

Sources: USA — A1, C2, F2

Rosa glauca (Red-leafed Rose)

Habit: Upright shrub, 5 ft (1.5m) tall and wide

Bloom: Spring

Other Interest: Showy hips, almost thornless

Special Uses: Border; thrives in full sun to partial shade

Hardiness: USDA zones 2–8, best in Northeast, Mid-Atlantic, Midwest, Rocky Mountain West, Northwest, upper Southeast, and higher altitudes of Southwest; Canadian zone 2

Pedigree: Native to central and southern Europe; cultivated prior to 1830

Other Names: *R. rubrifolia, R. ferruginea, R. giraldii*

Rosa laevigata (Cherokee Rose)

Habit: Upright, arching climber, 6–20 ft (1.8–6.0m) tall

Bloom: Spring

Fragrance: Moderate

Disease Resistance: Moderate

Other Interest: Decorative red hips

Special Uses: Climber

Hardiness: USDA zones 8–9, best in Southeast and Southwest; Canadian zone 9

Pedigree: Native to southern China; naturalized in southeastern North America by 1759

Other Names: *R. camellia, R. cherokeensis;* sometimes confused with *R. bracteata*

Blooming in late spring, *Rosa glauca* produces single, 1½ in (4cm), clear pink flowers with white eyes. Though not long-lasting, they produce attractive oval red hips that show up well against the colorful foliage, which is copper to purplish in sunny sites, silvery green in shade. The foliage color, enhanced by the purple hue of the young canes, makes this rose an unusual and eye-catching addition to a mixed border. Tough and hardy, this nearly thornless shrub performs particularly well in cold-climate gardens.

Sources: USA — A1, G1, R4; Canada — CaH1

Though of foreign origin, this rose is as much at home throughout the southeastern United States as were the people whose name it inherited. The Cherokee rose is almost evergreen in the warmer part of its range, and the glossy, dark green leaves are unusual in that each one has three leaflets, rather than the five or seven common among most roses. It flowers early, in April or May, bearing fragrant, single, white flowers 2½–3½ in (6.5–9.0cm) across, with showy yellow stamens. These blossoms are succeeded by large, decorative red hips.

Sources: USA — F2, H1, R1

Rosa nitida
(Shining Rose)

Habit: Low-growing, spreading, suckering shrub, 2 ft (.6m) tall

Bloom: Early summer

Fragrance: Moderate

Other Interest: Scarlet autumn leaf color, attractive prickles and hips in winter; tolerates poor soils, partial shade

Special Uses: Ground cover, erosion control

Hardiness: USDA zones 4–6, best in Northeast, Midwest, Rocky Mountain West, and Northwest; Canadian zone 5

Pedigree: Native to eastern Canada and northeastern United States; cultivated since 1807

Rosa nitida has earned its place in cold-climate gardens with its three seasons of display. In early summer, it bears fragrant, brilliant pink flowers. Then in fall, the glossy, narrow leaflets (which give this rose its name) turn a beautiful scarlet. Later, the bright red hips and reddish brown prickles provide winter interest.

Like most of the species roses, *R. nitida* is not a spectacular shrub, but instead one of quiet charms. It suckers readily, gradually forming a thicket of slender, reddish stems. Because of this spreading habit, *R. nitida* makes an excellent and self-sufficient ground cover for the outskirts of a garden — one that flourishes even in partial shade and poor soils.

Sources: USA — F2, H1; Canada — CaA1, CaH2

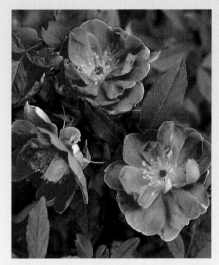

Rosa palustris scandens
(Swamp Rose)

Habit: Arching, almost weeping shrub, 4–6 ft (1.2–1.8m) canes

Bloom: Mid- to late spring

Fragrance: Moderate

Disease Resistance: Exceptional disease and pest resistance

Special Uses: Nearly thornless; tolerates wet soils

Hardiness: USDA zones 4–8, best in Northeast, Mid-Atlantic, Midwest, Rocky Mountain West, cooler parts of Southwest, and upper Southeast; Canadian zone 4b

Pedigree: Native to eastern North America; cultivated prior to 1824

Other Names: *R. hudsoniana scandens*

Few roses tolerate poorly drained soils; this shrub thrives on them. This makes the swamp rose a prize for gardeners in search of a shrub for a low-lying damp spot. Yet this rose need not be confined only to wet situations, for it also flourishes on ordinary, well-drained garden soils. In fact, the swamp rose, with its graceful, semiweeping form, is an asset to any landscape. Its nearly thornless canes bear fragrant, vivid pink, double flowers amid narrow, willowlike leaves. More gardeners should consider this easy, lovely shrub for gracing the edges of their ponds or streams.

Sources: USA — A1

Rosa sericea pteracantha (Wingthorn Rose)

Habit: Vase-shaped shrub, 6 ft (1.8m) tall, 4 ft (1.2m) wide

Bloom: Early summer

Fragrance: Insignificant

Disease Resistance: Outstanding

Other Interest: Enormous ruby thorns, ferny foliage

Special Uses: Specimen, hedge; tolerates poor, dry soils and seaside conditions

Hardiness: USDA zones 5–8, best in Northwest, temperate parts of Northeast and Canada, Midwest, Rocky Mountain West, and Mid-Atlantic; Canadian zone 6

Pedigree: Native of western China; in Western gardens since 1890

Other Names: *R. omeiensis pteracantha*

Everything about this rose is extraordinary. The rule for roses is that petals are borne in multiples of five, yet the wingthorn rose's small white blossoms have just four. Most gardeners, in any case, regard this rose's flowers as insignificant; instead they cultivate the shrub for the spectacular thorns, which may measure an inch (2.5cm) across the base and which are scarlet-colored and translucent on young canes. For the best display, the wingthorn rose should be cut back hard in spring to encourage abundant new growth. When less severely pruned, it can serve as a formidable barrier hedge. The fernlike foliage makes this an attractive shrub, and when set where the sun can backlight the jewel-like thorns, the effect can be magnificent.

Sources: USA — F2, G3, S1; Canada — CaH2, CaM1

Rosa setigera (Prairie Rose)

Habit: Sprawling shrub, 4–5 ft (1.2–1.5m) tall, 12 ft (3.6m) wide

Bloom: Midsummer

Fragrance: Rich

Disease Resistance: Good

Other Interest: Reddish canes, colorful hips, scarlet autumn foliage

Special Uses: Landscape, good for covering banks; tolerates sandy soils

Hardiness: USDA zones 4–9; Canadian zone 4

Pedigree: Native to eastern North America; cultivated since 1810

Ranging naturally from Ontario to Florida and Texas, this tough pioneer makes an excellent stabilizer for a sunny bank, and its tolerance for poor, dry soils makes it an outstanding highway planting. Its long canes can be trained up a trellis or pillar, but they look best when allowed to grow into a large shrub in a meadow or as a specimen at the edge of a substantial lawn. The single pink flowers appear later than those of other species roses, and the hips and vivid autumn foliage that follow make this an outstanding shrub for the landscape.

Sources: USA — A1, H2, L1, V1

Rosa spinosissima (Scotch Rose)

Habit: Spreading shrub, 3–4 ft (0.9–1.2m) tall

Bloom: Spring

Fragrance: Slight

Disease Resistance: Good

Other Interest: Abundant maroon-black hips

Special Uses: Tall ground cover, barrier hedge, erosion control, city plant; tolerates poor, sandy soil

Hardiness: USDA zones 3–8, best in Northeast, Midwest, Rocky Mountain West, and Northwest, also grows in Mid-Atlantic and at higher altitudes in upper Southeast or Southwest; Canadian zone 3

Pedigree: Native to Europe and western Asia; naturalized in northeastern United States; cultivated before 1600

Other Names: *R. pimpinellifolia*, burnet rose, Mary Queen of Scots rose

As the common name suggests, this rose is a native of Scotland, where it is often found growing wild on sandy banks. In mid- to late spring, it bears 2½ in (6.5cm) cream or white, single blossoms, and in general it is an extremely tough plant that suckers freely when grown on its own roots. This dense, thicketlike growth and the bristling armament of sharp, needlelike bristles make the Scotch rose outstanding material for a low-care barrier hedge or a tall, informal ground cover. Many hybrid roses have been bred from *Rosa spinosissima*; the best of these maintain its toughness but combine it with more mannerly growth. The Scotch rose's hips are distinctive, small, and maroon-black.

Sources: USA — F2, R4; Canada — CaH2

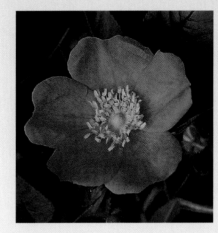

Rosa virginiana (Virginia Rose)

Habit: Dense, suckering shrub, 6 ft (1.8m) tall

Bloom: Late spring to early summer

Fragrance: Light

Disease Resistance: Excellent

Other Interest: Ornamental hips, fall leaf color, few thorns

Special Uses: Landscape

Hardiness: USDA zones 3–8, best in eastern Canada, Northeast, Mid-Atlantic, Midwest, Northwest, upper Southeast, flourishes with irrigation in Rocky Mountain West; Canadian zone 3

Pedigree: Native to northeastern North America; cultivated prior to 1807

Other Names: *R. lucida*

Despite its name, the Virginia rose grows wild far to the north and south of that state, for it ranges naturally from Newfoundland south to Alabama and west to Missouri. Wherever it grows, this rose offers year-round color: bronzy new foliage in spring; bright cerise-pink flowers with pale centers in midsummer; bright red hips and leaves that turn shades of red, yellow, and orange in fall; and arching red canes in the dead of winter. Such a tough, hardy shrub definitely deserves a spot somewhere in the garden, although it is especially useful for naturalized areas or slopes where few other roses would put on such a grand four-season display of color.

Sources: USA — F2, H1, R7; Canada — CaH2

Rosa wichuraiana (Memorial Rose)

Habit: 10–20 ft (3–6m) canes

Bloom: Early summer to midsummer

Fragrance: Pronounced

Disease Resistance: Outstanding

Other Interest: Glossy, nearly evergreen foliage

Special Uses: Ground cover, erosion control, climber

Hardiness: USDA zones 4–9, thrives in all but extreme Southeast and coldest parts of Northeast, Midwest, Rocky Mountain West, and Canada; Canadian zone 4

Pedigree: Native to Japan, eastern China, Korea, and Taiwan; introduced to North America in 1891

Rosa woodsii fendleri (Sierra Nevada Rose)

Habit: Dense shrub, 3–10 ft (0.9–3.0m) tall and wide

Bloom: Summer

Fragrance: Moderate

Other Interest: Decorative hips

Special Uses: Landscape; tolerates, drought, poor soil, some shade

Hardiness: USDA zones 4–8, best in Midwest, Rocky Mountain West, Northwest, and at higher altitudes in Southeast; Canadian zone 5

Pedigree: Native to British Columbia southward to western Texas and Mexico; first cultivated in 1888

Other Names: Mountain rose

The hardiness, vigorous growth, and sweet fragrance of *Rosa wichuraiana* made it a favorite cemetery planting, where it survived with only intermittent care. As a ground cover for gravesites, it won the name memorial rose; it has also been used as a climbing rose and is a parent of many fine hybrid climbers.

The pyramid-shaped clusters of white flowers open as late as August; each 1½–2 in (3.8–5.1cm) blossom has prominent yellow stamens and exudes a fruity fragrance. These are followed by small, ovoid, dark red hips. The glossy, dark green foliage can be almost evergreen in mild winters. The canes are moderately thorny, and when allowed to sprawl, they root where the tips touch the ground, giving rise to new plants; this makes *R. wichuraiana* the most effective ground cover rose.

Sources: USA — F2, H2; Canada — CaC1, CaH2

Rosa woodsii ranges over a wide area of central and western North America and has evolved a number of local variations. The form named *fendleri*, the one most often seen in gardens, is slightly taller than its relatives and has a more slender shape. The leaves are grayish green, and the flowers it bears in early summer are fragrant and lilac-pink with cream-colored stamens. These give rise to round, shiny, orange-red hips that cling to the canes well into winter. This is an excellent shrub for areas that have dry climates and cold winters.

Sources: USA — F2, H1; Canada — CaH2, CaP2

Introducing

TEA ROSES

It must have been some old Chinese connoisseur who first noticed that these roses can have a scent just like a cup of oolong. At any rate, it was as "tea-scented roses" that the ancestors of this class came to the West at the beginning of the 19th century.

They turned out to be superbly adapted to the American South. Practically immune to mildew and blackspot, the tea roses bloom from early spring through Christmas where winters are mild. Although they are not reliably cold hardy north of the southern part of USDA zone 7 (Canadian zone 8), tea roses are star performers down through zone 10, forming large, upright bushes that often flourish for decades without care.

Tea rose blossoms tend to be large, often 4 in (10.2cm) or more in diameter when completely opened, and full; and with their intriguingly different perfume they make unforgettable cut flowers. But don't try to arrange them as you would a long-stemmed hybrid tea. Tea roses typically have slender stems that bow over under the weight of the open bloom — a habit that the Victorians found particularly graceful. Outdoors, they make a fine contrast to the bronze-red new foliage.

From the 1830s until the turn of the century, the tea roses were the favorite florist's roses and the epitome of romance. These were the buds that a lady slipped into her hair before a party, and that a gentleman pinned to his lapel in the morning. They are also very practical roses, however, and deserve a spot in any garden where winters are not too harsh.

TEA ROSES

'Bon Siléne'

Habit: Upright, vigorous shrub, 4–5 ft (1.2–1.5m) tall

Bloom: Abundant, recurrent

Fragrance: Moderate

Disease Resistance: Good in warmer part of range

Special Uses: Specimen, outstanding cut flower

Hardiness: USDA zones 7–10; Canadian zone 8

Pedigree: Introduced before 1837

This early example of a tea rose makes a shrub that is often as wide as it is tall. The buds are long and pointed, unfurling into fragrant, deep pink, loosely double flowers on long stems. Few roses bloom as long or as lavishly, for this sturdy bush bears flowers profusely throughout the growing season. In addition, the foliage usually remains clean and healthy even during southern summers. Finally, this bush is a vigorous grower. Not surprisingly, 'Bon Silène' is an old favorite of southern gardeners and is often found as huge and thriving, though abandoned, bushes marking the sites of old homesteads.

Sources: USA — A1, C2, R1

'Duchesse de Brabant'

Habit: Upright, vigorous shrub, 3–6 ft (0.9–1.8m) tall

Bloom: Outstandingly recurrent

Fragrance: Powerful

Disease Resistance: Resistant to blackspot, prone to powdery mildew

Special Uses: Specimen, border

Hardiness: USDA zones 7–10; Canadian zone 8

Pedigree: Bernede, 1857

'Isabella Sprunt'

Habit: Upright shrub, 4–6 ft (1.2–1.8m) tall

Bloom: Reliably recurrent

Fragrance: Moderate

Disease Resistance: Good

Other Interest: Purple new growth

Hardiness: USDA zones 8–10; Canadian zone 9

Pedigree: Sprunt and Buchanan, 1855; sport of 'Safrano'

This was the rose that Teddy Roosevelt liked to wear in his buttonhole, and it's easy to understand why. 'Duchesse de Brabant' is the essence of luxury, with its heavily perfumed, large, cupped blossoms of soft pink. It is a generous bloomer, too, flowering from spring into fall and even winter in the southern part of its range. Unlike its rangy relatives, this tea rose makes a relatively compact vase-shaped shrub that is easily accommodated in the average garden. It's easy to grow, too — a healthy, vigorous shrub that in the South is often found as a survivor in abandoned gardens.

Sources: USA — A1, G1, R5; Canada — CaP2

This rose is a "sport" of the classic tea rose 'Safrano', which means that a bud on a bush of 'Safrano' spontaneously mutated, and a branch with different characteristics emerged from the parent bush. A nurseryman observed this and took a cutting from the mutated branch. Every bush of 'Isabella Sprunt' descends from that cutting.

Aside from that, every bush of 'Isabella Sprunt' is also a handsome shrub, mounded and as broad as it is tall, with clean, healthy foliage that is plum purple when new. This rose is almost always in bloom, bearing sulfur yellow, semidouble, fragrant flowers that, not surprisingly, resemble those of its parent in everything but color.

Sources: USA — A1, C2, R6

'Marie van Houtte'

Habit: Vigorous, upright shrub, 4–6 ft (1.2–1.8m) tall

Bloom: Recurrent

Fragrance: Moderate

Disease Resistance: Good

Special Uses: Specimen, landscape

Hardiness: USDA zones 8–10; Canadian zone 9

Pedigree: Ducher, 1871; 'Mme. de Tartas' × 'Mme. Falcot'

'Monsieur Tillier'

Habit: Upright shrub, 4–6 ft (1.2–1.8m) tall

Bloom: Recurrent throughout growing season

Fragrance: Moderate

Disease Resistance: Outstanding

Hardiness: USDA zones 7–9; Canadian zone 8

Pedigree: Bernaix, 1891

The Rose Rustlers of central Texas, a colorful and enthusiastic association of antique rose collectors, used to call this cultivar the "hole rose," because they first found it growing in a roadside depression beside an abandoned shed. It is a testimony to this rose's toughness that it coped so successfully in a climate that alternates between flood and drought, and did so in such a carefree way.

A vigorous tea rose that is inclined to sprawl, 'Marie van Houtte' bears large, round, very double, nodding, pale yellow flowers. A tinge of rose pink at the petal tips lends these flowers a special distinction. Any southern gardener in search of an easy rose can do no better than this healthy, attractive shrub, as the Rose Rustlers will testify.

Sources: USA — C2, G2, G3

An outstanding and accommodating rose for southern gardens, 'Monsieur Tillier' bears a steady stream of quartered, fragrant blossoms. Everyone who grows this rose describes the flower color differently, which indicates how complex and subtle is the blending of hues, and underlines the fact that rose color varies with exposure to sunlight and local climate. In general, though, the flowers of 'Monsieur Tillier' open carmine or dark pink with overtones of red, then fade to a brick red or coral pink touched with magenta. One thing is definite: the blossoms are memorable.

The foliage of this rose is a pleasant olive green, and the bush itself is relatively compact. Unlike some of its expansive tea relatives, 'Monsieur Tillier' is easy to work into a garden of ordinary suburban scale.

Sources: USA — A1, G3, R1, S2, V1

'Mrs. B. R. Cant'

Habit: Vigorous, upright shrub, 5–8 ft (1.5–2.4m) tall and wide

Bloom: Excellent recurrence

Fragrance: Strong

Disease Resistance: Good

Special Uses: Specimen, cut flower

Hardiness: USDA zones 8–10; Canadian zone 9

Pedigree: Cant, 1901

'Mrs. Dudley Cross'

Habit: Upright shrub, 3–5 ft (0.9–1.5m) tall

Bloom: Abundant, recurrent

Fragrance: Rich

Disease Resistance: Exceptional

Other Interest: Very few thorns

Special Uses: Specimen, cut flower

Hardiness: USDA zones 8–10; Canadian zone 9

Pedigree: Paul, 1907; parentage unknown

Though it will rapidly expand to fill a large proportion of a small garden, this exceptionally vigorous shrub is worth every inch it occupies. It blooms virtually all season and is a prolific producer of double, silvery pink blooms; the darker pink on the undersides of the petals creates an elegant contrast. These roses are as handsome in a vase as on the bush, for the blossoms of 'Mrs. B. R. Cant' are the best cut flowers among the tea roses. The ease with which this rose may be grown is proven by the fact that it is one of the South's most common graveyard roses; that is, it is often found flourishing on untended old gravesites.

Sources: USA — AI, HI, R6

In the shape and color of its blossoms, this rose suggests a daintier version of the famous hybrid tea 'Peace'. The sturdy shrub is compact, especially for the normally expansive tea roses, and its exceptionally disease-resistant foliage is reliably handsome. 'Mrs. Dudley Cross' is also close to thornless, and its pink-tinged, pale yellow flowers are excellent for cutting and indoor display. Like its tea rose relative 'Mrs. B. R. Cant', this rose is a survivor and is frequently found growing in abandoned gardens in the South. Because cuttings of this rose root easily, it is also one of the most commonly collected and shared of the southern heirloom roses.

Sources: USA — AI, HI, R6

'Perle des Jardins'

Habit: Upright shrub, 3–5 ft (0.9–1.5m) tall

Bloom: Recurrent

Fragrance: Moderate

Other Interest: Purple-red new growth

Special Uses: Specimen, landscape, cut flower

Hardiness: USDA zones 8–10; Canadian zone 9

Pedigree: Levet, 1874; seedling of 'Mme. Falcot'

'Safrano'

Habit: Vigorous, upright shrub, 4–6 ft (1.2–1.8m) tall

Bloom: Recurrent

Fragrance: Moderate

Disease Resistance: Good

Special Uses: Landscape, specimen, hedge

Hardiness: USDA zones 7–10; Canadian zone 8

Pedigree: Beauregard, 1838

A century ago, this was the standard yellow rose of florists, largely because the hefty stems are unusually sturdy for those of a tea rose, and they hold the blossoms erect. Even without this feature, these flowers would still be outstanding: straw yellow, large, fragrant, and very full, with the tips of the closely packed petals rolled to points. All in all, this is a remarkable rose for arranging in a vase.

Besides providing color for the house, 'Perle des Jardins' is a superb garden shrub — compact, healthy, vigorous, and in bloom almost all season. The new growth is wine red and the mature foliage dark green.

Sources: USA — C2, G3, VI

Anyone who has seen 'Safrano' at the peak of bloom — saffron- and apricot-colored petals just starting to fade to buff yellow — will never forget the sight, for this rose is one of the genuine glories of the South. But it is a regional institution as much for its durability as for its beauty. 'Safrano' is one of the toughest tea roses, an excellent choice for a landscape shrub or even a hedge virtually anywhere from USDA zone 7 south. The foliage is disease resistant, fresh, and attractive, and the bush, though naturally expansive, can be contained to a more modest size through pruning, if space is limited.

Sources: USA — C2, G3, SI

Introducing

CLIMBERS AND RAMBLERS

This is another category of convenience, the class into which rosarians have stuffed any type of rose that produces extra-long canes. Here you will find floribundas, polyanthas, hybrid teas, and even species roses. Often the distinction between bush and climber is blurred, as in the case of many of the English roses, which through pruning can be maintained as shrubs, or can be allowed to stretch their canes and be trained to climb up a trellis.

"Rambler" is a name commonly applied to those old-fashioned climbers that bloom just once a year. Most of these roses descend in one way or another from two tough species, *Rosa multiflora*, an Asian rose that has become a troublesome weed throughout much of the United States, and *R. wichuraiana*, the memorial rose (described on page 132). Northerners should watch for ramblers because they tend to be vigorous plants that tolerate cold and adverse conditions better than the other climbers. Ramblers also demand a somewhat different kind of pruning (*see p.191*) than other plants, and because they are so expansive, they are usually poor choices for small spaces.

As with the modern shrub roses, the miscellaneous nature of this class is an advantage. For among the 16 climbers and ramblers described here, there are sure to be some that will flourish in your garden no matter where you live. As these roses climb the sunny side of your garden wall or overtop the arch over your garden gate, they will add height as well as bloom to your landscape.

CLIMBERS AND RAMBLERS

'Dortmund'®

Habit: Vigorous shrub 12–20 ft (3.6–6.0m) tall

Bloom: Recurrent

Fragrance: Slight

Disease Resistance: Good

Other Interest: Dark green, glossy foliage; ornamental hips

Special Uses: Tolerates poor soils

Hardiness: USDA zones 4–8; Canadian zone 5b

Pedigree: Kordes, 1955; seedling × *Rosa kordesii*

Technically, this rose is one of the Kordesii shrubs (*see pp.113–114*), but because of its extreme vigor, it is nearly always grown as a climber. Like the other Kordesii shrubs, 'Dortmund'® descends from a cross between the memorial rose (*Rosa wichuraiana*) and *R. rugosa*, and so it is exceptionally hardy and disease resistant. Its glossy, hollylike foliage sets off the large, slightly ruffled, single, red blooms, each with a white eye surrounding the central knot of brilliant yellow stamens. Deadhead the flowers to encourage repeat bloom; leave them to wither on the stems in the fall so that you can enjoy the pretty orange hips. But beware of the jumbo thorns!

Sources: USA — AI, BI, R7; Canada — CaCI, CaH2, CaP2

'Fortune's Double Yellow'

Habit: Vigorous, vining shrub, 7–10 ft (2.4–3.0m) tall, 10–15 ft (3.0–4.5m) if trained as a climber

Bloom: One long flowering in spring

Other Interest: Extremely thorny

Special Uses: Cut flower

Hardiness: USDA zones 8–10; Canadian zone 7

Pedigree: Chinese garden rose brought to England by Robert Fortune in 1845

Other Names: 'Beauty of Glazenwood', 'Gold Rose of Ophir', *Rosa pseudindica*

'Gloire de Dijon'

Habit: Vigorous, climbing shrub, 12 ft (3.6m) tall

Bloom: Recurrent

Fragrance: Strong

Disease Resistance: Good

Special Uses: Cut flower; tolerates partial shade

Hardiness: USDA zones 6–10; Canadian zone 6

Pedigree: Jacotot, 1853; 'Souvenir de la Malmaison' × tea rose

The clusters of loosely double flowers of this popular old climber have been described as apricot with rose shades, salmon tinged with red, yellow tinged with copper, and so on. However you describe it, the colors are captivating and contrast nicely with the delicate, apple green foliage. It blooms heavily in springtime, and thrives in both the Southeast and the Southwest. Indeed, 'Fortune's Double Yellow' has escaped from cultivation to naturalize in southern California, which testifies to the ease with which this rose may be cultivated. Although it can be grown as a sprawling shrub, it is most effective as a climber; it is spectacular when the canes have been trained up into the limbs of an open-canopied tree, to spill back down to the ground in a curtain of golden blossoms.

Sources: USA — A1, C2, G3

Though classified as a climbing tea rose, this cultivar's blossoms have the look of its Bourbon rose parent, 'Souvenir de la Malmaison'. The flowers of 'Gloire de Dijon' are large, round, quartered, buff yellow with pink-apricot shading, and have a rich fragrance. This rose has also inherited something of the Bourbon's hardiness and will overwinter in USDA zone 6 if planted in a protected spot, such as the south side of a wall. 'Gloire de Dijon' begins the season with a heavy crop of flowers and then repeats well into the fall. It is a good source of cut flowers.

Sources: USA — G3, H4, R1; Canada — CaH2, CaP2

'Golden Showers'®

Habit: Vigorous, compact climber, 6–12 ft (1.8–3.6m) tall

Bloom: Excellent recurrence

Fragrance: Moderate

Disease Resistance: Susceptible to blackspot

Other Interest: Glossy foliage

Special Uses: Pillar; tolerates partial shade

Hardiness: USDA zones 6–9; Canadian zone 6

Pedigree: Lammerts, 1956; 'Charlotte Armstrong' × 'Captain Thomas'

'Goldstern'®

Habit: Bushy, upright shrub, 10 ft (3m) tall

Bloom: Recurrent

Fragrance: Slight

Disease Resistance: Good

Other Interest: Glossy foliage

Special Uses: Tolerates partial shade

Hardiness: USDA zones 4–8; Canadian zone 3

Pedigree: Tantau, 1966

Other Names: 'Gold Star'

This relatively short-caned climber bears large, ruffled, semi-double, daffodil yellow blooms with red stamens, providing a large flush of flowers in late spring or early summer, then faltering a bit and producing another big flush in fall. Although 'Golden Showers'® prefers full sun, it will tolerate some shade and so is a good choice when a rose is needed for a north-facing wall. By periodically pruning back the canes, this rose can be maintained as a large specimen shrub. It is somewhat cold sensitive and performs best in the Mid-Atlantic states and the South.

Sources: USA — BI, FI, OI; Canada — CaHI, CaH2, CaP2

An exceptionally hardy climber, 'Goldstern'® overwinters reliably even in USDA zone 4 and southern Canadian zone 3. Although this rose was bred by another German nurseryman, Matt Tantau, it descends from the Kordes nursery (*see pp. 113–114*). It is usually grown as a climber, though in a large spot and an informal planting, it could be allowed to sprawl. 'Goldstern'® is especially good for cold, exposed sites. It bears clusters of long, pointed buds that open into 4 in (10cm) fully double flowers that are flattened like architectural rosettes. The fragrance of the flowers is only slight. The leaves are medium green, glossy, and usually healthy. The new foliage is pale green edged with red, making a pleasant contrast.

Sources: USA — HI, R2, R5

'Henry Kelsey'

Habit: Vigorous, trailing shrub, 4 ft (1.2m) tall, 10 ft (3m) wide; 8–10 ft (2.3–3.0m) tall if trained as a climber

Bloom: Recurrent

Fragrance: Moderate

Disease Resistance: Some susceptibility to blackspot

Special Uses: Tolerates partial shade

Hardiness: USDA zones 3–7; Canadian zone 3

Pedigree: Svejda, 1984; *R. kordesii* hybrid × seedling

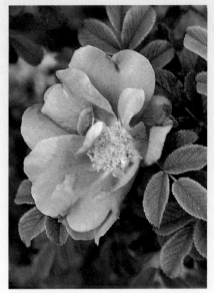

'Martin Frobisher'

Habit: Upright, vigorous shrub, 5 ft (1.5m) tall, 4 ft (1.2m) wide

Bloom: Recurrent

Fragrance: Moderate

Disease Resistance: Some susceptibility to blackspot and rust

Other Interest: Few thorns

Special Uses: Tolerates partial shade

Hardiness: USDA zones 2–7; Canadian zone 2

Pedigree: Svejda, 1968; 'Schneezwerg' × seedling

A superhardy climber from Agriculture Canada's explorer series of roses *(see pp.12–13)*, in early summer 'Henry Kelsey' bears a heavy crop of clustered, vivid red, semidouble blooms with showy golden stamens and a spicy scent. After slacking off in July, it returns with a strong showing in late summer and early fall. 'Henry Kelsey' has demonstrated some susceptibility to blackspot but otherwise seems quite disease resistant.

Given lots of room, this rose may be allowed to sprawl as a wide, arching shrub, but it is more often trained as a climber on a split-rail fence or trellis.

Sources: USA — CI, KI, R4; Canada — CaCI, CaHI, CaP2

The first of the Canadian explorer roses, this cultivar descends in part from the central Asian species *Rosa rugosa*, and in fact 'Martin Frobisher' is often classified as a hybrid rugosa. However you classify it, this rose shares its forebear's vigor and immunity to cold; at the Minnesota Landscape Arboretum in Excelsior, 'Martin Frobisher' has proven hardy to –22°F (–30°C). This rose may show some susceptibility to blackspot and rust, but in general it is a healthy plant.

The small, very double, soft pink rosettes are borne over a long season. Though 'Martin Frobisher' is technically a shrub, its narrow, upright habit lends itself to training along a fence or pillar.

Sources: USA — HI, R4, WI; Canada — CaCI, CaHI, CaP2

'Mermaid'

Habit: Extremely vigorous, trailing shrub, 6–25 ft (1.8–7.5m) tall

Bloom: Excellent recurrent bloom once established

Fragrance: Moderate

Disease Resistance: Good

Other Interest: Very thorny

Special Uses: Fast-growing screen or barrier; tolerates partial shade

Hardiness: USDA zones 6–10; Canadian zone 6

Pedigree: Paul, 1918; *Rosa bracteata* × yellow tea rose

'New Dawn'

Habit: Vigorous, rambling shrub, 6–10 ft (1.8–3.0m) tall

Bloom: Good recurrent flowering

Fragrance: Strong

Disease Resistance: Good

Special Uses: Well adapted to difficult sites; tolerates poor soils, partial shade

Hardiness: USDA zones 5–9; Canadian zone 6

Pedigree: Dreer, 1930; sport of 'Dr. W. Van Fleet'

This rose functions like floral white-out. Plant it next to an unsightly shed or an ugly fence and step back. 'Mermaid' will take a year or two to establish itself, but then it will bury the eyesore with awesome speed, especially in warmer climates. The huge (5 in [13cm]), single, canary yellow blooms have showy golden stamens that remain attractive after the petals have fallen. The impressive thorns make 'Mermaid' an effective barrier but also make pruning a chore; plant this rose where you can let it roam at will.

Sources: USA — AI, C2, VI; Canada — CaH2

This rose was regarded as so special when it was released onto the market that it received the first plant patent ever granted by the U.S. government. 'New Dawn' is an everblooming sport of an old, ironclad rambler named 'Dr. W. Van Fleet', and the offspring shares the parent's toughness. This rose bears pearl pink, cupped, semidouble blooms that fade to a rose-cream color with bright gold stamens once fully open. It may be maintained as an open, arching shrub, but because of its extraordinarily vigorous growth, 'New Dawn' is usually grown as a climber. It is especially beautiful when trained up into a tree and allowed to cascade back down. Because this rose tolerates less than ideal conditions, it's a good selection for a difficult site.

Sources: USA — AI, G2, G3; Canada — CaHI, CaH2, CaP2

'Prairie Dawn'

Habit: Vigorous, upright shrub, 5 ft (1.5m) tall, 4 ft (1.2m) wide; taller when trained as a climber

Bloom: Recurrent

Fragrance: Moderate

Disease Resistance: Good

Special Uses: Tolerates exposed, windy sites

Hardiness: USDA zones 3–7; Canadian zone 3b

Pedigree: Godfrey, 1959; 'Prairie Youth' × ('Ross Rambler' × ['Dr. W. Van Fleet' × *Rosa spinosissima altaica*])

'Sombreuil'

Habit: Vigorous, upright shrub, 8–12 ft (2.4–3.6m)

Bloom: Recurrent

Fragrance: Moderate

Disease Resistance: Good

Other Interest: Thorny

Special Uses: Pillar, wall, trellis

Hardiness: USDA zones 6–9; Canadian zone 6

Pedigree: Robert, 1850; seedling of 'Gigantesque' (hybrid perpetual)

One of the prairie roses bred at the Morden Research Station in Manitoba, this tall, superhardy shrub rose has suffered little damage even in the near-arctic winters at the Minnesota Landscape Arboretum. It has also demonstrated some susceptibility to blackspot and leaf spot in the rose trials there, but in general this is a heathy rose.

'Prairie Dawn' bears semidouble, radiant pink flowers in repeated flushes throughout the season. These flowers are of moderate size, roughly 3 in (7.6cm) in diameter, and are moderately fragrant. This is a terrific city shrub for fences or walls where the wind and exposure would kill other roses.

Sources: USA — M1, R1, R7; Canada — CaH1, CaH2, CaP2

One of the hardiest of the tea roses, 'Sombreuil' is a glory of the South that can also be enjoyed throughout much of the North. This graceful old climber bears large, very double, cream-colored flowers that are quartered and flat when fully open. After blooming heavily at the beginning of the season, it will rebloom dependably. The foliage is glossy and leathery, providing a nice foil for the pale flowers.

'Sombreuil' is a vigorous but mannerly rose that is easily controlled — but don't plant it near a walk, for it is very definitely thorny. Instead, 'Sombreuil' is at its best on a pillar, low wall, trellis, or any place you can enjoy its delicious tea scent in safety.

Sources: USA — C2, H1, M2; Canada — CaH2, CaP2

'Tausendschön'

Habit: Vigorous shrub, 8–12 ft (2.4–3.6m) tall

Bloom: Abundant bloom, one summer flowering

Fragrance: Slight

Disease Resistance: Somewhat susceptible to mildew

Other Interest: Few thorns

Special Uses: Pillar

Hardiness: USDA zones 5–9; Canadian zone 6

Pedigree: Schmidt, 1906; 'Daniel Lacombe' × 'Weiser Herumstreicher'

'Veilchenblau'

Habit: Vigorous, climbing shrub, 10–15 ft (3.0–4.5m) tall

Bloom: One summer flowering

Fragrance: Moderate

Disease Resistance: Somewhat susceptible to mildew

Other Interest: Nearly thornless

Special Uses: Tolerates partial shade

Hardiness: USDA zones 5–9; Canadian zone 6

Pedigree: Schmidt, 1909; 'Crimson Rambler' × 'Erinnerung an Brod'

Thousand beauties" is the translation of this rose's name, but that is an understatement. In fact, a well-grown specimen of this plant offers far more beauties than that when it buries itself under myriad clusters of small pompon blossoms for several weeks in early summer. These blossoms open a deep rose pink with white centers, then fade to a blushing white. As it's nearly thornless, it is a good choice for a pillar or arch in a high-traffic area. Use it as a living trellis for a clematis to extend the season of bloom. Or let 'Tausendschön' sprawl and use it as a ground cover.

Sources: USA — A1, R2, R3

This rose not only tolerates some shade, but it shows its best colors there. In a sunny spot, its reddish purple buds open to small, semidouble purple-violet flowers streaked with white and tufted with golden stamens. The scent of 'Veilchenblau' is that of oranges. In partial shade, the blossoms open lilac blue, as close to a true blue as you will find in a rose that has not been genetically engineered.

A vigorous climber, 'Veilchenblau' can be trained up a trellis, or the canes can be infiltrated into the branches of a small tree, where they will scramble up in a beautifully informal display. Providing good air circulation around this rose is particularly important in a shaded site if the foliage is to remain free of powdery mildew.

Sources: USA — H1, M2, R4; Canada — CaH2, CaP2

'William Baffin'

Habit: Upright, vigorous shrub, 5–8 ft (1.5–2.4m) tall, 8–12 ft (2.4–3.6m) tall if trained as a climber

Bloom: Recurrent

Fragrance: Slight

Disease Resistance: Highly resistant to blackspot and mildew

Special Uses: Tolerates exposed, difficult sites; partial shade

Hardiness: USDA zones 2–7; Canadian zone 2b

Pedigree: Svedja, 1968; seedling of *Rosa kordesii* × ('Red Dawn' × 'Suzanne')

'Zéphirine Drouhin'

Habit: Upright, vigorous climber, 8–12 ft (2.4–3.6m) tall

Bloom: Abundant, recurrent

Fragrance: Sweet, strong

Disease Resistance: Good

Other Interest: Thornless canes, purplish red new foliage

Special Uses: Pillars, fences, walls

Hardiness: USDA zones 6–9; Canadian zone 6

Pedigree: Bizot, 1868

Although all the Canadian explorer roses are tough, this one may be the toughest. Not only will 'William Baffin' tolerate winter temperatures that plunge to −50°F (−45°C), but it is also practically disease free when planted in the North. Although it can be grown as a tall shrub, this rose looks best when tied in and disciplined as a climber. It blooms steadily throughout the summer and into the fall, bearing large clusters of 3 in (7.5cm) strawberry pink blossoms with white centers marked by knots of showy yellow stamens. Remember this rose for your hour of need: it flourishes on the kind of windy, exposed sites where few other climbers will survive.

Sources: USA — AI, HI, R4; Canada — CaHI, CaP2

Parents of small children will appreciate this Bourbon rose's thornless stems; this characteristic also makes it a good selection for running up an arch over a busy path, since it won't snag passersby. Traditionally, 'Zéphirine Drouhin' has been espaliered against a wall or trellis, though it can also be allowed to sprawl as an outsize shrub in an informal cottage-type garden. Deliciously fragrant, loosely cupped, cerise-pink blooms appear almost continuously through the season. It has a delicious old-rose fragrance.

Sources: USA — MI, OI, R4; Canada — CaH2, CaPI, CaP2

Chapter Four

SHOPPING FOR ROSES

*"Rose is a rose is a rose is a rose," claimed Gertrude Stein,
which only proves that this great writer was not a great gardener. Any backyard
veteran knows that if you start with inferior stock, you cannot create a really fine
garden display. This is especially true in the case of roses.*

There are, sadly, careless wholesale rose nurseries that every year unload onto unsuspecting customers huge numbers of unhealthy and misidentified rosebushes. Often the customers of these wholesalers are local garden centers that innocently resell the defective plants to homeowners. If you acquire one of these inferior shrubs, you will be disappointed.

Fortunately, problem plants are the exception. And it's easy to identify and avoid them. The nursery industry as a whole works hard to enforce high standards among its members and ensure that products are of the very best quality. But benefiting from this quality control involves gaining a little education. In addition, learning how to shop for roses can save you a lot of money. Skillful shoppers will find many bargains. They also will find that the selection of roses available to them is much

greater. That will make their gardens not only more interesting but also more rewarding.

When to Plant and When to Shop

When ordering any kind of nursery stock, it's best to plan ahead. Those who wait until planting season to shop pay higher prices and often cannot obtain the cultivars they want. Instead, they have to settle for whatever the better-organized gardeners have not already purchased. So plan to begin shopping at least two months before planting time.

But when *is* planting time for roses? That depends on where you garden. In general, the ideal time for transplanting rosebushes is when the weather is moist and cool. Such weather is ideal because it promotes vigorous growth in a newly transplanted rosebush and so speeds its establishment in its new home. Cool, moist weather is also good because it does not stress the transplant by making demands on its traumatized root system.

Roots are traumatized during transplanting because the move from the nursery to the garden inevitably damages most of a bush's fine feeder roots. This damage temporarily cripples the plant's ability to absorb water from the soil and deliver it to the leaves and stems. So if you transplant a rose during hot, sunny weather, when moisture evaporates at a rapid rate from the leaves into the surrounding atmosphere, your new plant is guaranteed to suffer from dehydration. This can kill a transplant, or at least permanently stunt its growth.

Cool, moist weather typically comes twice a year in most of North America: in early spring to mid-spring and again in early fall. Spring planting is by far the most popular, and in the North, there is good reason for this. Throughout much of the northern half of the United States and in most of Canada, winter cold is the greatest threat to garden roses. New plantings need time to send their roots down into the soil, and new growth must be able to

mature before it is attacked by frost. Fall planting is possible but risky in such circumstances.

Throughout much of the South and Southwest, however, summer heat and drought are the principal threats to roses, and in those regions fall planting has the advantage. In warm-climate regions, winter is commonly a time of mild temperatures and increased rainfall. This means that a rose planted in fall has several months of ideal conditions in which to recover before it faces summer's stress.

Where temperatures are moderate year-round, as in much of the Northwest, British Columbia, and parts of the coastal northeastern and Mid-Atlantic states, both spring and fall are good planting seasons. Wherever you garden, though, set your planting by nature's calendar, not man's. Officially, spring may arrive on March 21 in North Dakota, but the soil is likely to be frozen then, or at least too wet from the recent thaw to dig. And although fall officially begins on September 21, summer's heat and drought are liable to last well after that date in the Deep South. So set your seasonal calendar (and

By the time your roses are in full bloom, the spring planting season for bare-root roses is past. Any additions to the garden now should be in the form of container-grown roses. In milder climates, fall brings another opportunity for bare-root planting.

your rose shopping) to the dates of the last spring frost and the first fall frost. A local nursery or the Cooperative Extension Service can tell you when these events usually occur in your area. The average date of the last spring frost marks midspring, while that of the first fall frost marks midfall.

Starting with Healthy Stock

As a gardener, you want to start your garden off right. You want to plant only top-quality rosebushes, the nursery's best. But how can you tell which those are?

Becoming a good judge of nursery stock is easy, but you have to understand what you are looking at. Nurseries package and sell roses in a number of different ways. The clues to quality vary considerably with the kind of packaging.

Bare-Root Roses

A generation ago, virtually all roses were sold "bare-root" — that is, the bushes were dug while dormant and placed in cold storage. Then they were shipped to the customer while still dormant, and without any soil around the roots. This may sound like a risky process, but if bare-root roses are shipped at the appropriate planting times in the customers' regions and the roses are planted promptly upon arrival, the survival rate is excellent.

Bare-root roses offer many advantages. Because roses packaged this way are light and easy to handle, the retail price tends to be much cheaper than for roses packaged in other ways. Often a bare-root rose will cost only half as much as other roses or even less. This kind of packaging also lends itself to mail-order sales, which means that a large nursery specializing in roses can sell bare-root plants directly to customers all over North America. Such specialist nurseries offer far more diverse selections of cultivars than local garden centers, so if you are looking for a particular type of rose, you are far more likely to find it as a bare-root plant.

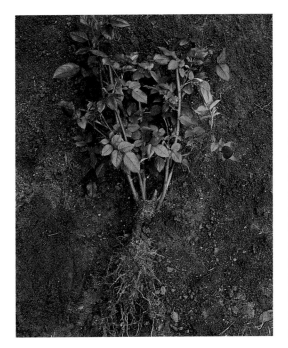

If bare-root roses arrive in full leaf, call the nursery and demand replacements or a credit. Bare-root roses withstand shipping and transplanting without harm, as long as they are dormant. Once they have resumed growth, however, this sort of handling causes unacceptable injury to the roots.

The disadvantages of bare-root roses are that they require a bit more care at planting time and the season for planting them is shorter. A rosebush in a pot of soil can sit in a nursery yard (or in your own backyard) without damage for several weeks; a bare-root rose must go into the ground within a few days of when it is taken out of cold storage and shipped to you.

When shopping by mail, you cannot, of course, inspect the plants before you buy them. The best guarantee of quality in these circumstances is the reputation of the nursery. Ask other gardeners in your area or the curator of the nearest public rose garden if they buy bare-root roses and which nurseries they recommend. You also should not hesitate to call the customer service number in a mail-order nursery's catalog. Ask which rootstock the nursery uses and make sure it is one adapted to your region (*see pp.*39-41).

Find out, too, the grade of the bushes that the nursery ships. Roses are graded according to the number and thickness of the canes as either No. 1, No. 1½, or No. 2. No. 1 is the top grade. No. 1½ roses are acceptable but should be markedly cheaper. Avoid No. 2 roses; such undersized plants

Roots emerging from the bottom of the pot, blackspot on the leaves, weed-infested soil, and one-sided branching are signs that the container rose to the right has been neglected and held in the pot too long. The evenly distributed outward-reaching canes on the rose to the left typify a healthy plant and a good buy.

Container-Grown Roses

These are an expensive alternative to bare-root roses, but container-grown bushes are becoming ever more popular because of the convenience and flexibility they offer. The name *container-grown* is actually a misnomer, since most such roses were not grown in their containers. According to the nursery industry definition, a rose need only have been in its pot for one month of active growth to qualify as container-grown. This means that most of the plants you find under this label were bare-root roses that the local retailer purchased and potted up sometime earlier in the spring. By the time you see the roses, though, they have broken dormancy and resumed growth both above and below ground. They can remain in the container for weeks or even months, and if planted carefully, they will suffer little trauma when transplanted into the garden. This makes container-grown roses the best bet for last-minute planting late in the spring.

Unfortunately, the trauma that can most seriously injure a container-grown rose often occurs before you buy the plant. If the nursery did a poor job of potting up the rose or gave it poor care subsequently, the bush may be permanently stunted, even though it looks healthy.

To make sure that a container-grown rose has received good care, first check the roots. If these are growing out through the drainage holes in the bottom of the container, the rose has been in the pot too long. Grasp the rosebush around the base of the canes, upend the pot, and slip out the root ball. Masses of roots running around the outside of the root ball are another sign that the rose has been in the pot too long. The tips of the roots should be visible, and they should be crisp and white. Blackened root tips are a sign that the plant was left out in a hot, sunny spot and the root ball became overheated.

Check the canes of container-grown roses, too. These should have been pruned so that the new

may be the result of poor growing conditions, and they will rarely recover to rival their huskier fellows.

Check bare-root roses upon arrival. The canes may be coated with paraffin, but underneath they should be smooth and green. Shriveled and blackened canes are symptoms of unhealthy plants. Each No. 1 plant should have three or four sturdy canes, and these should point outward so that the rose can develop an open, well-balanced structure of branches. If the dormant roses are lacking in any of these respects, call the nursery and ask for replacements or your money back.

Just as important as the quality of the canes is the state of the roots. These should be well branched and developed in a rounded, well-proportioned pattern so that the bush's root system won't be one-sided. Poorly developed roots and badly broken and damaged roots are both grounds for calling the nursery and demanding a replacement.

growth is directed outward. A rose with a dense mass of foliage and canes growing back through the center of the plant is not a good buy. Check under the leaves and along the stems for insects or insect eggs. If the nursery was careless about pest control, you may bring home problems on a container-grown rose that will cause an epidemic in your garden.

Boxed and Bagged Roses

Another common way to package roses for sale is to pack the roots of a bare-root bush in moist sphagnum peat and then enclose them in a cardboard box or plastic bag. This type of packaging seems to offer the same advantages as container-grown roses, and in the case of the boxed roses, even greater convenience, since the directions on the package recommend planting these roses box and all: just rip the top off the box and set it right into the soil.

Actually, though, this rarely works well. Typically, the rose's roots never emerge from their cardboard-enclosed cocoon, and so the bush remains stunted.

You can, of course, remove the rosebush from the box before planting; such treatment is essential when planting bagged roses. Usually, however, when you remove the box, the peat falls away from around the roots. If you are lucky, the rose will have remained dormant, and so you can plant it as if it had been shipped to you bare-root. Often, though, the rosebush has already broken dormancy and resumed growth while in the garden center or store. If this has happened, then the falling away of the peat will injure any new feeder roots. This setback will further slow the recovery of the plant from transplanting and may even cause its death.

All in all, boxed roses are the least desirable kind of nursery stock. Because they are easy to handle, however, they make up a large part of the roses that local garden centers sell. For this reason, you may find yourself with few alternatives if you want to pick up a new rosebush in a hurry. Keep in mind, though, that at the very least, the boxed or bagged rose will suffer more transplanting trauma and will almost certainly take longer to resume growth than other types of roses.

At local garden centers, the emphasis is on convenience, but that doesn't always serve the roses well. The "bagged" roses, far left, are bare-root plants whose roots were packed in sphagnum peat and enclosed in a plastic bag. Such roses are easy to handle for the retailer, but unbagging the roots when you plant is liable to injure them. The container roses, near left, are a better alternative. Just as easy to transport, they can wait in their pots for weeks and still be transplanted into the garden with little trauma.

Rooted Cuttings

Own-root roses and all miniature roses are reproduced by cuttings. That is, instead of grafting a bud of the garden rose onto a rootstock rose, the nursery takes a length of cane from the garden rose and encourages it to grow roots and develop into a plant of its own.

Usually such own-root roses arrive from the nursery as much smaller plants than grafted plants of similar age. In the case of miniature roses, the reason for this disparity is logical. With full-size shrubs, the smaller size of the own-root roses is due to the fact that their roots are typically less vigorous than those of the popular rootstock roses (*see pp.*39-41).

Own-root roses of the full-size classes are also slower to put on new growth once they are transplanted into the garden. Often, they spend the first year or two there extending their roots into the soil and making little visible growth above ground. Once they have settled in, however, own-root roses will usually equal grafted roses in vigor and prove much longer-lived. This is especially true of the roses developed by Agriculture Canada, which were specially bred to be grown own-root.

Before ordering own-root roses, you should decide whether you have the patience to work with these slower-developing plants. Those who garden in regions with challenging soils, such as areas where the soils are markedly alkaline, may also find that roses grafted onto well-adapted rootstocks perform better in their gardens than do garden roses grown on their own, less well-adapted roots.

An incurable virus causes the yellow "mosaic" streaking seen on these leaves. Often, though, infected roses betray no symptom other than a lack of vigor.

Avoiding Mosaic Viruses

A variety of viruses may afflict roses, causing a set of symptoms described as "rose mosaic." The leaves of infected plants may develop yellow streaks in a mosaic pattern (see below left). Sometimes, however, the viruses do not betray themselves with such visible symptoms. Infected roses gradually lose vigor, and although the viruses are not fatal, their debilitated victims become easy prey for winter cold, drought, and insect pests.

There is no cure, and infected plants, once identified, are best simply dug up and disposed of. Fortunately, prevention is easy. Mosaic viruses are spread almost solely by sloppy nursery work. Often they come to the rose through the rootstock. Rootstocks are commonly reproduced by cuttings, so if the "stock" plant from which the cuttings were taken is infected, all the cuttings will carry the virus, too, and will pass it along to any roses grafted onto them. Own-root roses also may carry the virus if the cuttings were taken from infected plants. In many cases, the problem may not originate with the retail nursery from which you bought the rose, but with the wholesaler who grew the bush.

In any case, you should make a point of buying roses only from nurseries that propagate from virus-free stock, or from retailers who insist on the same care from their wholesalers. All the nurseries listed in Appendix B are reliable sources of virus-free roses. The better-known wholesale rose growers such as Star Roses (Conard-Pyle) and Jackson & Perkins in the United States and Enderlein Nurseries in Canada, are also meticulous in this respect.

When searching for less common cultivars, you may be forced to patronize unfamiliar nurseries. You should feel free to call the growers and discuss your concern about viruses. Ask them what precautions they take to keep their roses virus free. Check with other gardeners in your area — the American and Canadian rose societies (*see p.*37) are excellent sources of such contacts — and see if they have had any experience with the nursery in question.

Sources

Where you get your roses is another important decision. It's one that will go far toward determining not only the price of new rosebushes and their quality but also the types that are available to you. As a resourceful gardener, you'll identify many different sources. With experience, you'll come to know where to turn no matter what your needs.

Commercial Sources

There are three basic types of commercial sources of roses, and each has its peculiar advantages and disadvantages. The dedicated shopper will use all three options.

• **Mail-Order Nurseries.** As mentioned earlier, these nurseries sell mainly bare-root roses. They offer the best selections of cultivars, often at excellent prices. The Canadian mail-order nurseries (*see p.213*) are particularly good sources of roses for northern gardens, since the Canadian growers use rootstocks adapted to northern soils and climates. In addition, any rose raised in a Canadian field has already been tested for cold tolerance. Southern gardeners are also more likely to find roses grafted onto rootstocks suited to their soils and climate at mail-order nurseries.

• **Local Nurseries and Garden Centers.** These offer smaller selections of cultivars and usually stock only container-grown and boxed roses. Generally, prices are somewhat higher, or even much higher, than those at mail-order nurseries. However, local nurseries offer convenience and a source of roses outside the early-spring and early-fall planting seasons. Often, too, the nursery can provide advice about types of roses that are successful locally.

For gardeners who like to personally inspect a rose before they buy it, the local garden center offers an obvious advantage over mail-order nurseries. Most often, the roses you will find there will be container grown, boxed, or bagged.

• **Discount Stores, Home Centers, Supermarkets.** Rosebushes appear in huge quantities at these outlets, usually in early spring. Generally, these roses come from reputable suppliers, but check the plants' labels to make sure they are No. I grade. Often the price per plant is very attractive at such outlets. The problem with these discount roses is that the plants have almost certainly been abused. They may arrive at the discount store or supermarket in good condition but thereafter are commonly stored at too high a temperature, subjected to unskilled and haphazard watering, and bounced around by careless sales personnel and hordes of shoppers. Always ask the manager when the roses were delivered to the store, and if they have been at that site for more than a few days, give them a miss.

Do-It-Yourself Roses

You don't *have* to buy your roses. Indeed, the roses you obtain locally for free are often the best performers. That's why, before sending off an order to some faraway rose grower, you should always take time to look around your own neighborhood. If you find a rosebush that is flourishing there with a minimum of care, chances are excellent that it will prove to be an easy rose in your garden, too.

Cemeteries and abandoned gardens are excellent places to look for hardy, self-sufficient roses, since any survivors in such sites have had to fend for themselves. If your neighbors have an outstandingly healthy and attractive rosebush, ask them what care the plant receives. Is it a carefree rose?

Once you've identified a promising rose and secured the permission of the owners, it's your job to propagate it. Often if you check around the base of the bush, you'll find suckers (rooted shoots) springing up in the surrounding soil. Compare the foliage and, if possible, the flowers of the sucker to those of the parent bush to make sure they are the same. If they differ, the sucker probably arises from a rootstock and isn't any kind of rose you want in your garden. Commonly, though, such old roses are of the own-root type. Even if the bush was originally a grafted one, roots may have sprouted from the base of the scion (the desirable top portion of the bush) if the rose was planted with the bud union below the soil surface.

If the sucker and the parent bush prove to be the same type of rose, you are in luck. But separating the sucker from the parent takes some care. The first thing you need to do is sharpen the edge of your spade with a file. Then slice down into the ground between sucker and parent to sever the connection between the two (*see p.*156). Carefully dig the sucker from the ground, retaining as much soil as you can around its roots, and replant it in an appropriate part of your garden as soon as possible.

More often than not, you'll find no suckers. In that case, you should take a cutting from the parent bush. Select a cane about as thick as a pencil — a mature shoot but one that is not yet too hard and woody. If you look in the early summer (in most areas, that's the best time to root a cutting), find a young cane with a blossom atop it. That cane is at the ideal stage of its development to turn into cuttings. With a sharp knife or pruning shears, cut the cane into pieces about as long as a pencil, making sure that each one has three to five leaves or buds on it. Store these in a plastic bag with a damp paper towel and keep them cool until you get home.

Upon arriving home, first make a rooting bed. Select an area that receives bright but indirect light, such as a bed at the foot of a north-facing wall. Then dig in an ample dose of sphagnum peat and coarse builder's sand so that the soil drains well and yet retains moisture. Next, take the cuttings out of the plastic bag and snip off all but the topmost leaf from each. Dip the bottom of each cutting into rooting-hormone powder (available at most garden centers) and shake off the excess. Poke a hole several inches deep into the rooting bed and drop in the cutting so that the bottom third rests below ground. Then with the tip of a pencil, firm the soil back in around the cutting.

ROOTING A CUTTING

1 To take a cutting from a mature rosebush, cut a cane with a flower — one whose stem is about as thick as a pencil. Cut just above an outward-facing set of leaves. Cut the cane into pencil-sized lengths, making sure that each piece has at least three leaves. Trim off flowers and store these cuttings for up to a day in a plastic bag with a damp paper towel.

2 With a sharp knife, cut all but the topmost leaf from each cutting. Then dip the base in rooting-hormone powder; shake off any excess.

3 Poke a hole in your rooting bed with a dibble or pencil, ease in the bottom third of the cutting, and then firm in the soil around the base of the cutting.

4 Water the cuttings well, then cover them with tops cut from two-liter plastic soda bottles. Check the cuttings every few weeks by giving a gentle tug; when the cutting resists removal from the soil, it has rooted.

The easiest way to secure a start of a care-free "found" rose is to locate a sucker, a shoot emerging from the roots of the rose. Check to make sure the sucker's foliage is identical to that of the parent shrub to avoid propagating rootstock. Then, with a sharp spade, slice down between the bush and sucker, and carefully lift the sucker out of the soil along with its roots. Replant promptly.

After lining out all the cuttings in the bed, water them well and cover each with an upended one-quart canning jar or a two-liter plastic soda bottle from which you have cut the bottom. Within four to six weeks, the cuttings should have begun to root. To test their progress, tug gently at the remaining leaf of each. If the cutting starts to slip out of the bed, it has not yet sprouted roots; push it back in and firm the soil around it. If the cutting resists removal, root growth has begun. Remove the jar or soda-bottle "greenhouses" from any rooted cuttings, but leave the cuttings in place until the following spring (or, in the South, fall), at which time you should transplant the cuttings to a sunny nursery area at the edge of your vegetable bed or cutting garden. In a year, they will be ready to transplant into their final location in the garden.

As always, there is a shortcut. At plant swaps sponsored by the garden club or other community groups, you may find already-rooted cuttings or suckers of roses. Ask about the care the parent roses have received before taking these youngsters home to your own garden, but chances are they will be easy roses. Although your neighbors may take visitors first to see their rarities, the roses they are most likely to share are the ones that are easy to grow and propagate.

First Aid for New Arrivals

To be dug from the earth, thrown in a truck, and then replanted in a new environment is a tremendous shock to any plant. Roses are more resilient than most plants and usually survive this experience with no permanent damage. Still, if you are going to take the time to search out appropriate cultivars and pay the money for premium nursery stock, it's only common sense to make the transition to your garden as stress free as possible.

Old-time gardeners insisted that this care began with preparation: you had to have the holes dug and ready for planting before the new roses arrived. Few of today's gardeners achieve that sort of meticulous organization. But a handful of precautions taken along the way — the work of minutes — are feasible and can make the difference between life and death for the roses.

With container-grown plants, the precautions begin at the nursery. After buying the plants, you should ask the nursery to water them before putting them in your car or truck. The ride back to your house is likely to be breezy. On the highway, the wind that blows through the car can easily reach gale strength. This will dehydrate the foliage unless the roots are well supplied with water. Don't stop for other errands on the way home; your roses won't appreciate an hour in a sun-heated car.

If you carry the roses home in the back of a pickup, the danger of dehydration is even greater. In that case, you should protect the roses by covering them with a tarpaulin.

Once the plants have arrived at your house, set them in a shaded or semishaded spot. Don't leave them out in the sun on the driveway to cook. And plant them promptly — ideally, the same day.

As disturbing as a move is to container-grown roses, it is vastly more so to bare-root plants. They need real first aid. Open the shipping carton as soon as it arrives, unwrap the roses inside, and check to make sure they are in good condition (*see p.*150). If the results of your inspection are satisfactory and you will be planting within a day or so, stand the roses in a bucket of water, making sure all the roots are covered.

If planting must wait for a few days, don't remove the roses from the shipping carton. Instead, moisten their roots with a mist of water, replace the shipping materials around the bushes, and put the box somewhere dry and cool but frost free. The customer service representative at Pickering Nurseries, Inc. (*see p.*213), a leading Canadian rose supplier, suggests that a refrigerator — "lots of people keep an old one in the basement" — is ideal. An unheated garage also works well; set the box of roses against an interior wall where the heat escaping from the house will moderate any nighttime dips in temperature. Another good storage space for dormant roses is the space found underneath an old-fashioned bulkhead door — the type that gives access to the basement from outdoors. Where winter climates are warm, an air-conditioned room on the north side of the house may provide the best conditions. In such climates, however, it is important to get the roses planted as soon as possible.

Usually nurseries take care to ship bare-root roses to customers around the correct planting date, but a late spring may throw off these calculations. You may find that your new roses arrive while the soil in your garden is frozen or still sodden from a recent spring thaw. Digging the soil while it is so

To store bare-root roses for any period longer than a week, heel them in. Dig a trench 12 in (30.5cm) deep and 18 in (45.7cm) across, and bury the roses at a 45-degree angle, covering all but the cane tips. Water well.

wet can destroy its structure and turn it into compacted mud. In such a situation, you may have to delay planting for a week or two. If so, find a spot to heel in the newly arrived rosebushes.

Heeling-in involves finding an area of thawed, well-drained soil. You are likely to find this in the vegetable garden, especially if you cultivate your edible crops in raised beds. An area up against the foundation of your house and sheltered by the eaves is another good spot. Once a suitable place has been located, dig a trench about 12 in (30cm) deep and 18 in (45cm) across. Lay the roses side by side in the trench so that their roots rest on its bottom and the canes point upward and out to the side at an angle of approximately 45 degrees. Then sift the soil back over the roses until the roots are buried and most of the canes are covered. Water well.

When stored in this fashion, your roses will remain safely dormant and intact as long as the weather stays cool. As soon as the weather warms, you will be ready to plant, at which time you can retrieve your bushes from their trench, digging carefully so as not to injure the canes or roots, and plant them like any other bare-root roses.

Differences among grades of hybrid tea roses are easily visible in this selection of bushes. The rose to the right, with the three husky canes emerging from the bud union, is of the highest, or No. 1 grade. The rose at center, with two strong canes, is rated No. 1½; the rose at left, with two spindly canes and only one strong cane, rates as No. 2.

Passing Grades

This grading system for roses was created by the American Association of Nurserymen, with the goal of providing buyers with a reliable standard of comparison when shopping for roses. Of course, it also protects the rose growers. Growers who produce a superior product — larger, huskier shrubs — can profit by their work because they can advertise their roses as belonging to a superior grade.

It is important to keep in mind, though, that the grade assigned to a rose reflects its size and quality at the time it was harvested. A rose that met all the qualifications for No. 1 grade then may have been so mistreated afterward that it becomes a very poor buy. In addition, you may encounter roses that don't make the grade and yet are still good buys. Own-root roses, for example, are typically slower growing than grafted roses. For this reason, nurseries commonly sell own-root roses at smaller sizes, so that they rarely meet the criteria for each rose type (*facing page*).

Among grafted roses, though, an inferior grade does generally reflect poorer quality. Likewise, a failure to label the roses with the grade is usually a caution flag. You may still decide to purchase the lower grade of rose, or the ungraded one, but you should ask the sales staff about this issue before you make your choice.

Grading Criteria

To make sure that you always get the most rose for your money, you have to understand the system by which rose plants are graded. Usually the plant label specifies the grade; if it doesn't, ask the nursery. Then check the plant to make sure that it does in fact conform to the standards listed at right. There's nothing wrong with purchasing a healthy rose of a lesser grade if that is reflected in the price. What you should avoid is paying a premium price for a plant of lesser quality. You don't want to pay for a No. 1 rose if you are actually getting only a No. 1½.

AMERICAN ASSOCIATION OF NURSERYMEN GRADING SYSTEM

Hybrid Tea, Tea, Grandiflora, Floribunda, Rugosa Hybrid, Hybrid Perpetual, Moss, and Climbing Roses

• No. 1: At least three strong canes $\frac{5}{16}$ in (8mm) in caliper,* branched not higher than 3 in (7.6cm) from the bud union.

• No. 1½: At least two strong canes $\frac{5}{16}$ in (8mm) in caliper, branched not higher than 3 in (7.6cm) from the bud union.

• No. 2: At least two canes, one of which shall be a strong cane $\frac{5}{16}$ in (8mm) in caliper and up. The second shall be ¼ in (6mm) in caliper, branched not higher than 3 in (7.6cm) from the bud union.

Caliper refers to the diameter of the cane.

Polyantha, Shrub, Landscape, and Low-Growing Floribunda Roses

• No. 1: At least three strong canes ¼ in (6mm) in caliper, branched not higher than 3 in (7.6cm) from the bud union.

• No. 1½: At least two strong canes ¼ in (6mm) in caliper, branched not higher than 3 in (7.6cm) from the bud union.

• No. 2: At least two canes, one of which shall be a strong cane ¼ in (6mm) in caliper and up.

Container-Grown Roses

These are classified by the grading systems listed above, but in addition they must meet certain criteria regarding the size of the container.

• No. 1: Pot height: minimum 7½ in (19cm)
Inside diameter, top: minimum 7½ in (19cm)
Inside diameter, bottom: minimum 6½ in (16.5cm)

• No. 1½ and No.2: Pot height: minimum 6 in (15.2cm)
Inside diameter, top: minimum 6 in (15.2cm)
Inside diameter, bottom: minimum 5 in (12.7cm)

For Oregon gardeners, a visit to the International Rose Test Garden in Portland (see p. 216) is the best preparation for rose shopping. Any rose gardener benefits from a visit to the nearest public rose garden; its staff can advise on the best rootstock for your immediate area and share experience with handling the different types of nursery stock.

Chapter Five

PREPARATION AND PLANTING

Rose gardening, if you are doing it the easy way, is like Chinese cookery.
A novice concentrates on what happens on the stove. The real master knows that the success
of the dish lies more in the care given to preliminaries: the selection of the ingredients;
the chopping, slicing, and seasoning.

So, too, in rose growing. The most important work takes place before the rosebush actually goes into the soil. How the rose is planted is crucial, too. Of course, proper maintenance is also important. But only a novice thinks that good maintenance can make up for bad preparation. Although careful preparation takes time, it is an excellent investment, for good soil and good planting will help a rose to be self-sufficient. The minutes you spend at the front end of the process, getting things right, can save hours of fussing later on.

Preparing the Soil

The rosarians of a generation ago were quite specific on this subject — and also quite discouraging. They insisted that a fertile loam was the only soil suitable for roses and prescribed that to prepare a new bed for planting, a gardener must excavate the soil to a depth of 3 ft (.9m). Into this pit was poured a layer of cinders or pebbles, and over that the sod that had been stripped from the area before it was dug. (The sod was laid on upside down, which supposedly speeded its decay.) Next the topsoil that had been dug from the area was mixed with manure and returned to the hole. Finally, over this was spread the subsoil, which also had been mixed with manure.

The wonder is that anyone grew roses at all.

Today's rose gardeners work, as much as possible, with the soil found on-site. As noted in Chapter One, a well-drained, fertile loam is an advantage but not a prerequisite. The checklist found on p.163 can help you cope with whatever soil your garden has, so that you may raise fine roses without having to rework your corner of the earth.

The right tool for digging (left to right): a curved-handled trowel for close work, a long handled shovel for big jobs, a Japanese soil knife for severing roots, a trowel for touching up, and a trenching spade for tight corners.

to the depth of another spade blade, for a total depth of about 18 in (45cm). Blend in any fertilizers, lime, compost, peat, or other materials indicated by the results of your soil test (*see pp*.33–37), adding them to both the forked-up subsoil and the topsoil. Afterward, replace the topsoil.

Obviously, if you are adding a rosebush to an existing planting of shrubs and annuals, you won't want to disturb the surrounding soil to this extent. Instead, skip forward to the planting instructions on p.165. The point is that to create a successful flower garden of the traditional type, you must provide a substantial bed throughout which the roses can spread their roots with no interference from other plants.

If, however, you are using the roses as landscape shrubs to be set out as accents or punctuation in the midst of a lawn, or if you are naturalizing the roses in a meadow or at the edge of a woodland or lawn, improving the soil in this fashion may actually stunt root growth.

In the past, the recommendation was to "put a 50¢ shrub in a $5.00 hole." In other words, gardeners believed that it was an advantage to the plant to set its roots in a wide and deep planting hole and to generously enrich any soil that was packed in around the roots in the planting hole. Over the past decade, however, research conducted at a number of agricultural universities has found that this treatment turns shrubs into what amounts to container plants.

The researchers observed that after planting, the new shrubs did indeed grow vigorously for a period. The roots threaded themselves all through the artificially enriched soil. But when they reached the edge of the planting hole, they failed to grow beyond it into the surrounding earth. Instead, the roots confined themselves to the area of improved soil. Eventually, this constriction hampered the shrubs' ability to find and absorb sufficient amounts of nutrients and water. This, in turn, slowed growth. It also left the shrubs more vulner-

Excavation is still recommended, but on a far more modest scale. The deep digging dictated by yesterday's gardeners is now known to be unnecessary. Indeed, depending on the type of display you are planning, "improving" the soil too lavishly may even be harmful to the roses.

If you intend to grow your roses massed in a formal bed, or if you are planting them as part of a mixed display of perennial and annual flowers and shrubs, you should dig and work the soil thoroughly throughout the proposed bed or border. The display you are planning is splendid, but to succeed it requires an extraordinarily rich stream of nutrients and water. To achieve this artificially brilliant display, you must provide an unnaturally rich environment, especially for the roots.

Begin by digging up and setting aside the topsoil to a depth of one spade blade. Then, with a spading fork, break up the soil remaining in the bed

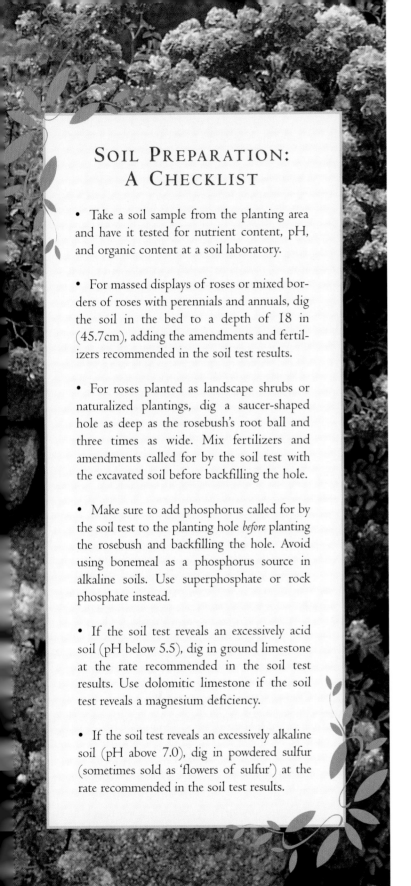

SOIL PREPARATION: A CHECKLIST

• Take a soil sample from the planting area and have it tested for nutrient content, pH, and organic content at a soil laboratory.

• For massed displays of roses or mixed borders of roses with perennials and annuals, dig the soil in the bed to a depth of 18 in (45.7cm), adding the amendments and fertilizers recommended in the soil test results.

• For roses planted as landscape shrubs or naturalized plantings, dig a saucer-shaped hole as deep as the rosebush's root ball and three times as wide. Mix fertilizers and amendments called for by the soil test with the excavated soil before backfilling the hole.

• Make sure to add phosphorus called for by the soil test to the planting hole *before* planting the rosebush and backfilling the hole. Avoid using bonemeal as a phosphorus source in alkaline soils. Use superphosphate or rock phosphate instead.

• If the soil test reveals an excessively acid soil (pH below 5.5), dig in ground limestone at the rate recommended in the soil test results. Use dolomitic limestone if the soil test reveals a magnesium deficiency.

• If the soil test reveals an excessively alkaline soil (pH above 7.0), dig in powdered sulfur (sometimes sold as 'flowers of sulfur') at the rate recommended in the soil test results.

able to drought. Because they were drawing on a smaller area of soil, they were quicker to exhaust the moisture in the soil when rainfall or irrigation were no longer available.

Actually, when the gardener has enriched the soil right around the roots with sphagnum peat, which is the most widely recommended practice, the shrubs become especially vulnerable not only to drought but also to wet weather. In times of low rainfall, water is sucked out of such loose, peaty soil into the finer-textured, unimproved surrounding soil. This means the rose, unless irrigated, actually dehydrates sooner than neighboring shrubs that haven't received such tender treatment. Nor is rainfall necessarily a benefit to roses planted in this fashion. Peat comes from bogs and will, if given the chance, soak up water like a sponge. When a prolonged rainfall or irrigation thoroughly moistens all the soil in the garden, the water tends to drain into the deep planting pits, turning them into quagmires that drown the rose roots.

Given these findings, the experts revised the planting recommendations for shrubs. Instead of the capacious planting pits of times past, current guidelines call for a saucer-shaped hole just deep enough to accommodate the existing roots. The hole should be broad, however; at least three times as wide as the root system of the shrub. For a miniature rose, that may mean a hole only 18–24 in (45.7–61.0cm) wide; a bare-root hybrid tea will need a hole 3–4 ft (.9–1.2m) wide. To encourage roots to penetrate the sidewall of the planting hole, that surface should be roughened with a pickax or spading fork. Above all, any soil used to backfill around the new shrub should be left substantially as it was when it was removed from the hole.

A modest amount of compost or well-aged manure may be added if the soil is really sandy or nutrient poor, but the addition should be no more than one-fifth the mix. You would do far better to save your organic matter and apply it to the soil over the roots as a mulch. Specifics on mulching can be found in Chapter Six. Suffice it to say that a mulch mimics the way nature applies organic matter — as a litter on the surface. To apply it in this way encourages the increase of earthworms and soil microfauna (beneficial bacteria and fungi), and it also keeps the top couple of inches of soil cool and moist, making it more hospitable to roots. That topmost layer is where the roots grow naturally, so improving it is especially beneficial to the plant.

If the soil test indicated a need for phosphorus, a couple of handfuls of bonemeal or superphosphate should be mixed into the backfill, too. Phosphorus is slow to move through the soil, and if it is applied to the soil surface after planting, it may stay out of the young roots' reach. Bonemeal is the phosphorus source preferred by organic gardeners, but it is alkaline and can cause problems in soils that are already markedly alkaline. Superphosphate has no effect on soil pH and would be a better choice in such a situation. Gardeners who use only natural materials should try rock phosphate, an unprocessed mineral that is available in the same state as it is mined from the earth.

Adjusting the pH

The importance of soil pH was discussed in Chapter One (*see pp.*33–35). As noted there, any efforts to alter the soil pH — to make your soil more acid or more alkaline — should be driven by the instructions included with the results of a soil test. Because soils vary dramatically in composition and structure, laying out a simple prescription for raising or lowering soil pH is not possible.

One simple rule does hold, however: you should adjust the pH *before* planting. This will demand continued attention. The natural factors that made the soil overly acidic or alkaline in the first place will continue to work on it, and you will have to re-treat the soil every few years. The initial treatment is the one that requires the most work, and it will be far more effective if you mix the correctives into the soil rather than just applying them to the surface.

What should you use to dose a soil that is too acid or too alkaline? Sphagnum peat is the classic corrective for a soil that is too alkaline. Peat of this type is distinctly acidic, and blending it into the soil in the planting hole will lower the pH of an alkaline soil and acidify it. Unfortunately, though, adding enough peat to achieve any substantial effect on the soil's pH can cause the problems outlined in the previous section. That is why it is better to acidify a too alkaline soil by mixing in powdered sulfur. The dose required will vary from 5 to 10 lbs (2.3–4.5kg) of sulfur per 100 sq ft (9.3m^2) of planting area, depending on the soil type. A dense, fine-grained clay, for example, or a soil that is rich in organic matter will likely

Southwest — Clair Martin III
SAN MARINO, CALIFORNIA

HOW HIGH DO YOU PLANT?

Once the recommendation was to set the bud union 3–4 in (7.6–10.2cm) above the soil, but that has proved to make bushes unstable and vulnerable to this region's strong winds. In addition, setting the bud union so high above the soil tends to ensure that new canes emerge only on the sunny side — exposure to sunlight has this effect on the dormant buds. Currently, Clair advises setting the bud union at ground level. This produces a more stable bush and keeps the bud union cooler and moister. It also encourages more even sprouting of new canes from all around the bud union.

PROBLEM SOILS:

Very sandy soils and heavy clays are both common in this area. In both cases, digging in lots of organic matter and applying organic mulches are the solutions. Also common in the Southwest (though not in his area, Clair notes) is caliche, a layer of concretelike hardpan that lies beneath the surface of the soil. If thin, this layer may be broken up with a crowbar before planting. If the caliche is thick and impenetrable, it is a good idea to increase the soil depth by building a raised bed.

require an extra-heavy dose, while a loose, sandy soil will usually respond to a lighter treatment.

To temper an excessively acid soil, you will need to dig in ground limestone. There are two types of limestone: calcitic limestone (calcium carbonate) and dolomitic limestone (calcium magnesium carbonate). In most cases, calcitic limestone will be adequate. But if your soil test indicates a magnesium deficiency, you should apply dolomitic limestone. Other forms of lime, such as hydrated lime and quicklime, may be found at local suppliers; but these should be avoided because they are caustic and can easily injure both people and plants.

Both sulfur and limestone take some time to work their magic, and it may be a year before the plants will enjoy the full benefits. Though slow-acting, they are also persistent and have a long-lasting effect, unlike some quicker fixes, which soon wash away. Two of these quick fixes can be useful as stopgaps, however, to be applied until the sulfur or limestone takes effect. Aluminum sulfate, an acidifying fertilizer, has a quick though short-lived tempering effect on alkaline soils. It should be used with caution, as it is nitrogen-rich and can stimulate leaf growth at the expense of the flowers. In excessively acid soils, a scattering of wood ashes from the fireplace will provide roses with some relief. The wood ashes also provide potassium, which is a major plant nutrient that promotes better flowering. It is important not to sprinkle the ashes onto rose leaves or to dig it in right around the roots at planting time, because it is caustic.

Planting

Once you have dug the soil and made the necessary adjustments, it's time to plant your new roses. The method you adopt for this depends on the type of rosebushes you have bought: bare-root, container-grown, or boxed.

Bare-Root Roses

If you haven't already dug the planting holes, do so now. A hole 12–18 in (30.5–45.7cm) deep and up to 4 ft (1.2m) in diameter is ideal for a landscape rose. If you are planting the rose into an established bed of flowers or shrubs, a broad planting hole may be impractical, as digging it would injure neighboring roots. In that situation, a 2 ft (.6m) hole is usually adequate.

Get the dormant bushes ready for planting by standing them in a bucket of water overnight. The roots should be completely covered. Canadian regional consultant Trevor Cole likes to give his plants an extra boost by adding a dose of soluble "plant starter" fertilizer such as formula 10-52-10 to the water. (For a definition of fertilizer formulas, see pp.184–185.) In any case, take the roses to the planting holes in the bucket. Having

Time spent on soil preparation and planting is the gardener's best investment. By promoting good health, a careful start reduces the need for maintenance later.

remoistened them, you do not want to expose them to the air and the sun any more than is absolutely necessary.

Before planting each rose, check its roots. With a sharp pair of pruning shears, snip off the ends of any damaged or broken roots. Leave the rest of the roots alone unless they are excessively long. Occasionally, a nursery may ship bare-root roses with roots a couple of feet (about 60cm) long. To plant these intact would require an enormous hole. In such cases, you should shorten the roots by one-half. Avoid unnecessary cuts, but don't begrudge the ones you have to make. Like pruning the branches above ground, root pruning, when done properly, encourages denser, more vigorous regrowth.

Check the rose's upper growth, too. Snip off any broken canes or thin, weak ones at their bases. Most roses are pruned at the nursery before shipping, and they usually don't require much pruning at this time. Do make sure, however, that the bushes have the skeleton of an open, spreading shape. Remove any canes or branches that are growing back through a bush's center, and if the rose presents a crowded bunch of stems, cut away those in the center to leave just three to five outward-trending canes.

To plant, push loose soil into a broad, shallow cone in the center of the planting hole. Set the rosebush down over this mass, arranging the roots around it in a loose skirt. If the rose's top growth is unbalanced, rotate it so that the side with the fewest canes faces in the direction from which the bush will receive the most sun. This will stimulate extra growth on that side and help to give the rosebush a full shape as it matures.

Make sure, too, that the bud union — the swollen spot where the canes emerge from the rootstock — is at the proper height. In cold-winter regions, the bud union should stay from 1 to 4 in (2.5–10.2cm) below ground level to protect it from freezing. In warm regions, gardeners usually set the bud union at the soil surface, or an inch or two (2.5–5.1cm) above it. This encourages the emergence of new canes from the base of the bush and helps protect the bud union from infection with crown gall, a bacterial disease (*see p.203*). Even in the South, however, some gardeners set the bud union below ground level. These gardeners prefer own-root roses but have had to buy grafted ones to get the cultivars they want. By setting the bud union a couple of inches underground, they hope to encourage the rose to send out roots directly from the bases of the canes and so turn a grafted plant into an own-root one. (For advice on planting heights in your area, see the comments from the regional consultants placed throughout this chapter.)

After arranging the plant in the hole, replace the excavated soil. It's often recommended that you pack this soil in around the roots with the heel of your shoe. Don't. Instead, work the soil in with your fingers as you add it to the hole. You shouldn't leave any air pockets around the roots; you want to leave the soil firm but uncompacted.

Once the soil is in place, water the rose well. Let the first watering drain into the ground, then water again.

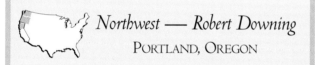

Northwest — Robert Downing
PORTLAND, OREGON

HOW HIGH DO YOU PLANT?

Bob's practice used to be to set the bud union at the soil surface, but he found that the International Rose Test Garden lost a lot of roses in cold winters. Now he plants in raised beds to prevent waterlogging of the soil, and he sets the bud union 1 in (2.5cm) below the surface of the soil.

PROBLEM SOILS:

With the constant rain that characterizes this region, soils tend to become waterlogged, especially in winter. Bob recommends raising planting areas by adding soil and organic matter; this improves drainage. He strongly discourages traditional deep digging, since that creates a trough into which water naturally drains and therefore exacerbates waterlogging.

PLANTING A BARE-ROOT ROSE

1 Soak the roots of a bare-root rose in water overnight before planting. Protect them against dehydration by carrying the bush out to the planting site in a bucket filled with water.

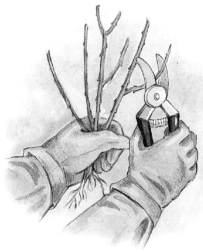

2 With a sharp pair of pruning shears, snip off broken or spindly canes and damaged roots.

3 Spread the roots like a skirt over a mound of soil in the bottom of the planting hole. Add more soil and raise the rose, if necessary, so that the bud union (swelling at base of stem) rests at the recommended height above, at, or below the soil surface (see consultant box for your region).

4 Replace the excavated soil in the planting hole. Use your fingertips to work the soil in among the roots and eliminate air pockets. When finished, water the newly planted rose, and when the first watering is absorbed into the soil, water again.

Container-Grown Roses

Once again, begin by excavating the planting hole. Make it as deep as the rose pot and at least three times as wide, or a minimum of 2 ft (.6m).

Turn the rose on its side and slip the root ball from the container. If it sticks, don't try to force it out; get a pair of shears and cut the container open. Next inspect the roots. If the rose has been in the container for some time, it may be pot-bound. That is, the roots may have begun to wrap themselves around the outside of the ball of earth. If so, take a sharp knife and score the root ball shallowly from top to bottom four times at even intervals around the perimeter. Check the bottom of the root ball, too. If the roots have begun to form a mat there, tease the ends out gently with the end of a pencil or the tip of a hand cultivator.

Set the root ball in the hole, taking care to adjust the bud union to the right height: typically a couple of inches (5cm) below the surrounding soil in cold climates, even with the surface in temperate ones, and slightly above the surface in warm climates (see consultant box for your region). Return the excavated soil to the hole, firming it around the root ball with your fingertips. Water thoroughly and let the water soak in, then irrigate again.

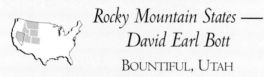

Rocky Mountain States — David Earl Bott

BOUNTIFUL, UTAH

HOW HIGH DO YOU PLANT?

Local practice in this region varies with the climate and therefore with the altitude. In the mountains, the bud union is usually set 1 in (2.5cm) below the soil surface. On the plains, it is set even with the soil surface.

PROBLEM SOILS:

Alkaline soils, or "alkali," are a common problem in the Rocky Mountain West. To acidify the soil, David mixes sphagnum peat into the planting area; horticultural research indicates that powdered sulfur should be used too. Acidic mulches such as pine bark also help.

Boxed Roses

Neither fish nor fowl, these roses are more susceptible to root damage than bare-root roses and yet have not formed a firm root ball like a container-grown rose.

If you are planting a boxed rose early in spring, before its buds have started to swell, it's best to remove it from the box and treat it exactly as you would a bare-root rose. If the rose has started to awaken from dormancy, however, you must handle it more carefully. Cut down the side and around the bottom edge of the box with a sharp knife or shears. Don't remove the box until you have set the rose in the planting hole and at the correct height for the bud union (see the previous section). Once the rose is in place, carefully peel away the cardboard, taking care to disturb the roots as little as possible. Leave the bottom of the cardboard box underneath the rose; the roots will grow around it. Backfill carefully around the rose with the soil from the hole, then water thoroughly. After the first watering has soaked in, water again.

Aftercare

Immediately after planting the rose, bank up soil or mulch around the bud union, if it was set above the soil surface, and several inches up the base of the canes. Leave this soil in place for a couple of weeks to protect the bush from dehydration while it begins the process of reestablishing its roots.

Watering

Dehydration is the greatest threat to any new rosebush. Water extra conscientiously: the infant roses should get a deep, soaking irrigation every third day or so in dry weather. In doing this, try to avoid wetting the rose foliage, because that fosters fungal diseases such as mildew and blackspot. For this reason, a soaker hose or bubbler or a drip-irrigation system is a far better irrigation device for roses than a sprinkler. Likewise, it is better to water in the

PLANTING A CONTAINER-GROWN ROSE

1 Excavate a bowl-shaped hole, as deep as the rose container and at least three times as wide as the container, or a minimum of 2 ft (.6m). Adjust the depth of the hole so that the rose's bud union (swelling at base of stem) will stand at the level above, at, or below the soil surface recommended for your region (see consultant box).

2 If the rose's root ball does not slide easily from the container, cut the can or plastic pot open with a pair of shears.

3 If the roots have wrapped themselves around the root ball, score them with a sharp knife. Slice the root ball shallowly from top to bottom, at even intervals around the perimeter.

4 Replace soil in the planting hole, working out any air pockets with your fingertips. When finished, water the new rose, and when the first watering is absorbed into the soil, water again.

morning or early afternoon than in the late afternoon or evening. Any inadvertent wetting of the leaves soon dries in the midday or late afternoon sun; foliage still wet at sunset is likely to remain wet all night and serve as a nursery for fungal spores.

Fertilization

Feeding should start at or soon after planting, when you can give your new roses a dose of some balanced soluble fertilizer with a formula such as 20-20-20. (For an explanation of fertilizer formulas, see pp.184–185.) Mix the formula with water at half the strength recommended on the label. Organic gardeners can substitute manure "tea," made by soaking a bucketful of composted manure in a barrel of water. In any case, this is one time to ignore the rule against wetting the foliage. Let the liquid fertilizer run down over the leaves, which will absorb nutrients directly into their tissues and benefit from the feeding almost instantly.

Shelter

Circumstances may force you to transplant a rosebush outside the ideal planting season. You may wish to rescue a fondly remembered bush from a family home before it is sold, or you may be snatching a found rose out of the path of a bulldozer. Whatever the reason, you may find it necessary to transplant a rosebush in a time of heat and drought. If you do, you should take special precautions.

First, cut the rose canes back by one-half or more to reduce the total leaf surface. A rosebush sweats in hot weather much as we do, and it loses most of this moisture through its leaves. Reduce the number of leaves, and you reduce the water loss, thus easing the pressure on the injured roots. Of course, you also should take extra care with the watering of the newly moved rose.

Besides cutting back and watering the bush, the most helpful thing you can do is to provide some temporary shade. This is easily improvised using a sheet of burlap supported by a few stakes. If you leave a sprinkler playing over the homemade awning for the first few days after transplanting, you will furnish not only shade but also air-conditioning to further reduce the stress on the traumatized plant.

Roses transplanted in fall in northern regions also benefit from shelter, of a sort. The easy rose gardener does not, as a rule, indulge in the kind of winter protection that traditional rose gardeners use, but rules are made to be broken. Fall-planted roses should be hilled up the first year. That is, as the cold weather settles in, you should protect a transplanted rose by piling soil around and over the base of the bush to a depth of 8–12 in (20.3–30.5cm). Remove this overcoat as the soil thaws and temperatures begin to moderate in early spring.

Planting for Special Purposes

Not all new roses will go into a garden bed. Because they are such functional shrubs, they will surely find their way into other niches — as container plantings, hedges, ground covers, or even part of a kitchen garden. To succeed there, however, your roses may require somewhat different treatment.

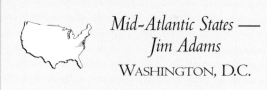

Mid-Atlantic States — Jim Adams
WASHINGTON, D.C.

HOW HIGH DO YOU PLANT?

Although the Mid-Atlantic region's climate is typically mild, hard freezes occur regularly. At planting time, Jim sets the bud union just below the soil surface.

PROBLEM SOILS:

Dense clay soil is a common complaint in this region. Cover the planting area with 2–3 in (5.0–7.6cm) of compost or other decomposed organic material and dig it in with a garden fork. Dig at least one fork length deep, preferably two.

Containers

Usually we think of roses as garden shrubs, and yet many kinds make outstanding container plants. Virtually any rose will adapt to life in a pot or tub, but the larger types will require containers of an inconveniently large size. For this reason, you will find it more practical to stick with the more compact types of roses, such as the polyanthas, the compact hybrid rugosas such as 'Snow Owl', the smaller floribundas such as 'Escapade'® or 'Sun Flare', and any of the miniature roses.

Once you discover the advantages of growing in containers, you are likely to cultivate more and more of your plants this way. For example, because we like to frame our houses with trees, most yards have few truly sunny spots. You can grow roses in areas of light shade, but unless you choose your cultivars carefully, you will find the roses to be shier with their bloom there and more prone to diseases. But even on the most wooded site, a driveway cuts an opening through the canopy. A rose set in a tub at the edge of the blacktop is likelier to find the sun it craves and better air circulation, which will help to protect the leaves against fungal infection. Decks, terraces, and balconies are other rose-friendly sites.

Some gardeners like to test types of roses that they have never grown before by keeping them in a

Miniature roses flourish in containers, and container plantings offer great flexibility. They can be moved to find the sun or suit your mood, and provide bloom for areas without soil.

tub for a year or two. If they prove well adapted to the climate and site, the roses can be planted in the garden. If the roses do not perform well, they can be removed without leaving any gaps in the landscaping and traded off to a less choosy neighbor in return for a trash bag full of pachysandra cuttings or a basket of tomatoes.

Roses growing in containers do have some special needs, however. Above all, they need to be started off right, and this involves several factors.

The size and type of container is crucial. Large pots are sorted by volume at most garden centers; for most miniature roses, a 2-gal (7.6L) container is best. (This is just a bit smaller than the average bucket.) The smallest cultivars, such as 'Cinderella', can make do with a smaller container, such as a hanging basket 10 in (25.4cm) in diameter, though underpotting in this fashion will mean that you must water more frequently. For roses of the bigger classes, such as polyanthas, you'll need larger pots or tubs. Generally, a 7-gal (26.5L) pot is adequate for these.

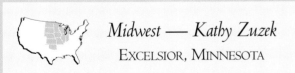

Midwest — Kathy Zuzek
EXCELSIOR, MINNESOTA

HOW HIGH DO YOU PLANT?

Given the intense winter cold experienced in this region, Kathy advises protecting the bud union by setting it 3 in (7.6cm) below the soil surface.

PROBLEM SOILS:

Cold, not quality, is the soil-related problem in the prairie states. A couple of inches (about 5cm) of organic mulch insulates and helps to prevent the cold from penetrating down to kill roots.

Just as important as the size of the container is the material from which it has been fashioned. You want a pot or tub that will keep the soil around the roots cool and moist, yet well drained, and is rot resistant, so that it doesn't require continual maintenance or replacement. Wooden tubs should be made of some naturally rot-resistant timber such as cedar or redwood or from lumber that has been pressure treated with a wood preservative.

An advantage of wood is that it provides excellent insulation: in summer it helps to keep the heat of the sun out, and in winter it helps buffer the roots against sudden freezes or thaws. Protection against heat is especially important. On a sunny summer day, the temperature of the soil inside even a large pot may rise above 100°F (37°C), especially in the drier areas around the outside of the rose's root ball. Above 104°F (40°C), the roots start to die.

Metal, fiberglass, and plastic are poor insulators, and containers made of these materials perform poorly for this reason. Clay provides some insulation but is likely to crack if exposed to intense cold. In addition, unglazed clay pots, such as the terra-cotta ones imported from Italy, lose water through the sidewalls, which means that you have to irrigate more frequently. Watering can become nearly a constant task in summer.

Price and durability, however, make heavy-duty plastic pots a practical choice, and they can be made both more functional and more attractive by hiding them inside a decorative container. Make sure there is at least an inch of clearance all around the plastic pot, and fill this space with polystyrene foam packing "peanuts." If you set the inner pot low, so that its lip rests a couple of inches (about 5cm) below that of the outer container, you can cover the gap and styrofoam with a layer of an organic mulch such as shredded bark.

An alternative way to buffer rose roots is to use just one container per rose but to line the pot with two or three layers of ¼ in (6.4mm) foam carpet padding. Similarly, straight-sided containers can be lined with sheets of ½ in (12.7mm) rigid foam insulation. Another simple way to protect rose roots in summer is to paint the containers a light, reflective color so that they absorb less solar radiation.

Make sure that the container has adequate drainage holes in the bottom. Refrain, however, from lining the container's bottom with pebbles or bits of broken clay pots ("crocks"). Traditionally, this was done to enhance the drainage of the soil in the pot. In fact, research has found that this practice creates a perched water table within the root ball and that it actually impedes the flow of water out through the bottom of the pot. Instead, just line the bottom of the container with a sheet of fiberglass window screening. That will keep the soil inside from washing out and will let excess water pass freely through the container's drainage holes.

Because a rose in a tub or pot cannot send its roots out through the surrounding soil in search of water and nutrients, the quality of the soil inside the pot is especially important. A mixture of one part loam, one part compost or sphagnum peat, and one

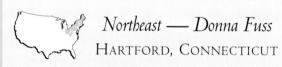

Northeast — Donna Fuss
HARTFORD, CONNECTICUT

HOW HIGH DO YOU PLANT?

Winter cold is a concern in New England, and Donna likes to protect the bud union by letting it rest just below ground. She finds that rosebushes settle slightly after planting, so she places the bud union even with the soil surface and depends on gravity to pull it a little bit lower.

PROBLEM SOILS:

Glaciers dumped sand in many regions of New England during the last ice age. Such poor, dry soils need lots of compost or other organic matter dug into them. Another common problem throughout New England is rock ledge running close to the surface. This creates shallow soils that dry out quickly and yet also may drain poorly. In a soil of that type, raised beds are the most effective way to grow roses.

A cedar tub (top right) insulates rose roots from temperature extremes. Hiding a durable but ugly plastic pot inside a more attractive container (bottom left) and filling the intervening space with packing "peanuts" offers similar protection.

part "sharp" builder's sand is excellent. (Sharp sand is the coarse, gritty type used in concrete mixes. It doesn't compact like the finer, more rounded sand dug from riverbeds or beaches for use in sandboxes.) If you buy the soil, specify loam and do not accept mere "topsoil." Topsoil is actually just the top few inches (cm) of any soil, so this term can include muck skimmed off nearby wetlands or the depleted clay from a farmer's exhausted field.

Be sure to test the pH of your potting mix. This can be done with an inexpensive test kit from the local garden center. Adjust the pH as necessary with lime or sulfur, then retest. If you have to, adjust again. Keep at it until you have achieved a pH between 5.5 and 7.0.

To plant a rose in a container, first line the container's bottom with fiberglass window screening and then pour in a couple of inches (about 5cm) of potting mix. Leave enough room to accommodate the roots of your new rosebush, keeping in mind that you want the bud union to rest about an inch (2.5cm) below the top of the pot. That will mark the top of the potting soil; you should leave the top inch (2.5cm) of the pot empty so that you can irrigate without having water slop out over the container's edge.

If you are planting a bare-root rose in the container, form a cone of soil within the container over which you can drape the roots. If the roots are too long to fit in the container, trim them back; don't coil them up in the container's bottom. A container-grown rose should be planted exactly as if you were setting it into a hole in the ground.

 *Southeast — Peter Haring*
SHREVEPORT, LOUISIANA

HOW HIGH DO YOU PLANT?

To keep the bud union up and away from soilborne pests and diseases, Peter sets it 1–2 in (2.5–5.1cm) above ground at planting time.

PROBLEM SOILS:

Poorly drained soil is a common problem. Peter recommends enhancing drainage by raising the level of the soil that is to be planted. To do so, frame the planting area with landscape timbers stacked 8 in (20.3cm) deep. Then rototill it, digging in several inches (6cm) of sharp builder's sand and several inches of some organic material such as composted pine bark, adding enough material to raise the soil to the top of the frame.

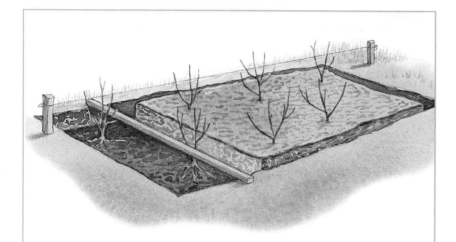

To promote strong growth and minimize weeding, plant rose hedges in a long, narrow bed. Dig two spades deep, mixing in a 2½ gal bucket of compost per square yard (10L per m²) as well as bonemeal or superphosphate, lime or sulfur as called for by a soil test *(see p.33)*. Use a pole stretched across the bed to help set the rosebushes at the proper height, and space the bushes at intervals equal to two-thirds to one-half of their predicted spread at maturity. Where space permits, plant a double row with bushes staggered to make a more secure and more impressive hedge.

Water the rose well immediately after planting. If it is still dormant, cover it with a large clear plastic bag. Insert bamboo stakes around the rose to ensure that the plastic doesn't actually rest on the rose. Tuck the edges of the bag into the soil around the rim of the pot or weight it down with pebbles to make sure it doesn't blow away. In a week or so, when the rose's buds start to swell and break dormancy, poke a few air holes in the bag. As the leaves emerge and expand, enlarge the existing holes and poke a few more. When the new shoots have reached a length of 2 in (5.1cm), remove the bag entirely.

Hedges

A row of rosebushes can be not only colorful but also practical: they can make an intruder-proof fence that is both rustproof and self-repairing. To furnish all these practical benefits, the plants must be started out right. The individual bushes must be set close enough together that the tips of

the branches merge into a continuous wall of shrubbery. The roses should not be so crowded, however, that foliar diseases are encouraged, and the roots of each bush must be given adequate room to expand.

To plant a hedge, begin by creating a long, narrow bed. As with a regular flower bed or mixed border, the soil should be excavated two spades deep, about 18 in (45cm). Suit the width of the bed to the size of the rose: a bed 18 in (45cm) wide is fine for miniature roses, but 2–3 ft (.6–.9m) is better for a full-size shrub, depending on the vigor of the species or cultivar you have chosen.

Proper spacing is the key to establishing a dense, continuous hedge. Generally, the interval between shrubs should be about one-half to two-thirds the predicted spread of the rose. For example, if you intend to plant a hedge of the hybrid rugosa 'Frau Dagmar Hartopp', you'll find its spread listed as 3–4 ft (0.9–1.2m); set these bushes at an interval of 18–32 in (45.7–81.3cm). The shrub rose 'Morden Ruby' spreads to a width of 5 ft (1.5m); set bushes of this cultivar at an interval

Canada — Trevor Cole
KINBURN, ONTARIO

HOW HIGH DO YOU PLANT?

Noting the wide variety of climates in his country, Trevor recommends adapting the planting to local conditions. In his own region, southern Ontario, he plants so that the bud union rests an inch (2.5cm) or so below ground level. In the harsher climates of the central and northern regions — Edmonton, Alberta, for example — Trevor would recommend setting the bud union as much as 4 in (10.2cm) below the soil surface.

PROBLEM SOILS:

Heavy clay soil can be a challenge in Ontario. When confronted with this, Trevor advises digging down to break up the subsoil and mixing in sharp builder's sand or fine gravel to coarsen and loosen the soil's texture.

Why plant privet, when you can have a hedge that combines blossoms with the security of natural barbed wire? Use own-root roses for this planting, and your display should last decades.

of 2½–3 ft (.8–.9m). Setting the bushes closer together will help the hedge form a solid wall more quickly, but if you intend to let the hedge grow tall, the greater planting interval is recommended.

As a rule, own-root roses are recommended for hedge planting. They are longer-lived, and the suckers that own-root roses send up from the roots can be left to grow and add density to the hedge. If you choose to plant grafted bushes, set the bud unions 2–3 in (5.1–7.6cm) below the surface of the soil so that roots may sprout from the bases of the canes and the bushes will gradually convert themselves to own-root and lose their dependence on the rootstocks. This transformation leaves the rootstocks intact, however, and they often live on, so any suckers arising from such converts are suspect.

Also keep in mind when planning and planting a hedge that, where space permits, a double row in which the bushes are staggered makes a much more impressive and impermeable living fence.

Ground Covers

As with hedges, spacing is crucial with ground-cover roses. You want the roses close enough that the canes mesh into an unbroken sheet of foliage, but you don't want to crowd the plants. Before planting, check the predicted spread of the cultivar you have chosen. Reduce that figure by one-third and use this as the spacing between the shrubs. Thus, if you have selected the shrub rose 'Flower Carpet Pink'™ as your ground cover, you will find that the predicted spread of each plant is 3 ft (.9m). Set the roses 2 ft (.6m) apart.

One word of warning: don't expect roses, on their own, to provide the kind of solid, weed-proof ground cover that pachysandra or ivy makes. Weeds will spring up through a sheet of roses. Pulling the weeds by hand can be a bloody business, and any chemicals that will kill the weeds also will harm the roses. You can avoid this situation with careful preparation before you plant.

Begin by eliminating weeds, as much as possible, from the whole area to be planted. This can be done

Mulch furnishes an attractive setting for these ground-cover roses. It also hides the underlying landscape fabric, an essential protection against weeds.

landscape fabric. This is sold under a variety of brand names and essentially it is a toughly woven sheet of plastic fibers that allows water and air to penetrate down into the soil but prevents the emergence of weeds. Pin the fabric in place with hoops made from lengths of heavy wire and cover it with 1 in (2.5cm) of shredded bark mulch.

To plant the roses, just push aside a patch of mulch, cut a pair of crossing slits into the landscape fabric, and plant right through it. Plant the ground-cover roses just as you would any other landscape roses. After planting, tuck the edges of the fabric and the mulch back in around the roses.

Naturalizing

The object of this kind of planting is to give the roses a spontaneous look; it should appear that they found their own way into your meadow. If you plant several bushes together, put them in an irregular grouping rather than a geometrically dictated bed. Usually, in naturalizing roses, it is more effective to use them singly, as specimens.

Plant as you would for a landscape shrub (*see p.165*), but take extra care in stripping away the sod or ground cover from the area you excavate for a planting hole. Above all, remove from the soil all roots of perennial weeds. Leaving bits of them in the soil will allow the weeds to resprout, and they will quickly choke young roses.

This is another instance in which grafted roses should be set extra deep, with the bud union 2–3 in (5.1–7.6cm) underground. Encouraging the transformation of the grafted rose into an own-root bush will help to withstand nibbling deer and rabbits and all the other natural calamities that are more likely to befall the plant in a naturalized setting, because an own-root bush will regenerate true to type even if all the aboveground growth is destroyed.

After planting, blanket the area over the planting hole with some unobtrusive but effective mulch. Shredded leaves, which you can make by running the lawn mower over the piles you rake up in autumn,

by spraying the area with glyphosate, an herbicide that kills any plant it contacts but typically is rapidly neutralized by the organic matter in the soil and so does not run off to harm plants and wildlife outside the targeted area.

In order to accomplish the same thing without the use of chemicals, wait until a period of warm, sunny weather arrives and then rototill the area that is to be planted. Rake it smooth, water it well, and cover it with a sheet of clear plastic. Bury the edges of the piece of plastic to seal off the planting area, and leave the plastic in place for one to two months. The plastic will act as a solar collector, trapping sunlight to heat the soil below and cook most weeds, weed seeds, and soilborne diseases and insect pests.

After clearing out the weeds, keep them from recolonizing the planting area by covering it with blend in with a natural setting and are quite good at suppressing weeds and preserving soil moisture.

Kitchen Gardens

Roses can make a handsome addition to a kitchen garden, although you should be sure to select disease- and pest-resistant types that won't need spraying with toxic chemicals. When placing and planting the roses, keep in mind one fact: roses are shallow-rooted shrubs, and any digging or hoeing around their bases is likely to injure them.

This means that you shouldn't set roses in the middle of a vegetable bed, unless you surround each shrub with a circle of mulch that extends out beyond the predicted spread of the rose canes. Generally, it makes far more sense to locate the roses in a decorative area of the garden. Set one amid your perennial herbs, or among the nasturtiums you raise to provide flowers and buds for your salads. Or espalier the rose on the wall or fence that surrounds the garden. A hedge of roses can be a nice divider in a kitchen garden, but leave room for the rose roots to run, and flank the hedge with paths.

As vigorous as it is beautiful, 'New Dawn' quickly climbs an arch to shroud it in glossy foliage and blush-pink, repeat-blooming flowers. Its fragrance is best appreciated in a kitchen garden such as this, where the rose perfume mingles with the aromas of the herbs. 'New Dawn' possesses another essential attribute of a kitchen garden rose: it flourishes without spraying.

Chapter Six

EASY MAINTENANCE

"How does she do it? Oh, she has a green thumb."
How often have you heard a gardener's accomplishments dismissed with that comment?
Yet really, there is no such thing as a green thumb. Healthy plants and lavish flowers are not the results
of any magic, empowering touch. On the contrary, what brings these rewards is giving your roses
what they need, when they need it. Only with that help can the bushes do the rest themselves.

You have to select the right roses and start them off right. But given these prerequisites, the difference between your glorious roses and your neighbor's sickly runts lies in the caliber of the care. Providing superior care also has another advantage. Remember that expert maintenance is easy maintenance. If you learn to use your head, you'll rely less on your back.

Healthy Soil for Healthy Plants

Although you can't see most of it, a good garden soil teems with life. An acre (.4ha) of healthy loam may be home to as many as 500,000 earthworms, and given a microscope and sufficient time, you could identify 1,000 different organisms in just one square yard (about one square meter) of the

leaf and twig litter spread out beneath the trees in your woodland garden. Just like the life above the soil, the life within it is an ecosystem. As in any ecosystem, the different elements of this one are all interdependent. Exterminate a certain species of fungus, and a tree, shrub, flower, or grass may cease to thrive because its roots normally work in partnership with that fungus. Without it, the roots do not function properly.

Of course, you usually can compensate for a gap in the soil's ecosystem by supplying artificially the various nutrients and other substances that the missing microorganism would normally supply. It's as if you were feeding your plants intravenously.

This style of gardening can be successful, at least in the short run. But it is hard work. By short-circuiting the ecological balance within the soil, this approach sets the garden up for a portfolio of plagues and disasters. The wonder plant food, for example, may in time upset the soil's pH, so that the rose roots cannot absorb the jolts of nutrients that the fertilizer supplies. Regular dosing with sulfur or lime then becomes necessary. Meanwhile, the disruption of the soil's invisible life allows disease pathogens and insect pests to flourish out of control, causing the chemical gardener to have to drench the plants with pesticides and fungicides. This treatment massacres helpful as well as harmful organisms, making the plants even more dependent on the artificial stimulation of synthetic foods. As the soil loses its vitality, its structure collapses, so irrigation and fertilization have more trouble penetrating to the roots and thus have less and less effect.

Does this mean you should avoid the use of synthetic fertilizers and other chemical products altogether? No — but look upon them as something like the multivitamin you swallow in the morning, or the aspirin you take when you are running a fever. These products are convenient, and they can help solve problems. But they do not substitute for a healthy diet and regimen.

Organic Advantages

What is a healthy diet for your roses? For the best

In a humus-rich soil, the particles clump together in "crumbs." This lets water drain through and enables oxygen and fertilizers to penetrate to the roots.

performance, the diet must include fertilizers of some sort, but fertilizers are not the basis of the diet. The foundation is always the organic portion of the soil, that is, the decomposed plant and animal matter making up what is called humus. If you maintain the

humus at an adequate level — and with a little help, the soil will do most of the work required itself — many other gardening tasks will be reduced or even eliminated.

Keep the organic content of the soil between 5 and 20 percent, and the soil will produce most of the nutrients your rosebushes (and other plants) need. It will absorb water faster and retain it better so that the need for irrigation will be lessened. Yet the soil also will drain better, so your roses will develop a stronger root system. The soil pH will tend toward neutral, and the pH will react less to acid rain and other disturbances such as the acidifying action of some synthetic fertilizers. Among the many forms of life found in an organic-rich soil are various predators, and these make a garden naturally resistant to soilborne pests and diseases. In addition, an organic-rich soil produces robust roses that are better able to resist blackspot, powdery mildew, and other infections.

Mulching: Maintaining the organic content of your soil is simple. Just blanket the area over the roots of the rosebushes with 2–3 in (5.1–7.6cm) of an organic mulch. As this material decomposes, the earthworms and other soil-dwelling creatures will devour it and carry it down into their burrows with them. And unlike digging in sphagnum peat or compost, this method of replenishing the soil won't injure rose roots.

Mulch provides many other benefits. By conserving soil moisture, it can reduce by one-half the need for irrigation, one of the gardener's most time-consuming chores. Mulch keeps the area near the soil surface cooler and moister in summer, and so it encourages roots to grow right up through the top layer of soil, increasing the roses' total root mass. The right mulch can even help acidify excessively alkaline soils. Any sort of evergreen needles will work this way, although spruce needles are especially potent.

Your choice of mulch will probably depend largely on what is available at little or no cost in

Other mulch materials may provide similar practical benefits, but shredded bark is unrivaled in appearance as a setting for roses. If you find the cost of blanketing the whole garden in this material prohibitive, you may still elect to use it in a particularly visible bed.

your region. Pine needles, or "pine straw," is a favorite in the Southeast and Southwest, where pine woods extend over millions of acres. Shredded, semicomposted leaves make an excellent mulch, too, and are available for free every fall throughout the Northeast, most of the Midwest, and the Northwest. If there is a riding stable in your neighborhood, you can stack its manure by the compost heap for a couple of months, then spread it over the root area of your rose bushes as a most effective mulch. Spent compost from a nearby mushroom farm, peanut shells, and ground-up corncobs — there are all sorts of regional bargains available to those with some imagination. And if all else fails, bags of shredded bark are sure to be available at the local garden center.

Some mulches, though inexpensive and effective, are too unattractive to use around roses. Grass clippings, for example, once they have dried, make a very effective mulch, but their straw color doesn't set off roses well. The local arborist may be willing to dump a load of wood chips in your driveway, and these will provide the same benefits as other organic mulches. But the chips weather to a rough gray and should be used only as a last resort.

A few organic mulches can actually be harmful to your roses. Clippings from lawns that have been treated with herbicides can poison roses. Redwood mulch also has a toxic effect on most plant life. Pecan hulls can be had cheaply in certain areas of the Southeast, but they release substances that are harmful to other plants as they decay. Shredded cypress mulch, popular in the Lower South, should be avoided for environmental reasons: buying this product encourages the destruction of the already threatened Southeastern swamps. Hay (except for salt hay) brings weed seeds. Sphagnum peat is often recommended as a mulch, but it is reluctant to absorb water once it has thoroughly dried, and because it is so light when dehydrated, it may blow away.

You are sure to hear one common criticism of organic mulches: They rob the soil of nitrogen, a major plant nutrient, as they decay. If you don't compensate with increased doses of fertilizer, your roses are going to starve. In fact, this warning is half true. Coarser organic mulches, such as wood chips, do absorb nitrogen as they decay. But the humus they produce when they have finished decaying rereleases the nitrogen into the soil. For the first year or two after you mulch, you *should* increase the rate of fertilization. Gradually, though, the situation will correct itself as repeated mulching builds up a layer of humus-rich topsoil, and the need for extra nitrogen will subside. Indeed, that is when you begin to realize a surplus. As you continue to replenish the mulch, the layer of humus increases, and its nitrogen release increases, too, feeding to the plants the years' worth of fertilization that has been absorbed by the mulch.

One final word on organic mulches: in regions where humidity fosters fungal diseases, a mulch that drains quickly, maintaining a dry surface, is healthiest. Pine needles have this quality, which helps make them a superb mulch for the Southeast.

You want a mulch that not only is effective but also looks good, and nothing could look better than

The Best Plants for a Living Mulch

Because you don't want the "mulch" to compete with the roses, you should use only shallow-rooted flowers for a living mulch. Perennial flowers may gradually develop a dense mat of herbage around the roses, depriving their roots of air and water, and they may prove *too* successful, turning into weeds. Annual flowers are a better choice because the first frost will clear them from the area for you. Two of the best annuals for this purpose are sweet alyssum (*Lobularia maritima*) and portulaca (*Portulaca grandiflora*). Both work well as spring plantings in the North and fall plantings in the South.

a carpet of flowers. Cover the soil below your roses with a planting of annual flowers, and you will realize many of the benefits that a conventional mulch supplies. The plants will insulate the soil and protect it against erosion and compaction. They'll also keep the area weed free, and if you hoe them into the soil after the fall frosts cut them down, you'll add organic matter to the soil. The greatest benefit is visual. When the mulch blooms, it can make a superbly dramatic setting for the roses.

To plant your living mulch, rake away any other mulch from the area and scratch the soil's surface with a cultivator. Then scatter the seeds and water over the soil. For aesthetic reasons, it's best to avoid seed mixes that include strains of different colors. That creates a busy background that distracts the eye from the beauty of the roses. Solid colors provide a more effective setting for the roses. A carpet of white-flowered annuals is especially dramatic.

Unlike a conventional mulch, a living one does not help with water conservation. On the contrary, it will substantially increase the amount of irrigation that area of your garden demands. At the same time, it doubles the harvest of color.

Fertilizing: In the wild, roses forage quite successfully for nutrients on their own. So it might seem that feeding your bushes should be unnecessary.

In fact, if you are naturalizing species roses, the need for fertilization will be modest. An early-spring meal of some slow-release (often called timed-release) synthetic fertilizer, or an organic fertilizer formulated for shrubs, should be all that your species roses will need.

In most garden situations, however, we place unnatural demands on our roses. We want them to be green and fresh right through the summer heat, to bloom heavily and as continuously as possible, and to bear hips in the fall. If we are going to expect all that from a bush, we have to help it out with extra fuel — another feeding in early summer, and in southern regions and the Pacific Northwest, where the growing season is long, an early fall feeding as well. Beware of such a late-season fertilization in cold-winter regions, however. It will encourage the roses to keep producing tender new growth when they should be hardening the new growth they already have in preparation for dormancy and freezing temperatures.

Feeding is a simple process. If you are using a dry, granular fertilizer, you measure out the amount recommended for each bush. Then you sprinkle the fertilizer in a ring around the bush and scratch it into the soil with a hand cultivator or hoe, taking care not to dig so deeply that you injure the rose's roots.

One disadvantage of many synthetic fertilizers is that they release their nutrients very quickly. That

Most effective of the synthetic fertilizers are the "timed-release" formulas. These polymer-coated pellets release nutrients into the surrounding soil over a period of weeks.

is, their nutrients are highly water soluble, so when you sprinkle them onto the soil surface, they dissolve and wash into the soil with the first irrigation or rainstorm. Unfortunately, they wash out as quickly as they wash in. Instead of benefiting the plants, most of your fertilizer ends up as pollution in the nearest stream.

For this reason, you should use fertilizers that are designed to release their nutrients gradually, at a rate that the rosebushes can absorb. There are a number of slow-release synthetic fertilizers on the market in which the actual nutritional matter has been treated so that it dissolves into the soil gradually. Look for these products when you shop. Or use so-called organic fertilizers, most of which are naturally slow-release. This use of the word *organic*, though very common, is in fact misleading and incorrect when applied to the chemistry of fertilizers. In such an application, organic really describes a particular kind of chemical structure, and organic compounds may be made in a test tube as readily as in the gut of a cow or horse. Organic gardeners, however, have changed this term to connote only an unprocessed fertilizer of natural origin and include in this category pulverized stone as well as manure. Since this usage has become generally accepted by gardeners, we will use it here.

A Caution for Northern Gardeners

In colder climates, organic decomposition is slower. That's why regional consultant Trevor Cole advises Canadian gardeners to apply organic fertilizers well ahead of the time that the plants actually need the nutrients. A spring feeding, for example, might be better applied in late fall.

Regional consultant Donna Fuss claims the same problem for New England. She fertilizes in spring and early summer but gives her roses a 10-10-10 formula that combines 60 percent fast-acting nitrogen (which provides an immediate feed) and 40 percent organic nitrogen (for longer-lasting benefits). Regional consultant Bob Downing in Portland, Oregon, also favors a blend: 60 percent slow-release and 40 percent fast-acting nitrogen. This gives his roses a steadier, more even supply of nutrients.

Plants don't care about the provenance of the nutrients they absorb through their roots. They don't care if a fertilizer came from a factory or a barnyard. However, organic fertilizers (using the term as organic gardeners do) have an advantage in that most of them are based on crude plant and animal wastes. The basic nutrients in these wastes are contained in more complex compounds, and they must be digested by soil bacteria and fungi before the nutrients can infiltrate the earth and become available to roots. This ensures a more gradual release; it also helps synchronize the fertilizer's nutrient flow with the needs of the plants. Organic fertilizers are digested most quickly when the soil is warm and moist, because that's when the bacteria and fungi are most active. That's also when the rose roots are most active. As the soil becomes hot and dry, or really cold, the roots go dormant, but so too do the fertilizer digesters.

Cottonseed meal is an excellent organic source of nitrogen, and also supplies limited amounts of phosphorus and potassium. Because it is acidic, cottonseed meal should not be applied to soils with a markedly acidic pH. However, its acidity makes cottonseed meal doubly beneficial in regions such as the Southwest, where soils are often alkaline. Alfalfa meal is a better choice in acid soil regions. If you can't find it among the fertilizers in your garden center, look among the rabbit foods at your local feed store or pet supply store.

Chances are, if you fertilize with organic fertilizers, you will have to apply more than one type. In shopping for rose fertilizers, either organic or synthetic, you should be sure to buy a product or a combination of products that provides a feeding that is both complete and balanced.

A fertilizer that is complete is one that furnishes all three of the major plant nutrients: nitrogen, phosphorus, and potassium. You can identify such a product by the series of three numbers you'll find on the label, such as 5-10-5 or 20-20-20. These numbers indicate the percentage (by weight) of the

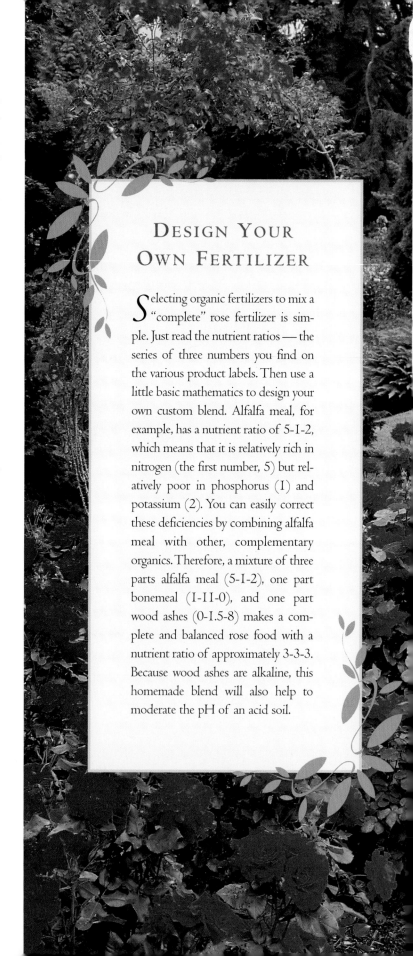

DESIGN YOUR OWN FERTILIZER

Selecting organic fertilizers to mix a "complete" rose fertilizer is simple. Just read the nutrient ratios — the series of three numbers you find on the various product labels. Then use a little basic mathematics to design your own custom blend. Alfalfa meal, for example, has a nutrient ratio of 5-1-2, which means that it is relatively rich in nitrogen (the first number, 5) but relatively poor in phosphorus (1) and potassium (2). You can easily correct these deficiencies by combining alfalfa meal with other, complementary organics. Therefore, a mixture of three parts alfalfa meal (5-1-2), one part bonemeal (1-11-0), and one part wood ashes (0-1.5-8) makes a complete and balanced rose food with a nutrient ratio of approximately 3-3-3. Because wood ashes are alkaline, this homemade blend will also help to moderate the pH of an acid soil.

three major nutrients. Each of these is essential to healthy growth, and a fertilizer is "complete" only if it provides all three. Most organic fertilizers do not furnish adequate amounts of all three major nutrients. As a result, when fertilizing organically, you usually must apply two or three different fertilizers at the same time. For example, you might blend a nitrogen-rich fertilizer with one that is a good source of phosphorus and potassium.

There is no rule of thumb for the amount of fertilizer you should give to your roses. In this, you should be guided by the results of your soil test. If, when you submit your soil sample, you specify that you are growing roses, the laboratory should include recommendations for a feeding program with its results. Because soil tests are so inexpensive, it makes sense to include them as part of your annual spring maintenance program.

Micronutrients: Any fertilizer you select as the basis of your feeding program should supply not only the three major plant nutrients but also micronutrients, such as iron, manganese, zinc, and copper. Plants use only traces of these (indeed, they are usually described on fertilizer labels as "trace elements"), but these minute quantities are essential. Often what a gardener thinks is a disease is really a plant's reaction to a deficiency in the soil of one of the micronutrients (*see p.*201).

One of the best sources of micronutrients, with the advantage of being a natural product, is seaweed. If you live near the coast, you can collect seaweed from the beach and stack it on the driveway to let the rain wash the salt out of it. Then add it to your compost heap. For most of us, though, it is more convenient to purchase a seaweed extract (often labeled as "kelp extract"). These extracts are available from most garden supply stores that stock organic gardening products.

Other commercial "plant tonics" can be used to replenish the soil's supply of micronutrients and trace elements, and many complete fertilizers include trace elements in their formulas. But sea-

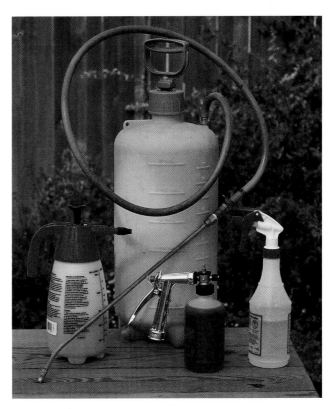

A hose-end sprayer (bottom center) is the most efficient device for feeding the foliage of large numbers of roses. Hand-pumped compressor sprayers (top and left), and simple hand-pump sprayers (right) are more convenient for smaller collections of one or a few bushes.

weed extract seems to be superior in at least one respect. Among the ingredients of the extract is a carbohydrate called mannitol, which not only helps make available to plant roots the micronutrients that the seaweed supplies but also helps free the micronutrients already present in the soil.

Feeding the Foliage: Seaweed extracts are most easily applied with an inexpensive hose-end sprayer, and they should be sprayed right onto the rose foliage. Generally, two applications, one in spring and the other in fall, are sufficient. Fall feeding with seaweed extracts won't harm northern roses, because the extracts do not contain appreciable amounts of the major plant nutrients and so do not encourage a burst of new growth. On the contrary, many northern gardeners claim that the extra vigor that a fall feeding of seaweed extract gives their roses results in a substantial increase in their cold tolerance. Likewise, gardeners in regions with irregular rainfall claim an increased tolerance for drought in seaweed-nourished roses.

A drip-irrigation system consists of suspended pipes with openings at regular intervals. The water drips slowly directly onto the soil, keeping the leaves dry and thus less susceptible to fungal diseases.

Watering

Depending on where you live, watering your roses may be only an occasional chore or a regular part of your gardening routine. Throughout much of the Northwest, for example, rainfall supplies almost all the irrigation roses need, and you may need to irrigate only a handful of times each summer. By contrast, in most of the Southwest regular irrigation is what makes rose growing possible.

If you live in a dry climate, you can limit your watering by cultivating native species roses. For instance, the Sierra Nevada rose, *Rosa woodsii fendleri*, is notably drought tolerant and in many western landscapes will flourish with little more than the natural irrigation of rain and snow. Some types of garden hybrids also are relatively drought tolerant, such as the China roses and the hybrid rugosa roses. You can stretch whatever water you do give your roses by mulching, which slows evaporation. But for continuing bloom throughout the summer, you will have to irrigate in all but the moistest climates.

When to Water

The amount of water you must provide and the frequency with which you irrigate will depend on the local climate. Regional consultant Clair Martin waters deeply twice a week during the summer in San Marino, California. Regional consultant Bob Downing may not water for weeks on end in Portland, Oregon.

The old rule for watering roses is that the bushes should get at least 1 in (2.5cm) of water, either from rainfall or from the hose, every week during the growing season. Some growers recommend doubling or even tripling that allowance. Lavish watering, when combined with heavier doses of fertilizers, can prompt spectacular growth and flowering. But when pushed this way, the bushes become soft and too lush — easy prey for diseases and pests. Your goal should be to maintain healthy but compact growth.

You may have to boost your irrigation a bit above the average if you are gardening in sandy soil, since soils of that sort dry out more quickly than clay or loam. When you water, water deeply, so that the moisture penetrates all the way through the area of soil infiltrated by the roots of your roses. One deep watering will be far more beneficial than several superficial sprinklings.

In arid climates, especially in areas with severe air pollution, you should make a point of washing rose foliage early in the day, weekly with a forceful spray from the hose. This not only cleanses, but it also helps wash away spider mites, a particularly serious pest in hot, dry conditions. In areas where heat combines with humidity, you should avoid wetting the foliage of your rosebushes when irrigating, as that promotes fungal diseases. A leaky hose or a drip-irrigation system is a better solution than a sprinkler in such areas. For watering a mixed bed that includes perennial and annual flowers as well as roses, a sprinkler may be the only practical device. In that case, you should take care to water in the morning so that the strong midday sun will dry the rose foliage promptly.

If you do water your roses with a drip-irrigation system, resist the urge to let an electronic timer take over all the watering for you. Such a device can be a true lifesaver for your roses when you go away on vacation, but it administers water by the clock, not by the roses' need. When the time comes to water, the timer turns the system on, even if the soil is already moist. That's not only wasteful, it's also harmful to the rose roots and the soil. So when you are at home, switch off the timer and water only when the soil around the roses becomes dry.

Water Quality

One final note about irrigation: be sure to check with your municipal water board to determine the quality of the water it is delivering. In many regions, tap water is markedly saline. If that is the case with your water, lavish irrigation will salinate the soil and eventually poison your roses. Gardeners with saline water should definitely install drip-irrigation systems. Because such a system delivers water right to the soil, it is more efficient than conventional sprinklers and uses less water to moisten the root zone of your plants. That means it also puts less salt into the soil. Planting in raised beds is also helpful in regions of saline water, because this makes it easier for the rain to wash through the soil and flush out any salt that has accumulated there.

Pruning

No other aspect of rose growing so intimidates the beginner. It's easy to understand why. Over the generations, rosarians have turned pruning into a complex ritual. Every cut is prescribed, and all must be done in the correct sequence at the correct season. The instructions a beginner gets are about as user-friendly as the stack of manuals the store hands you when you buy a computer. It seems that the real object is to make the beginner feel stupid.

If you remember two things, this task will cease to intimidate. First, roses are fast-growing shrubs. If your bushes are healthy, most mistakes will repair themselves within a few weeks, or at worst within a single growing season. Second, roses are fundamentally just another kind of flowering shrub. If you feel reasonably confident about your ability to prune your other shrubs, you will have no trouble with your roses.

Reasons for Pruning

Start your pruning by forgetting all those rules of traditional rose pruning. The goal of that type of pruning was to force from the rosebushes a few exhibition-quality flowers, and if these blooms were borne on ugly shrubs, that was fine. Your goal should be to encourage the healthy growth that produces a bigger and finer crop of flowers.

Pruning promotes this in two ways. First, by stimulating new growth, it forces the roses to continually renew themselves. It helps them stay young and vigorous. Second, by clearing away damaged or infected branches, pruning beats back diseases and pests.

Tools

Three tools should take care of all your pruning needs. You'll need a pair of pruning shears to cut

A folding pruning saw and bypass pruning shears make the clean cuts good gardeners require. Thorn-proof leather gloves, by making the work less painful, promote more thorough pruning.

PRUNING A BUSH-TYPE ROSE

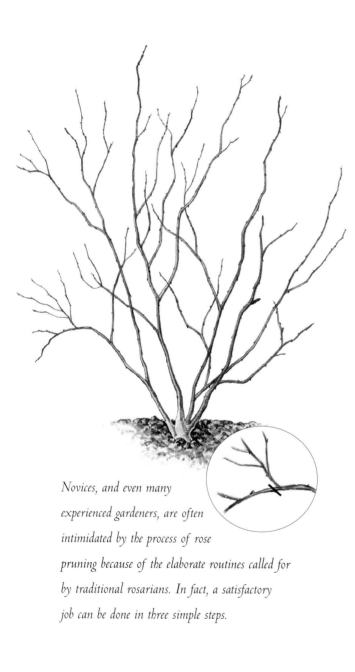

Novices, and even many experienced gardeners, are often intimidated by the process of rose pruning because of the elaborate routines called for by traditional rosarians. In fact, a satisfactory job can be done in three simple steps.

1 Begin pruning a bush-type rose by removing the three D's: dead, damaged, and diseased branches. Also remove weak, spindly branches.

2 Prune crossing branches that rub against others, wounding the bark and creating entry points for diseases. Cut ones that grow inward through the bush's center, because they create congested growth more susceptible to blackspot and mildew.

3 Shorten remaining canes by one-third. Make all your pruning cuts at an angle, ¼ in (6.4mm) above a bud that faces outward from the center of the bush. This encourages spreading, open growth.

canes up to ½ in (12.7mm) in diameter, a pair of lopping shears for larger canes, and a pruning saw for removing large stubs and canes at the base of the bush.

The shears should be of the "bypass" type; that is, they should cut like a pair of scissors, with one blade sliding past the other. There are straight-bladed models, but the ones that feature a hooked blade to grab the branch and a curved one to cut it are easier to use because they cut without slipping.

Low-priced pruning shears tend to be of the "blade-and-anvil" type, which cut by squeezing the branch between a sharp-edged blade and a broad-edged flat one. These crush and injure the tissue as they cut and cannot remove a branch without leaving a stub. Bypass shears are more expensive, but they do a far better job. The very best models feature replaceable blades made of surgical steel; these cut cleanly for years.

Make sure your long-handled lopping shears are of the bypass type, too. The models with light-weight metal alloy handles are lighter and easier to wield; they are stronger and more durable, too. Good lopping shears also sport rubber bumpers, or shock absorbers, inside the handles, right behind the pivot that connects the two arms. These bumpers are basic protection for your knuckles —

when you snap the blade through a branch, the bumpers keep the handles from slamming together and crushing your fingers.

Shop for a pruning saw with a short blade — 7–8 in (17.8–20.3cm) is ideal — and a thin, pointed tip that you can insert into narrow crotches. A fine-toothed saw, one with eight teeth to the inch, makes cleaner cuts and is best for roses. Most often you'll find that the folding saws — the ones in which the blade folds into a wooden or plastic handle like a jackknife blade — best fit this profile.

One other tool that many gardeners find essential in rose pruning is a pair of gloves. "Fruit-picker gloves," which are coated with a thorn-proof plastic and have long gauntlets stretching up over the wrists and forearms, provide the most effective protection. Any thorn-proof leather glove will work too.

When to Prune

As with any kind of pruning, how and when you make the cuts should be based on the way the plant grows. Roses follow one of two patterns. Everblooming roses — the types, such as hybrid teas, that rebloom more or less continuously through the summer — produce the best flowers on "new wood," branches and stems produced during the current year's growth. To encourage the

 A Pruning Tip from the Southwest Regional Consultant

The winter weather that Clair Martin experiences at the Huntington Botanical Gardens in southern California lacks significant chilling. Although the temperature may (rarely) drop into the 20s (below 0°C), the cold is never persistent enough to trigger a period of true dormancy among his roses.

This might sound like a blessing to northerners, but it can create problems. By stripping the foliage from roses, winter in other regions also strips away most of the rose pests and exposes the remaining ones and their eggs, making them more vulnerable to a late-winter spray of horticultural oil. Over-wintering foliage also harbors spores of fungal diseases,

perpetuating those infections. In addition, the Huntington Botanical Gardens' most famous attraction is their unmatched collection of historic roses, and many of these require a period of winter dormancy if they are to bloom.

Clair has found that timely pruning can reproduce many of the effects that winter produces elsewhere. He prunes all his roses in late January or February, cutting them back by one-third to one-half. At the same time, he strips (by hand) all the remaining leaves from the bushes. By March, his roses are covered with clean new growth and are making buds for a new display of flowers.

maximum production of new wood, everbloomers should be cut back right as the current year's growth starts, when the bushes are emerging from their winter dormancy and the buds are swelling.

This means that you'll start pruning as early as late winter in the South and in early spring in the North. In cold climates, where a cold snap can bring freezing weather late in the spring, you may want to delay pruning a bit longer, until the new shoots have emerged on their own and stretched to a length of an inch or so (about 2.5cm). Pruning stimulates new growth, and if you prune too early in the spring, you may prompt the rose to accelerate its emergence from dormancy. This will make the bush more vulnerable to any late frosts that should occur.

Once-blooming roses — a group that includes most of the species roses and the older classes of garden roses such as alba roses and gallica roses — bloom most heavily, or even solely, on "old wood," branches and stems produced during the previous year. If you prune these roses at the beginning of the season (as you would an everbloomer), you cut off the old wood before it has a chance to bloom. Winter-killed branches should be removed as soon as growth resumes in the spring, but aside from that, postpone pruning the once-bloomers until just after they have flowered.

This rule also applies to the other types of cold-hardy old roses, such as Bourbons and hybrid perpetuals. Although these roses do rebloom to some extent, most of their flowers come in the first flush, the one that is borne in late spring or early summer. Wait until after that period of bloom subsides to prune these shrubs.

Regional Considerations: In the Southeast and Southwest, you'll have to do a second round of pruning. Those two regions have an exceedingly long growing season that may last 9 or 10 months. Indeed, because the summer heat forces the roses into a second period of dormancy, most southern regions actually experience two growing seasons in any given year: one in spring and another in fall. So

in these regions, it makes sense to prune everblooming roses again (lightly) in late summer, just before the fall growing season begins.

Adapting for Different Types of Roses

Just as the timing varies from one type of rose to another, so should the style of your pruning. In this case, however, the important distinction lies in the natural shape of the roses. You prune shrub roses one way, to enhance their naturally bushy form; you give a different sort of treatment to climbing roses, one calculated to create a full and graceful fountain of bloom. Ground-cover roses receive yet another treatment. Always, though, the key is to work with the natural inclination of the rose.

Clean Cuts for Shrub Roses: When you take out your pruning shears, keep reminding yourself that your goal is to produce a handsome shrub. Don't cut the rosebushes back to stubs, in the traditional manner. Instead, begin by removing the three D's: dead, diseased, and damaged wood. Any canes that were killed by the winter or that have been nibbled by rabbits or deer should go, as should any that show evidence of canker infestation (*see p.203*). Cut below the affected areas or cut the whole canes off cleanly at their bases.

Next, remove any spindly, weak branches and canes, as well as any ingrown canes — branches or shoots that instead of reaching outward have grown back through the center of the bush. Thin the bush by removing one of any two branches or canes that are crowding each other or rubbing against each other. Finally, to encourage compact, sturdy growth, shorten the remaining canes by one-third.

A good rule of thumb is to make all your cuts ¼ in (6.4mm) above a vegetative bud or branch that faces outward from the center of the bush, as this will promote a spreading, open structure. This not only gives the rose a more graceful appearance, but it also contributes to the bush's health. Air circulates more easily through an open, spreading rosebush. As it does so, it evaporates any water sitting

on the surface of the canes and foliage and blows away fungal spores. Careful pruning is one of the chief defenses against blackspot, mildew, and other fungal diseases.

To some degree, you will have to modify your pruning to suit the style of each cultivar. A rose that naturally produces upright growth, like most of the hybrid teas, cannot be forced to adopt a low, bushy shape. Nor can a sprawling shrub such as one of the Canadian explorer roses be given a compact silhouette. To lop back such a rose's long, arching canes would destroy its natural grace. Enhancing nature, rather than fighting it, should be the goal of any sensible gardener.

Pruning Climbing Roses: Like shrub roses, climbing roses divide into everbloomers (such as the climbing hybrid teas) and once-bloomers (a group that includes most of the old ramblers). Again, the timing of the pruning depends on the pattern of the flowering. Everbloomers receive most of their pruning at the beginning of their season of growth, because this encourages the production of new shoots, which on these roses are the ones that flower most heavily. With the exception of the removal of deadwood (which may be done at any time), once-blooming climbers are pruned only after they bloom, as are any of the old-fashioned climbers that rebloom sporadically (such as the climbing form of the Bourbon rose 'Souvenir de la Malmaison').

Whatever the timing, pruning a climbing rose begins as with a shrub rose, by removing any dead, damaged, or diseased branches and any spindly, crossing, or ingrown growth. Finish the first pruning by cutting back the side shoots, the branches that extend more or less horizontally from the long

Regular pruning is essential to maintaining the floral display of climbing roses such as this miniature, 'Jeanne Lajoie'. As the vertical canes age, they eventually lose vigor and bear fewer blossoms. Such senile stems must be replaced with new canes, but to avoid traumatizing the rose, you should replace only one each year.

PRUNING A CLIMBING ROSE

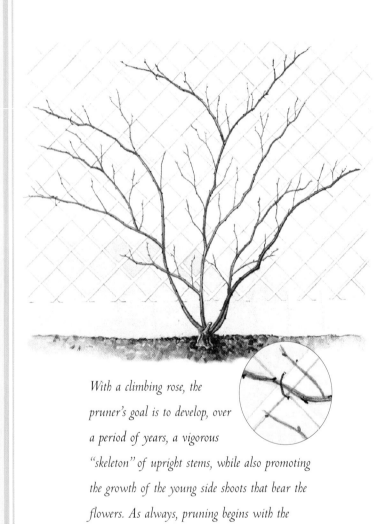

With a climbing rose, the pruner's goal is to develop, over a period of years, a vigorous "skeleton" of upright stems, while also promoting the growth of the young side shoots that bear the flowers. As always, pruning begins with the removal of dead wood in early spring.

1 On everblooming climbers, the side shoots are cut back by half as the rose emerges from dormancy. With once-blooming climbers, and cold-hardy old-fashioned types such as Bourbon roses, this operation is delayed until after the main early summer bloom.

2 After the first flush of blossoms in early summer is a good time to renew the skeleton of both everbloomers and once-bloomers. If an old, woody vertical cane is showing signs of declining vigor and reduced bloom, cut it off at the base. Try not to remove more than one vertical cane a year.

3 Select a flexible new shoot as a replacement for the missing vertical cane. Tie it into place loosely but securely with a length of soft twine.

vertical canes, by one-half. Once-bloomers get much the same treatment, although in their case, the pruning should wait until after they bloom.

Right after the first flush of roses has ended is also a good time to work on the structure of your climbing roses. Unlike shrubs, climbers must develop a skeleton. That is, they need a framework of upright canes that serve as the trunks from which the flower-bearing side shoots emerge. The number of vertical canes you allow the rose to develop will depend on the vigor of the rose and the expanse of wall, trellis, or fence you wish to cover. But keep in mind that climbing roses, like ordinary shrub roses, are healthiest when the stems don't crowd one another and air can circulate through the plant.

If tied into place loosely but securely with soft twine, these vertical canes often will grow vigorously and flower well for several years. Eventually, though, as they become thick and woody, their vigor will decline and they will bear fewer blossoms. Then it's time to replace them.

To replace one of the main trunks, select a vigorous new cane that springs from the crown of the rosebush, at or just above the bud union. Remove the old cane by cutting it off at the base. Then tie the young, flexible cane into the spot once occupied by the old cane.

Try to manage your climbing roses so that you don't need to replace more than one vertical cane annually. Removing several of the vertical canes at the same time forces the rose to replace a great many branches all at once and at the same time deprives the plant of much of the foliage that converts sunlight into energy. Drastic pruning of this sort depletes a rose, not only reducing bloom but also leaving it especially vulnerable to diseases, pests, and winter damage.

Pruning Ground-Cover Roses: In many cases, ground-cover roses are just climbers that have been encouraged to spread their canes along the ground rather than up a trellis. The difference in orientation, from upright to prone, dictates a somewhat different style of pruning. For example, if you want 'Red Cascade' to cover a sunny bank, you must treat it differently from the way you would if you wanted to espalier it up the garden wall. This different style of pruning also requires an additional kind of equipment. To get into the center of a ground-cover rose without injury, you need not only thorn-proof gloves but also high-top leather or rubber boots.

When you use long-caned climbing roses as ground covers, your goal is to induce a more or less solid sheet of growth. You can accomplish this by letting each rose produce a denser skeleton of canes than you would permit when growing the rose as a climber. After all, the climbing rose cannot spread itself over an arc of more than 180 degrees, while the ground-cover plant must spread in every direction, over 360 degrees.

Besides permitting the rose to make a fuller skeleton, you should also encourage it to make more side branches by cutting back the tips of each of the skeleton's "ribs." Do this at the end of the dormant period with everblooming roses and after the first flush of bloom with once-bloomers and most of the old-fashioned roses.

The finer textured foliage and flowers of miniature roses, such as 'Red Cascade', make them most decorative as ground covers. This example is soon to need careful pruning, as it spills onto the walkway.

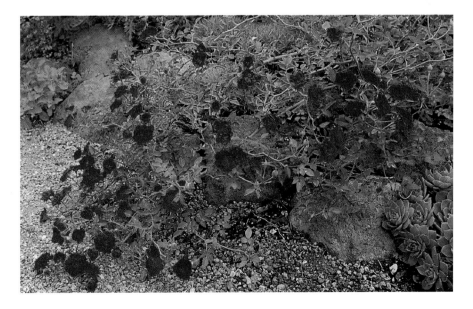

To promote cold-hardiness, northern gardeners should stop deadheading at midsummer and let the roses set a crop of hips. Though this slows flower production, the colorful rose fruits provide a subtler show more in harmony with the autumn season.

If your ground-cover roses are bush-type cultivars, such as 'Scarlet Meidiland'™, pruning should be limited to removing dead, damaged, and diseased branches as they appear, and also thinning the shrubs judiciously if they become choked with branches. If your ground-cover roses have the habit of throwing out high, arching canes, you can give them a neater profile by pinning the canes to the ground. Fashion wire clothes hangers into giant staples that will penetrate 8 in (20.3cm) or more into the ground, then use them to pin down the unruly stems. Suppressing canes in this fashion causes new shoots to emerge from every bud along the length of the pinned cane, and these shoots should bear an extra-heavy crop of flowers.

Deadheading

This is a gardener's term for the practice of snipping off old blossoms as they wither and start to go to seed. The only motive for applying this treatment to once-blooming roses is a desire for neatness —

the spent flowers look messy. But removing the blossoms means that the bushes will bear no hips.

Deadheading can, however, improve tremendously the display you get from reblooming roses. When such roses set seed, their flower production slows drastically; it's almost as if the plant undergoes a hormonal change. Aborting the seeds by deadheading the old flowers can keep your roses in bloom weeks longer.

This is not always an advantage, though. Gardeners in northern regions, for example, should stop deadheading by midsummer. Letting the bushes set seed at that time seems to help them mature. Roses that are allowed to bear hips in the fall seem to slip into dormancy more easily and suffer less winter damage.

Promoting Hardiness

Traditionally, this subject was the rose fancier's obsession. The reason was that hardiness, which is loosely defined as the ability to cope with the extremes of the local weather, was so often lacking in garden roses. The fault for this lay not in the plants, but in the gardeners: they selected roses primarily for their ability to please the eye rather than for their adaptation to the regional climate.

To compensate for their poor choices, gardeners developed elaborate methods of protecting their roses from the weather. This was especially true in the North, where devoted fanciers would build insulated shelters around their roses to bring them through the winter, or even dig them up and bury them in deep trenches until spring.

As any southern gardener will testify, however, summer hardiness can be far more important than winter hardiness, depending on where you garden. Obviously, the two sets of problems are very different. But the solutions are not.

The secret to protecting your roses against the extremes of summer or winter weather is really threefold. First and most important, you must plant roses that are adapted to your climate and soil. But even if your roses are naturally adapted to your region, you have to make sure they have all they need for sturdy, healthy growth. Adequate irrigation is essential both in summer heat, when the sun will parch drought-stricken roses, and in winter cold, when arid winds can dehydrate frozen shrubs just as quickly. Good nutrition is also essential, and an annual spring soil test, which allows a gardener to fertilize accurately, will pay for itself many times over in the increased longevity of your rosebushes.

But giving your roses too much encouragement is liable to prove as harmful as giving them too little. Overly generous fertilization and too-frequent waterings will incite overactive growth. The result will be roses that are impressive in size but soft and unable to withstand either summer heat or winter cold. You want roses that are vigorous but sturdy, and ready to follow the season's hints and drop into dormancy when they need to. This can happen only if you respect the natural growth cycle.

Because pruning encourages new growth, you must prune at a time when the rose would naturally be producing new shoots. Fertilization also promotes growth, so you should feed at a time when growth is natural; you should not fertilize when growth would naturally be slowing.

The schedule for these operations will vary with the region, but the strategy and the results remain the same. Attentive, well-timed maintenance, not special tricks, is the secret to hardier roses.

The best way to simplify maintenance is to choose carefully the roses that you plant. This 'Henry Kelsey', for example, a Canadian explorer rose, combines disease resistance with exceptional cold hardiness; and it flourishes without fussing in California, where this picture was taken, as well as in the chilly north. Traditional rosarians defied nature; today's gardeners look to it for direction.

Chapter Seven

PROBLEMS AND PRESCRIPTIONS

*If their basic needs are met, easy roses will behave just that way.
You should remember, though, that easy does not mean trouble free. Every plant, no
matter how hardy and self-reliant, eventually experiences some sort of problem.*

*T*here are many reasons why a plant that has been outstandingly healthy can suddenly fall sick. Perhaps, over time, nutrients have washed out of the soil around its roots, so that some crucial mineral is lacking. Or a prolonged period of harsh weather may reduce the plant's vigor, so that it becomes unusually vulnerable to disease. Just as you are more likely to catch a cold when you are tired, so a rose may become more susceptible to blackspot when stressed by summer heat or by drought. Insect populations are cyclical, too, and in a year when such a population is peaking, the customary host plants may not be enough to support the pest, so it attacks other plants that it otherwise would leave alone.

The development of symptoms does not necessarily mean that you made a poor choice of cultivar or that the rose must be replaced. But it does mean that the time has come to act, and fast. The speed with which you recognize and respond to a problem will have a strong impact on the rose's recovery. If you treat the problem while it is still in its initial stages, before it has exhausted the strength of the bush, the rose is likely to recover quickly. If you wait until the rose is half defoliated, nursing it back to health will be a long, difficult process.

Targeting the Treatment

Although speedy treatment is important, reacting with too much haste can lead to trouble. That's because to treat a problem effectively, you must first take the time to identify exactly what that problem is. Otherwise, you are likely to do more harm than good.

Unfortunately, there is a common impulse toward the preemptive strike. As soon as you notice spots appearing on the leaves, you reach for the cure-all: some preblended mixture of insecti-

High encircling walls and fences may protect your garden from rabbits and deer, but they also inhibit air circulation, and that makes your roses more susceptible to fungal diseases.

Even spraying the roses with a "miticide," a chemical designed to kill mites, often proves harmful because some of the most effective predators of spider mites are other species of mites. Knowing this, Peter stopped applying all insecticidal and miticidal sprays several years ago. Now, though neighboring gardeners battle mites continuously, his roses do not suffer significant damage from this pest.

Another problem of the preemptive strike is that it is launched with the assumption that an insect or disease is what is troubling the roses, when actually the problem may well be cultural. Yellowing leaves, for example, may be a sign of a nutritional deficiency, something lacking in the soil. Spraying cannot correct that deficiency, unless you spray the roses with a fertilizer.

Still, there are situations where your roses may need the protection that a spray, either organic or synthetic, provides. Even then, an accurate diagnosis is important. Knowing exactly what you are treating will allow you to select the least harmful treatment. If you identify the mold on your rose's leaves as powdery mildew, for example, you needn't resort to toxic synthetic fungicides. You can cure a case of powdery mildew with a spray of ordinary baking soda (*see p.*200). In addition, knowing the identity of the pest or disease allows you to treat it at the stage in its life cycle when it is most vulnerable, so that whatever measures you take will be most effective.

A Troubleshooter's Guide

The following is an illustrated guide to 20 of the most common rose pests, diseases, and cultural problems. To make identification easy, these have been grouped by the type of symptom, and each problem is illustrated with a photograph. If you find your rose's leaves perforated with holes, you can turn to the section of the guide that deals with leaf problems and look for a match between an illustration and what you observe on your bush.

cides and fungicides that you hope will kill everything. Although it may not accomplish that, it is sure to have a devastating effect on garden fauna, thoroughly upsetting the natural balance within your landscape. By such indiscriminate slaughter, you may indeed kill whatever it is that was troubling your roses. At the same time, you will most likely kill predatory insects that have been keeping various other pests in check.

That's why Peter Haring, our Southeast regional consultant, has stopped applying insecticides to his roses. Spider mites, nearly invisible relatives of the more familiar spiders, are one of his region's most persistent rose pests, sucking the juices from leaves and stems and sapping the plants' vitality. Because they are not insects, they are not vulnerable to most insecticides. In fact, the more common combination sprays will actually encourage spider mites by killing the insects that prey on them.

In some cases, you may find that your rose symptoms resemble a couple of the diagnostic photographs. If so, read the text that accompanies both of them; the descriptions of the problems should enable you to decide which one is afflicting your roses. For example, attacks of the various pests and diseases tend to be seasonal. This means that if a symptom first appears in midsummer, it is unlikely that a pest or disease that flourishes in the cool weather of spring and fall is the cause.

After helping you to identify your problem, the guide recommends remedies. In general, these recommendations begin with the treatment that is least likely to have a negative impact on garden wildlife and the environment. Often you will find that adjusting the way you care for your roses can eliminate the problem. Because stronger measures are sometimes necessary, however, recommendations for the use of pesticides are also included.

If you should choose to use these pesticides, you should first take the time to read the product label in full and observe all precautions recommended there. In some cases, you may find that the use of certain chemicals is not permitted in your area. In that case, you should check with your local Cooperative Extension Service (affiliated with land-grant universities; see your phone book) to identify approved alternatives. In Canada, contact Health Canada's Pest Management Regulatory Agency at 1-800-267-6315.

Leaf Symptoms

A rosebush manufactures the food that supplies it with energy in its leaves; because it is so nutrient rich, the foliage is a favorite target of insects and diseases. Commonly, these biological food-factories are the first part of the bush to show the effects of environmental problems such as a soil deficient in minerals. For these reasons, it is especially important to diagnose leaf symptoms quickly and accurately.

Discoloration

Blackspot: A fungal disease that causes round, fringed, black spots to appear on the upper sides of leaves from spring through summer, especially during periods of high humidity or persistent rain. Eventually, infected leaves yellow and fall from the bush. Severe infestation can completely defoliate the bush, sometimes killing it.

Regional notes — Prevalent in the Northwest, Rocky Mountain West, Midwest, Southeast, Mid-Atlantic region, Northeast, and eastern and Pacific Coast regions of Canada.

Suggested treatments — Where blackspot is common, plant only disease-resistant roses. Set rosebushes in breezy, open spots and thin by pruning to keep the bushes from becoming congested. Water in the morning so that foliage dries quickly and avoid as much as possible wetting the foliage. Rake up any fallen leaves and dispose of them off-site. When symptoms appear, spray with neem, an extract of the seeds of the tropical neem tree, as directed on the product label, or apply an approved fungicide such as mancozeb as directed on the product label.

Miscellaneous Other Leaf Spots: A variety of other fungi, such as spot anthracnose, may also cause spots of various colors (red, brown, or purple) to appear on upper leaf surfaces. In the case of spot anthracnose, the centers of the spots turn gray or white and often fall out, leaving a shot hole appearance. Heavy infections can cause leaves to yellow and drop off the bush.

Regional notes — Especially serious in the upper Midwest, according to regional consultant Kathy Zuzek, and common in moist climates throughout North America.

Suggested treatments — Avoid wetting foliage, as that spreads the disease spores. Rake up fallen rose foliage and dispose of it off-site. If infection becomes widespread, spray with an approved fungicide such as mancozeb.

Powdery Mildew: A white or gray powdery fungus that spreads across new growth and over flower buds. This disease may cause leaves to twist and fold, and often fall from the bush. It may also abort  the blossoms. Powdery mildew is especially common during spring or other periods when high relative humidity combines with a sequence of warm days followed by cool nights. In Canada, these conditions, and powdery mildew, occur mostly in late summer.

Regional notes — Common throughout North America. Peter Haring, our Southeast regional consultant, cited this as a springtime problem. All our other consultants mentioned powdery mildew as among the most serious problems in their regions throughout the growing season.

Suggested treatments — As with other fungal diseases, protect roses by planting disease-resistant cultivars and setting them in open sites where air can circulate around them. Thin bushes by pruning to prevent congestion. Strip infected leaves from the bushes and spray with a mixture of 1 tablespoon (15ml) baking soda and 1 tablespoon (15ml) light horticultural oil in 1 gal (3.8L) water at weekly intervals; apply in the early morning or late evening when the sun is least intense. Alternatively, you can apply an approved fungicide such as mancozeb as directed on the product label.

Rose Rust: A fungal disease that causes yellow to brown spots on the upper surfaces of leaves and powdery orange spots on the undersides of leaves. Young twigs may also be  affected. Infected leaves become twisted and dry and may drop from the plants. Periods of moist weather (fog or rain) and moderate temperatures (55°–75°F [13°–24°C]) promote the spread of this disease.

Regional notes — Most common in the Southwest, Northwest, and Pacific Coast of Canada. Clair Martin, our Southwest regional consultant, cited this as a particular problem in the Los Angeles area.

Suggested treatments — Plant disease-resistant cultivars where rust is prevalent. When symptoms appear, strip infected leaves from the plants and dispose of them off-site. Spray with an approved fungicide such as ferbam or mancozeb as directed on the product label.

Viruses: Yellow or brown rings or yellow blotches on the leaves are usually a symptom of infection by any one of a number of viruses. Look also for puckered and curling new leaves and malformed flower  buds. A decline in vigor and gradual stunting are also typical.

Regional notes — Common throughout North America.

Suggested treatments — There is no effective treatment, and viruses can be spread from plant to plant by sucking insects like leafhoppers and thrips, so remove and destroy infected plants. Viruses are more commonly transmitted during propagation when careless nurserymen use rootstocks cloned from infected plants. If you find a virus among your roses, you should contact the nursery that sold you them.

Chlorosis: This con-  dition is marked by yellowing of the younger leaves in the areas between the leaf veins; the veins remain darker green. A symptom of iron deficiency, chlorosis most often derives from a problem with soil pH. Soil that is excessively acid or alkaline prevents rose roots from absorbing the iron present in the soil.

Regional notes — May occur throughout North America, particularly common in western regions with strongly alkaline soils.

Suggested treatments — Test soil pH with an inexpensive kit available at your local garden centersand add ground limestone or sulfur to bring it within the desirable 5.5 to 7.0 range. If the condition persists, treat the soil with chelated iron (available at most garden centers) as directed on package label.

Soil Deficiencies:  NITROGEN — leaves smaller than normal, stems thin, reduced new growth; foliage yellows, then dries to a light brown and subsequently drops off.

PHOSPHORUS — growth slows; foliage is dark green, then turns purplish or, less often, yellow between the veins.

POTASSIUM — lower leaves begin yellowing at the margin and then gradually toward the center; eventually margins turn brown and curve under and leaves drop.

MAGNESIUM — *older* leaves develop symptoms of chlorosis, often curling up or down or developing a puckered effect.

Regional notes — Occurs locally throughout North America.

Suggested treatments — Send a soil sample to a laboratory for testing and incorporate amendments into the soil as recommended in the test results.

Spider Mites: Leaves  that are stippled or bronzed are commonly the result of an infestation of these tiny relatives of the spider. Fine, silken webs on the undersides of leaves and on new growth are another symptom. For a positive identification, tap an affected leaf over a sheet of white paper and look for moving red, green, or yellow specks. Mites are especially common during hot, dry weather.

Regional notes — Present throughout North America, particularly common in the Southwest, Rocky Mountain West, and Southeast, according to regional consultants for those areas.

Suggested treatments — Wash mites off bushes weekly with a forceful stream of water, or apply an approved miticide such as Aphid-Mite Attack, an insecticidal soap, as directed on the product label. Horticultural oils may also be used.

Holes in Leaves

Japanese Beetles:  These brownish or metallic green beetles attack the foliage, riddling it with holes, and often eat their way into flower buds. Appearing in late spring or early summer, the beetles lay their eggs and usually disappear in late summer.

Regional notes — Often reach plague proportions in the Northeast, Mid-Atlantic, and Southeast. Beetle infestations are also cited as a serious problem by Trevor Cole, our regional consultant in Canada.

Suggested treatments — Neem extract provides an effective repellent when sprayed on the bushes as directed on the product label. Insecticides that kill the beetles have little effect because during their season, new beetles will fly in to reinfest.

Rose Slugs: Attacking in spring, these pests eat out the interior leaf tissue from between the leaf veins, leaving a translucent, lacy leaf. The pests themselves are brown-headed, pale green to metallic green,  sluglike worms up to ¾ in (19mm) long.

Regional notes — Common on the Pacific Coast, in the Mid-Atlantic region, and in the Northeast.

Suggested treatments — Insecticidal soap and neem extract both provide effective control.

Flower Problems

Rose Chafers: These beetles feed on flowers during the late-spring and early-summer blooming period. They are about ½ in (13mm) long and have tan bodies and reddish brown heads.

Regional notes — Common throughout the Northeast, upper Midwest, and southeastern Canada. Cited as a special problem by Trevor Cole, our regional consultant in Canada.

Suggested treatments — Handpicking may be enough to control a slight infestation. For more serious outbreaks, spray the bushes with neem extract, or dust or spray them with pyrethrin.

Rose Midge: When rosebuds and shoots blacken and wither, look closely, and you will probably find them infested with these tiny white maggots.

Regional notes — Common in the Southeast, Mid-Atlantic region, lower Northeast and Midwest, and Southwest.

Suggested treatments — Prune off and dispose of or destroy the affected buds and shoots. Spray the bushes with insecticidal soap or some approved insecticide such as acephate.

Thrips: The most dramatic damage that these insects cause is to the flowers of the rose, although the foliage is also damaged. When attacked by thrips, buds are deformed and usually 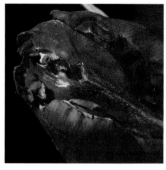 fail to open. Petals of open blossoms are marked with brown flecks and streaks, and young leaves are distorted and flecked with yellow. Pull apart a streaked or deformed flower over a sheet of white paper, and you may see the tiny yellow or brown insects against the paper.

Regional notes — Common throughout North America, but cited as a particular problem by Clair Martin, Southwest regional consultant, and David Earl Bott, Rocky Mountain West regional consultant.

Suggested treatments — Remove and destroy infested buds and blossoms. Neem extract and insecticidal soap provide some control if sprayed three times at an interval of 7–10 days. Thrips are persistent, however, and may require treatment with an approved insecticide. Systemic insecticides such as acephate, which are absorbed and transported through the plant tissues, are most effective against thrips.

Stem Problems

Caneborers: If the tip of a seemingly healthy rose cane suddenly wilts and the foliage begins to die, look for a swollen band of tissue at the base of the dieback and a hole in the cane's tip. These  are signs of a caneborer's attack, and if you split the dead cane open with a knife, you will find it hollow, with a white or yellow grub hiding inside.

Regional notes — A problem locally throughout North America, with damage caused by a number of different insect larvae. Cited as a special problem by David Earl Bott, our Rocky Mountain West regional consultant.

Suggested treatments — Prune off and destroy infected canes. Sealing all cut stem ends with a dab of white glue after pruning also deters borers.

Canker: A number of different fungi can cause this sort of infection, which often results in the death of affected stems. The identifying symptoms are sunken areas of yellow, red, or brown discoloration on  the stems. Usually canker enters a stem during periods of wet or humid weather through wounds caused by pruning or the rubbing together of two stems.

Regional notes — Prevalent throughout North America, except in the desert Southwest.

Suggested treatments — Prune off any infected stems at a point at least 5 in (12.7cm) below the affected area; you will need to disinfect your pruning shears with rubbing alcohol after each cut. Reduce the incidence of infection by pruning to eliminate rubbing stems and by making clean cuts that leave no stubby ends or ragged edges.

Crown Gall: Large, corky galls, or tumors, form at the base of the plant at the bud union and on stems and roots. Though it is not fatal, this disease will weaken the bush. It is  more commonly found on grafted roses than on own-root roses.

Regional notes — Common throughout North America and a serious pest in some locations; cited as a special problem by David Earl Bott, Rocky Mountain West regional consultant.

Suggested treatments — There is no cure for this soilborne bacterial disease. Infected plants should be dug up and discarded, and the soil from the root area should be replaced before a rose is replanted there. Avoid injuring the roots or crown when planting roses in areas where crown gall is prevalent.

Mossy Rose Gall: These galls may look like some sort of exotic fruits, but in fact they are a reproductive device of a type of wasp. The adult lays its eggs on the stems of the rosebush, and  when the eggs hatch in early spring, the larvae secrete a chemical that causes the stems to produce abnormal, tumorlike growths in June and July. The larvae overwinter in the galls, emerging as adults the following spring. Though interesting from an ecological point of view, these growths drain the strength from a rose. Indeed, a heavy infestation may kill a bush. Hybrid rugosa roses are especially susceptible.

Regional notes — Cited by Midwest regional consultant Kathy Zuzek as a particular problem.

Suggested treatments — In fall, after the leaves have fallen from the rosebushes and the galls are clearly visible, prune them off the stems, then dispose of them.

Rose Stem Girdlers: Actually the larval form of a small green beetle, this grub excavates a spiral tunnel under the bark of the rose stem, causing the bark to swell and split.

Regional notes — Most common east of the Mississippi River; cited as a special problem by Kathy Zuzek, Midwest regional consultant.

Suggested treatments — Prune off and dispose of infected stems, cutting below the affected area.

General Insect Problems

Aphids: Tiny green, white, or pink, pear-shaped sucking insects that cluster on new growth and flower buds. If left unchecked, they cause the distortion of leaves and buds and may abort the flowers.

Regional notes — Common throughout North America. Cited as a special problem by Trevor Cole, Canadian regional consultant; Donna Fuss, Northeast regional consultant; Kathy Zuzek, Midwest regional consultant; and Clair Martin, Southwest regional consultant.

Suggested treatments — Wash aphids from the stems with a strong jet of water, or spray with insecticidal soap. An aphid infestation may be an indication that there has been excessive fertilization with nitrogen.

Scale: These insects can be white, gray, or brown and cling to the stems and leaves like small barnacles, sometimes forming a crust.

Regional notes — Occurs throughout all of North America.

Suggested treatments — With slight infestations, cut off the stems below the area of infestation. Or rub off adults with a toothbrush, then spray with insecticidal soap to kill the young.

Pesticide Application

Safety — your own and that of your family, neighbors, pets, and wildlife — must be your first concern when using any kind of pesticide. This holds true whether you are applying synthetic products or so-called organic sprays. Usually organic gardening remedies such as pyrethrin have a less persistent effect on the environment, but their acute toxicity, which is their immediate effect, may be lethal if they are misused.

A Few Simple Rules

• Whatever you are applying, begin by reading the product label carefully. Take all the recommended safety precautions, and if the label calls for mixing the pesticide with water, follow the prescribed formula. Resist the temptation to make the spray "extra strong," since that can transform a safe product into a harmful one.

• When mixing and using sprays, wear all the protective gear recommended on the product label. Rubber gloves, protective clothing, a respirator face mask, and a waterproof head covering are standard precautions.

- Do not store and save leftover spray solutions. Try to mix only as much spray as you need for a given application. Dispose of any extra by spraying it on the target plants.

Targeting Sprays More Effectively

- If your water is alkaline, add 1 tablespoon (15ml) white vinegar per 1 gal (3.8L) water when mixing solutions of chemical pesticides. This will boost their effectiveness.

- Add a few drops of liquid dishwashing detergent to each gallon (3.8L) of homemade sprays, such as the baking soda, oil, and water mixture recommended for powdery mildew (*see p.*200). By reducing the surface tension of the water, dishwashing detergent helps to spread and "stick" the spray. This is not necessary with commercial formulas, which generally include a "spreader-sticker."

- Early morning or evening is usually the best time to spray. The air tends to be still and cool then, and bees are less active, so they will escape exposure to the toxins. Don't spray on windy days, and avoid the hottest part of the day, since many sprays will harm the plants if applied then.

- Applying pesticides by dusting is an attractive option because it requires little or no application equipment. In general, however, dusting is far less effective than spraying, and because dusts are likely to drift and blow about in the breeze, they cause far more unintentional damage to innocent bystanders.

Timing

If the product label recommends a series of sprayings, be sure to follow the schedule precisely. Many sprays, especially the less toxic ones such as insecticidal soaps, kill adult pests but may not kill their eggs. The successive sprayings are intended to kill the emerging young before they can mature and reproduce. Often as many as three sprayings are needed to control an infestation.

A compression sprayer with a long wand allows you to spray the undersides of the leaves, for thorough coverage.

A product label may warn against spraying when the temperature outside has risen above 85°F (29°C). The reason for this is that the product may injure the plants if applied then. By ignoring that warning, you may cause more damage with your remedy than the pest or disease will ever cause.

Equipment

Pump-type compression sprayers are the most accurate in their delivery of pesticidal sprays. However, hose-end sprayers are less expensive, and they are more efficient in dealing with large numbers of plants. Hose-end sprayers screw onto the end of your hose and use water pressure to mix and deliver the spray solution. Because hose-end sprayers tend to apply more spray, responsible gardeners may prefer to use hand-pump models when applying the more toxic synthetic insecticides and fungicides to their plants.

Thorough Coverage

When applying sprays to rosebushes, the tendency is to soak the surfaces that you can see and ignore the rest. In fact, the parts of the rose that are commonly hidden from view — the undersides of the leaves and the areas where the leaf stems attach to the canes — are often more important targets, since that is where the pests tend to hide and lay their eggs.

Take time to wet both the tops and undersides of the foliage thoroughly, to the point where the solution begins to run together and drip off the leaves. Wet the stems and canes, too. Thorough coverage is essential for effective control of a pest or disease. That's why serious gardeners rarely bother with pesticidal or fungicidal dusts. Puffing a cloud of toxic particles around a bush is not only hazardous to the environment, it is also ineffective. Unlike liquid sprays, whose droplets can be precisely directed, dusts settle wherever the wind blows them. It is extremely difficult to achieve thorough coverage of an infested rosebush with a dust.

Rabbits, Deer, and Rodents

In many areas, the most serious pests the rose gardener faces are the four-legged kind. Deer and rabbits feed on shoots and buds during the growing season,

The parallel strands of wire topping this fence, one electrified and the other a ground, make this an effective bar against deer. To secure the garden against rabbits, the fence's lower section should be lined with chicken wire, with the base of this finer barrier run down underground.

and voles and mice may gnaw the bark from around the bases of bushes, girdling and killing them.

Wire-mesh barriers are effective at excluding all these pests. Hardware cloth, a relatively fine wire mesh, will exclude mice and voles. A 3-ft-high (.9m) fence of 1-in-mesh (2.5cm) chicken wire will frustrate rabbits. Use 4-ft-high (1.2m) chicken wire and bury the bottom 12 in (30.5cm) in the ground, running it 6 in (15.3cm) down and then 6 in (15.3cm) outward to stop burrowers. For deer, the fence must be 8 ft (2.4m) high to be really effective.

Not only is such fencing expensive, but it is also unsightly, which defeats the purpose of your landscaping efforts. For this reason, pest repellents, which are sprayed onto the rosebushes, are usually a better alternative. A number of commercial preparations are available at garden centers, and these provide adequate protection in most cases. You can make your own animal repellent spray by mixing five eggs with 5 qt (4.7L) of water.

Mixing repellents with antitranspirant sprays such as Wilt-Pruf before application helps to prolong their effectiveness. Generally, you will have to reapply the repellent periodically throughout the growing season. Start your treatments early in the spring and be conscientious in your spraying. Animal marauders are creatures of habit, and if they become accustomed to dining on your rosebushes, it will be hard to stop them.

Another trick that provides temporary protection against rabbits and deer is to peg down swaths of black plastic bird netting over your rosebushes. Obviously, this doesn't offer as much of a barrier as wire, but unlike a wire barrier, the plastic netting is virtually invisible at a distance of a few feet (about 1.5m).

To bar deer from the garden without electrification, you must make your fence fully 8 ft (2.4m) tall; alternatively, you may surround the garden with two parallel, 4-ft-tall (1.2m) fences, set 4 ft apart. Careful construction (as here) can make even 8 ft fences less unsightly.

APPENDIX A - ZONE MAPS

U.S. CLIMATE ZONES

Published by the U.S. Department of Agriculture in 1990, this hardiness map is a revision of an earlier version that was first published in 1965. It divides the United States into eleven hardiness zones, taking as its criterion the average minimum winter temperature of each region. If a rose (or any other plant) is described as "hardy to USDA zone 7," that means that it has proven proof against the winter temperatures in this map's zone 7, where (on average) the lows are in the range of 0° to 10°F (−18° to −12°C).

This system for rating hardiness has obvious limitations. Microclimates are likely to make a particular garden warmer or colder than the surrounding area, and so your yard may not entirely agree with the zone assigned to it by this map. In addition, this map doesn't take into account the threat that summer heat may pose to a plant's survival in the southern states. To remedy that, this book lists both the most northern and the most southern zone suitable for each rose.

Despite its limitations, this method of rating plant hardiness does provide a simple and fairly reliable guide to the adaptation of plants to your climate. Because the USDA map has been accepted as the standard hardiness index by the U.S. nursery industry, it is also the most convenient guide; you'll generally find the zone of hardiness listed for each type of rose in the better catalogs.

AVERAGE MINIMUM WINTER TEMPERATURE

	Fahrenheit	Celsius
Zone 1	below −50°	below −46°
Zone 2	−50° to −40°	−46° to −40°
Zone 3	−40° to −30°	−40° to −34°
Zone 4	−30° to −20°	−34° to −29°
Zone 5	−20° to −10°	−29° to −23°
Zone 6	−10° to 0°	−23° to −18°
Zone 7	0° to 10°	−18° to −12°
Zone 8	10° to 20°	−12° to −7°
Zone 9	20° to 30°	−7° to −1°
Zone 10	30° to 40°	−1° to 4°
Zone 11	above 40°	above 4°

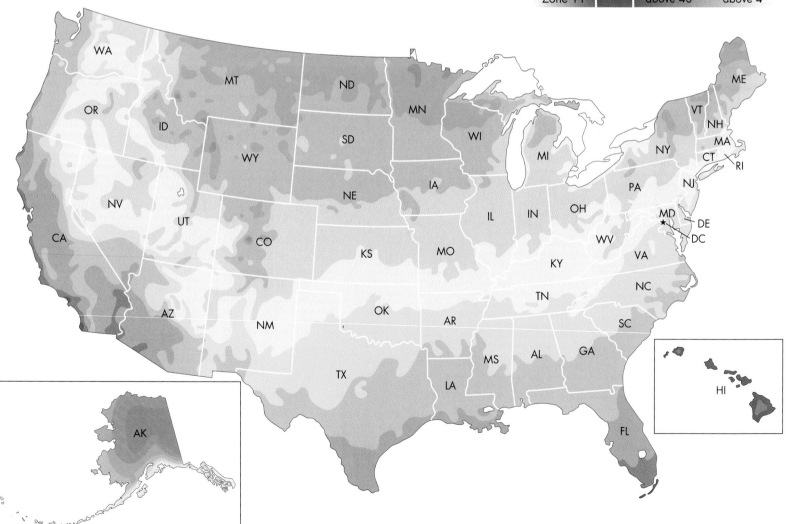

CANADIAN CLIMATE ZONES

This map is similar in conception to the USDA map on the facing page, in that it divides the whole of Canada into a series of zones based on regional climate. Like the USDA map, the Canadian map distinguishes the different zones partly on the basis of minimum winter temperatures. However, it has used the survival of certain "indicator plants" in each zone to adjust the meteorological data. In addition, the Canadian hardiness map divides each of its nine zones into colder (a) and warmer (b) regions.

As with the USDA map, local and personal experience may cause you to adjust the guidance that the map provides. A microclimate that makes your garden warmer or cooler than the surrounding area may cause you to assign a lower or higher zone number to your yard than the one indicated by the map — or, at least, you may wish to affix a "b" to your zone number rather than an "a" (or vice versa). In general, gardens in towns are somewhat warmer than those in nearby open countryside.

Summer heat is not, typically, a serious threat to plant survival in Canada. As a result, this book lists each rose's hardiness with just a single zone number — in general, a rose that survives the winter in that zone will survive in a zone of a higher number.

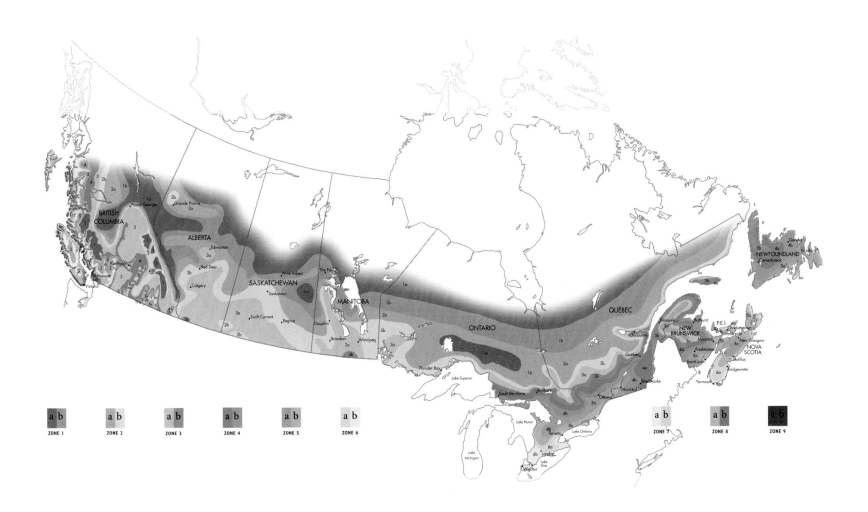

APPENDIX B
SOURCES

*T*here's no value in identifying the ideal rose for that certain spot in your garden if you cannot find that cultivar and buy it. This is a real possibility if your only source of roses is the neighborhood garden center. The local retailer may be a fine source of plants, and you should begin your search for roses there. But simple economics prevents a local supplier from stocking even a significant fraction of the thousands of different roses currently on the market.

For those determined to plant just the right rose — the easy rose — shopping by mail is essential. Only in the catalogs of specialist rose nurseries will you find all the roses you want. Unfortunately, though, shopping by catalog can be a slow and intimidating process. The huge selection of roses to be found in mail-order catalogs is their attraction, but it can also make finding the particular rose you want like searching for the proverbial needle in a haystack.

To simplify the process, this appendix includes a source for every rose recommended in this book. In addition, the Gallery of Roses (Chapter Three) tells you how to find exactly which nurseries offer the cultivar that interests you. At the end of each rose entry in the Gallery, under the heading "Sources," is a series of letter and number codes, such as "J1" or "CaH1." These indicate mail-order nurseries listed in this appendix. "J1," for example, is the letter code for the Oregon-based nursery Jackson & Perkins, the first nursery listed under the letter J. "CaH1" is the letter code for a Canadian nursery, Hardy Roses for the North. (Codes for all the Canadian nurseries cited here begin with "Ca.") Finding a particular nursery or nurseries in this appendix is easy, too. The code for each of the 50 nurseries listed here is included above the nursery's name and address. The nurseries and their codes follow alphabetical order, so locating any one is just a matter of running up or down the list until you arrive at the one you want.

Because you may prefer to order roses from your own geographic region, nurseries located in the United States are listed separately from those in Canada. Most Canadian nurseries will ship roses to customers in the United States, but in those cases in which a Canadian nursery does not ship to the United States (or vice versa), this fact has been noted in its entry.

Note: Unless a price is given, catalogs are available free of charge.

A1

The Antique Rose Emporium
9300 Lueckemeyer Road
Brenham, TX 77833
409-836-9051
Catalog $5.00; does not ship to Canada

B1

Bay Laurel Nursery
2500 El Camino Real
Atascadero, CA 93422
805-466-3406
Does not ship to Canada

B2

Bridges Roses
2734 Toney Road
Lawndale, NC 28090
704-538-9412
Does not ship to Canada

B3

W. Atlee Burpee & Co.
300 Park Avenue
Warminster, PA 18991
800-888-1447
Does not ship to Canada

C1

Carroll Gardens
444 East Main Street, P.O. Box 310
Westminster, MD 21157
410-848-5422
800-638-6334
Catalog $2.00; does not ship to Canada

C2

Chamblee's Rose Nursery
10926 U.S. Highway 69 North
Tyler, TX 75706
800-256-7673
Does not ship to Canada

D1

Donovan's Roses
P.O. Box 37800
Shreveport, LA 71133
318-861-6693
Does not ship to Canada

E1

Edmund's Roses
6235 SW Kahle Road
Wilsonville, OR 97070
503-682-1476
888-481-7673

F1

Henry Field's Seed & Nursery Co.
415 North Burnett
Shenandoah, IA 51602
605-665-9391
Does not ship to Canada

F2

Forestfarm
990 Tetherow Road
Williams, OR 97544
541-846-6963
Catalog $3.00

G1

Garden Valley Ranch Nursery
498 Pepper Road
Petaluma, CA 94952
707-795-0919
Does not ship to Canada

G2

Giles Ramblin' Roses
2968 State Road 710
Okeechobee, FL 34974
941-763-6611
*Send self-addressed stamped envelope for rose list;
does not ship to Canada*

G3

Greenmantle Nursery
3010 Ettersburg Road
Garberville, CA 95542
707-986-7504
*Send self-addressed stamped envelope for rose list
(catalog $3.00); does not ship to Canada*

H1

Heirloom Old Garden Roses
24062 Riverside Drive NE
St. Paul, OR 97137
503-538-1576
Catalog $5.00; does not ship to Canada

H2

Heritage Rosarium
211 Haviland Mill Road
Brookville, MD 20833
301-774-6890
Catalog $1.00

H3

High Country Roses
P.O. Box 148
Jensen, UT 84035
435-789-5512
Does not ship to Canada

H4

Historical Roses
1657 West Jackson Street
Painesville, OH 44077
440-357-7270
*Send self-addressed stamped envelope for rose list;
does not ship to Canada*

H5

Howerton Rose Nursery
1656 Weaverville Road
Allen Township
Northampton, PA 18067
610-262-5412

J1

Jackson & Perkins Co.
One Rose Lane
Medford, OR 97501
800-872-7673
Does not ship to Canada

J2

Justice Miniature Roses
5947 SW Kahle Road
Wilsonville, OR 97070
503-682-2370
Does not ship to Canada

K1

Sam Kedem Greenhouse and Nursery
12414 191st Street East
Hastings, MN 55033
612-437-7516
Catalog $2.00

L1

Lowe's Own Root Roses
6 Sheffield Road
Nashua, NH 03062
603-888-2214
Catalog $3.00

M1

Mary's Plant Farm
2410 Lanes Mill Road
Hamilton, OH 45013
513-894-0022
Does not ship to Canada

M2

Mendocino Heirloom Roses
P.O. Box 670
Mendocino, CA 95460
707-937-0963

M3

Michigan Miniature Roses
45951 Hull Road
Belleville, MI 48111
734-699-6698
Does not ship to Canada

N1

Nor'East Miniature Roses, Inc.
P.O. Box 307
Rowley, MA 01969
978-948-7964
    or
P.O. Box 473
Ontario, CA 91762
909-984-2223
Does not ship to Canada

O1

The Old Mill Nursery
806 South Belt Highway
St. Joseph, MO 64507
816-279-7434
800-344-8107
Does not ship to Canada

P1

Petaluma Rose Co.
P.O. Box 750953
Petaluma, CA 94975
707-769-8862
Does not ship to Canada

R1

Regan Nursery
4268 Decoto Road
Fremont, CA 94555
510-797-3222
800-249-4680

R2

Ros-Equus
40350 Wilderness Road
Branscomb, CA 95417
707-984-6959
Catalog $1.50; does not ship to Canada

R3

The Rose Ranch
P.O. Box 329
La Grange, CA 95329
209-852-9220
*Send self-addressed, stamped envelope for rose list;
catalog $3.00*

R4

The Roseraie at Bayfields
P.O. Box R
Waldoboro, ME 04572
207-832-6330
Does not ship to Canada

R5

Roses of Yesterday & Today
802 Brown's Valley Road
Watsonville, CA 95076
408-724-3537
Catalog $3.00

R6

Roses Unlimited
Route 1, Box 587
North Deer Wood Drive
Laurens, SC 29360
864-682-7673
Does not ship to Canada

R7

Royall River Roses
P.O. Box 370
North Yarmouth, ME 04096
207-829-5830

S1

Sequoia Nursery
2519 East Noble Avenue
Visalia, CA 93292
209-732-0190
Does not ship to Canada

S2

Sweet Briar Farm
14825 You Win Court
Grass Valley, CA 95945
530-477-7346

T1

Teas Nursery Co., Inc.
4400 Bellaire Boulevard
Bellaire, TX 77401
713-664-4400

V1

Vintage Gardens
2833 Old Gravenstein
Highway South
Sebastopol, CA 95472
707-829-2035
Catalog $5.00; does not ship to Canada

W1

Wayside Gardens
1 Garden Lane
Hodges, SC 29695
800-845-1124
Does not ship to Canada

W2

White Flower Farm
P.O. Box 50, Route 63
Litchfield, CT 06759
800-503-9624
Does not ship to Canada

Canadian Nurseries

CaA1

Au Jardin de Jean-Pierre
1070 RR 1 Ouest
Sainte-Christine, PQ J0H 1H0
819-858-2142
Catalog $5.99; does not ship to United States

CaC1

Corn Hill Nursery, Ltd.
RR 5
Petitcodiac, NB E0A 2H0
506-756-3635
Catalog $2.00

CaH1

Hardy Roses for the North
Box 2048
Grand Forks, BC V0H 1H0
250-442-8442
Catalog $5.00

CaH2

Hortico, Inc.
723 Robson Road
Waterdown, ON L0R 2H1
905-689-6984
Catalog $3.00

CaM1

Mach Rose Farm
26746 13th Avenue
Aldergrove, BC V4W 2S4
604-856-2631
Catalog $1.00

CaM2

Mori Miniatures
Box 772
Virgil, ON L0S 1T0
905-468-0315
Does not ship to United States

CaP1

Carl Pallek & Son Nursery
Box 137
Virgil, ON L0S 1T0
905-468-7262
Does not ship to United States

CaP2

Pickering Nurseries, Inc.
670 Kingston Road
Pickering, ON L1V 1A6
905-839-2111
Catalog $5.00

CaR1

Roses By Walter Lemire
2900 Highway 3
Oldcastle, ON N0R 1L0
519-737-6788

APPENDIX C
PUBLIC ROSE GARDENS

*I*n rose growing, as in any other branch of gardening, nothing is so valuable as local experience. The best place to find that is at a local public rose garden. The gardeners there are likely to have among them decades of experience in dealing with the peculiarities of the local climates and local soils, and generally they are glad to pass along their wisdom to the gardening public. Often, too, in a public garden you can examine firsthand roses that you would otherwise know only from catalog descriptions.

Usually you do not have far to look to locate a public display of roses. Your municipal parks department may be able to help you locate such a planting in your own hometown. If you wish to tour a really outstanding rose display, however, you may wish to consult the list of gardens below.

Every U.S. garden included in this list is an accredited display garden of the All-America Rose Selections (AARS) committee. This is a nursery industry group that was founded to select the best roses from each year's crop of introductions. Because the AARS has focused primarily on hybrid tea and floribunda roses, and because it is not interested in regionally adapted types, its "All-America Roses" are not always the easiest roses to grow. However, as a guide to rose gardens, its accreditation is perhaps the best of all, since the organization annually inspects all the gardens in which it displays its new award-winning roses, and it insists on a high level of cultivation. An AARS accreditation ensures prospective visitors that they will find the roses in that garden well cared for and properly labeled.

Unfortunately, not every state in the United States offers an AARS accredited rose garden. However, among the 61 U.S. gardens — and 19 Canadian gardens — listed in this appendix, you are sure to find some that have a climate and gardening situation similar to your own.

U.S. Gardens

ALABAMA

David F. Hemphill Park of Roses
Springdale Plaza
Airport Boulevard
Mobile, AL 36606
334-479-3775

The Formal Rose Garden
Birmingham Botanical Gardens
2612 Lane Park Road
Birmingham, AL 35223
205-879-1227

ARIZONA

Valley Garden Center Rose Garden
1809 North 15th Avenue
Phoenix, AZ 85007
602-252-2120

ARKANSAS

State Capitol Rose Garden
Arkansas State Capitol
Little Rock, AR 72201
501-682-3533

CALIFORNIA

Exposition Park Rose Garden
701 State Drive
Los Angeles, CA 90037
213-748-4772

Golden Gate Park Rose Garden
Golden Gate Park
Section 7
San Francisco, CA 94117
415-666-7003

The Huntington Botanical Gardens
1151 Oxford Road
San Marino, CA 99108
818-405-2160

Pageant of Roses Garden
3900 South Workman Mill Road
Whittier, CA 90601
562-699-0921

COLORADO

Longmont Memorial Rose Garden
Roosevelt Park
700 Longs Peak
Longmont, CO 80501
303-651-8446

CONNECTICUT

Elizabeth Park Rose Garden
150 Walbridge Road
West Hartford, CT 06119
860-722-6543

DISTRICT OF COLUMBIA

The George Washington University
2033 H Street NW & 830 21st Street
Washington, DC 20052
202-994-6412

United States National Arboretum
3501 New York Avenue NE
Washington, DC 20002
202-245-2726

FLORIDA

Sturgeon Memorial Rose Garden
13401 Indian Rocks Road
Largo, FL 34644
813-595-2914

GEORGIA

Atlanta Botanical Rose Garden
Piedmont Park at the Prado
Atlanta, GA 30309
404-876-5859

HAWAII

University of Hawaii
Maui County Research, CTAHR
209 Mauna Place
Kula Maui, HI 96790
808-878-1213

IDAHO

Julia Davis Rose Garden
Julia Davis Drive
Boise, ID 83706
208-384-4327

ILLINOIS

The Bruce Krasberg Rose Garden
Chicago Botanic Garden
Lake Cook Road, (½ mile east of
Edens Expressway)
Glencoe, IL 60022
847-835-8331

INDIANA

Lakeside Rose Garden
Lakeside Park
1401 Lake Avenue
Fort Wayne, IN 46805
219-427-6402

IOWA

Greenwood Park Rose Garden
Greenwood Park
4802 Grand Avenue
Des Moines, IA 50310
515-263-8725

Vander Veer Park Municipal Rose Garden
215 West Central Park Avenue
Davenport, IA 52803
319-326-7894

KANSAS

E. F. A. Reinisch Rose Garden
Gage Park
4320 West 10th Street
Topeka, KS 66604
913-272-6150

KENTUCKY

Kentucky Memorial Rose Garden
Kentucky State Fairgrounds
937 Phillips Lane
Louisville, KY 40232
502-267-6308

LOUISIANA

American Rose Center
8877 Jefferson-Paige Road
Shreveport, LA 71119
318-938-5402

MAINE

City of Portland Rose Circle
Deering Oaks Park
High Street Extension
Portland, ME 04101
207-756-8383

MASSACHUSETTS

James P. Kelleher Rose Garden
Park Drive
Boston, MA 02118
617-635-7381

The Stanley Park of Westfield, Inc.
P.O. Box 191
400 Western Avenue
Westfield, MA 01085
413-568-9312

MICHIGAN

Michigan State University
Horticulture Demonstration Gardens
Horticulture Department
East Lansing, MI 48823
517-353-4800

MINNESOTA

Lyndale Park Municipal Rose Garden
4125 East Lake Harriet Parkway
Minneapolis, MN 55409
612-370-4900

Minnesota Landscape Arboretum
3675 Arboretum Drive
Chanhassen, MN 55317
612-443-2460

MISSISSIPPI

The Jim Buck Ross Rose Garden
Mississippi Agriculture & Forestry
Museum
1150 Lakeland Drive
Jackson, MS 39216
601-354-6113

MISSOURI

Gladney & Lehmann Rose Gardens
Missouri Botanical Garden
4344 Shaw Boulevard
St. Louis, MO 63110
314-577-5190/577-9404

MONTANA

Missoula Memorial Rose Garden
Blaine & Brooks Streets
Missoula, MT 59833
406-523-2751

NEBRASKA

Boys Town AARS Constitution Rose Garden
Father Flanagan's Boys Home
Boys Town, NE 68010
402-498-1104

Memorial Park Rose Garden
58th & Underwood Avenue
Omaha, NE 68132
402-444-5497

NEVADA

Reno Municipal Rose Garden
2055 Idlewild Drive
Reno, NV 89509
702-334-2270

NEW HAMPSHIRE

Fuller Garden Rose Gardens
10 Willow Avenue
North Hampton, NH 03862
603-964-5414

NEW JERSEY

Rudolf W. van der Goot Rose Garden
Colonial Park
Mettler's Road
East Millstone, NJ 08873
908-234-2677

NEW MEXICO

Prospect Park Rose Garden
8205 Apache Avenue NE
Albuquerque, NM 87110
505-857-8650

NEW YORK

Cranford Rose Garden
Brooklyn Botanic Garden
1000 Washington Avenue
Brooklyn, NY 11225
718-622-4433

Maplewood Rose Garden
100 Maplewood Avenue
Rochester, NY 14615
716-647-2379

The Peggy Rockefeller Rose Garden
New York Botanical Garden
Bronx, NY 10467
718-817-8700

NORTH CAROLINA

The Biltmore Estate
1 Biltmore Plaza
Asheville, NC 28803
800-543-2961

Reynolda Rose Garden of Wake Forest University
100 Reynolda Village
Winston-Salem, NC 27106
910-758-5593

OHIO

Columbus Park of Roses
3923 North High Street
Columbus, OH 43214
614-645-6640/645-3350

OKLAHOMA

Tulsa Municipal Rose Garden
Woodward Park
21st & Peoria
Tulsa, OK 74114
918-596-7275

OREGON

International Rose Test Garden
400 SW Kingston Avenue
Portland, OR 97201
503-823-3636

PENNSYLVANIA

Hershey Gardens
P.O. Box 416, Hotel Road
Hershey, PA 17033
717-534-3493

Robert Pyle Memorial Rose Garden
Routes 1 & 796
West Grove, PA 19390
610-869-2426

SOUTH CAROLINA

Edisto Memorial Rose Garden
200 Riverside Drive
Orangeburg, SC 29115
803-533-6020

SOUTH DAKOTA

Rapid City Memorial Rose Garden
444 Mount Rushmore Road
Rapid City, SD 57702
605-394-4175

TENNESSEE

Memphis Municipal Rose Garden
750 Cherry Road
Memphis, TN 38117
901-682-6188

TEXAS

El Paso Municipal Rose Garden
1702 North Copia
El Paso, TX 79901
915-541-4331

Fort Worth Botanic Garden
3220 Botanic Garden Boulevard
Fort Worth, TX 76107
817-871-7686

Tyler Municipal Rose Garden
420 South Rose Park Drive
Tyler, TX 75702
903-531-1200

UTAH

Salt Lake Municipal Rose Garden
1602 East 2100 South
Salt Lake City, UT 84010
801-295-7960

VIRGINIA

Norfolk Botanical Gardens
Azalea Garden Road
Norfolk, VA 23518
757-441-5830

WASHINGTON

Manito Park — Rose Hill
4 West 21st Avenue
Spokane, WA 99203
509-625-6622

Point Defiance Rose Garden
5400 North Pearl
Tacoma, WA 98407
253-591-5328

Woodland Park Rose Garden
5500 Phinney Avenue North
Seattle, WA 98103
206-684-4803

WEST VIRGINIA
The Palace Rose Garden
RD 1, Box 319
Moundsville, WV 25701
304-843-1600

WISCONSIN
Boerner Botanical Garden
5879 South 92nd Street
Hales Corner, WI 53130
414-425-1131

Canadian Gardens

Rose gardening is at least as popular in Canada as in the United States, and despite the rigors of a northern climate, many fine rose gardens are open to the public. Because the Canadian nursery industry offers no organization comparable to the All-America Rose Selections committee, we have depended on recommendations from our Canadian consultant, Trevor Cole. The following are gardens that he finds to be widely acknowledged as outstanding.

ALBERTA
Calgary Zoo Botanical Garden and Prehistoric Park
1300 Zoo Road, N.E.
Calgary, AB T2E 7V6
403-232-9300

Olds College Rose Garden
Conference Services
4500 50th Street
Olds, AB T4H 1R6
403-556-8330

St. Albert Botanic Garden
c/o Richard Plain
39 Bellevue Crescent
St. Albert, AB T8N 0A5
403-459-8062

BRITISH COLUMBIA
Agriculture and Agrifood Canada Research Center
4200 Highway 97
Summerland, BC V0H 1Z0
250-494-6385

Butchart Gardens
Box 4010
Victoria BC V8X 3X4
250-652-4422

VanDusen Botanical Garden
5152 Oak Street
Vancouver, BC V6M 4H1
604-878-9274

MANITOBA
Agriculture and Agrifood Canada Research Center, Unit 100
Morden, MB R6M 1Y5
204-822-4471

Assiniboine Park
2799 Roblyn Boulevard
Winnipeg, MB R3R 0B8
204-986-5537

NEW BRUNSWICK
Le Jardin Botanique de New Brunswick
Box 1629
Saint Jacques, NB E3V 1A3
506-737-5383

NEWFOUNDLAND
Memorial University Campus
Elizabeth Avenue
St. John's, NF A1Z 5S7
709-737-7600

NOVA SCOTIA
The Annapolis Royal Historic Garden
Box 278
441 St. George Street
Annapolis Royal, NS B0S 1A0
902-532-7018

Haliburton House
414 Clifton Avenue
Windsor, NS B0N 2T0
902-798-2915

Halifax Public Garden
Halifax Parks and Natural Services
Box 1749
Halifax, NS B3J 3A5
902-490-4894

ONTARIO
Canadian National Exhibition Park
Lakeshore Road West
Toronto, ON M6K 3C3
416-392-2379

Central Experimental Farm
Prince of Wales Drive
Ottawa, ON K1A 0C6
613-828-5264
(Call Tuesday or Thursday)

Niagara Parks Botanical Gardens
School of Horticulture
Niagara Falls, ON L2E 6T2
905-356-8554, extension 225

Queen Elizabeth Gardens
Jackson Park
2450 McDougall Avenue
Windsor, ON N8X 3N6
519-253-2300

Royal Botanical Gardens
Box 399
Hamilton, ON L8N 3H8
905-527-1158, extension 243

QUEBEC
Le Jardin Botanique de Montreal
4101 Sherbrooke Street East
Montreal, QC H1X 2B2
514-872-1400

Index

Italic page numbers refer to illustrated entries in Chapter Three ("A Gallery of Easy Roses").

Photographs

Front cover: M. Thonig / H. Armstrong Roberts

Back cover: bottom Crandall & Crandall; right Albert Squillace/Positive Images

Spine: P.A. Haring

p.2 Terry Wild Studio; p.8 Jackson & Perkins; p.10 Crandall & Crandall; p.11 Malcolm (Mike) Lowe; p.12 Albert Squillace/Positive Images; p.13 Alan & Linda Detrick; p.14 Jerry Pavia ; p.16 Jim Adams; p.17 Kathy Zuzek; p.18 left David Earl Bott; p.18 right P. A. Haring; p.19 left Claire Martin III; p.19 right Donna Fuss; p.20 Bob Downing; p.21 Trevor Cole; p.22 William Welch; p.24, p.25 G. Mike Shoup; p.27 Karen Bussolini/ Positive Images; p.28, The Conard-Pyle Co.; p.34 Malcolm (Mike) Lowe; p.36, p.37 Saxon Holt Photography; p.38 Allan Mandell; p.41 Allan Mandell; p.40 Arena Rose Company; p.42 Richard Shiell; p.44 Jerry Pavia; p.45 Diane A. Pratt/Photo Designs 1998; p.46 Saxon Holt Photography; p.47 Janet Loughrey Photography; p.48 Jerry Howard/Positive Images; p.49 Jerry Pavia; p.50 The Conard-Pyle Co.; p.51 G. Mike Shoup; p.52 Margaret Hensel/Positive Images; p.53 Jerry Howard/Positive Images; p.55 Jerry Pavia; p.56 Allan Mandell; p.58 Crandall & Crandall; p.59 The Conard-Pyle Co.; p.60 Richard Shiell; p.61 left Jerry Pavia; p.61 right Malcolm (Mike) Lowe; p.62 P. A. Haring; p.63 left G. Mike Shoup; p.63 right P. A. Haring; p.64 Malcolm (Mike) Lowe; p.65 left P. A. Haring; p.65 right Malcolm (Mike) Lowe; p.66 P. A. Haring; p.67 left P. A. Haring; p.67 right P. A. Haring; p.68 left Malcolm (Mike) Lowe; p.68 right Jerry Pavia; p.69 P. A. Haring; p.70 left Malcolm (Mike) Lowe; p.70 right Jerry Pavia; p.71 Albert Squillace/ Positive Images; p.72 right Albert Squillace/Positive Images; p.72 left Jerry Pavia; p.73 both photos P. A. Haring; p.74 left Crandall & Crandall; p.74 right P. A. Haring; p.75 left P. A. Haring; p.75 right Dency Kane; p.76 left Richard Shiell; p.76 right Jerry Pavia; p.77 P. A. Haring; p.78 both photos P. A. Haring; p.79 left Bill Johnson; p.79 right P. A. Haring; p.80 Jerry Pavia.; p.81 left Malcolm (Mike) Lowe; p.81 right Albert Squillace/Positive Images; p.82 P. A. Haring; p.83 left Ben Phillips/Positive Images; p.83 right Jerry Pavia; p.84 left Malcolm (Mike) Lowe; p.84 right Alan & Linda Detrick; p.85 Jerry Pavia; p.86 left Albert Squillace/Positive Images; p.86 right Malcolm (Mike) Lowe; p.87 Alan & Linda Detrick; p.88 left Dency Kane; p.88 right Richard Shiell; p.89 left Alan & Linda Detrick; p.89 right Malcolm (Mike) Lowe; p.90 left P. A. Haring; p.90 right Janet Loughrey Photography; p.91 left Malcolm (Mike) Lowe; p.91 right Jackson & Perkins; p.92 Richard Shiell; p.93 left P. A. Haring; p.93 right Alan & Linda Detrick; p.94 left Crandall & Crandall; p.94 right Albert Squillace/Positive Images; p.95 left Saxon Holt Photography; p.95 right Terry Wild Studio; p.96 left Albert Squillace/ Positive Images; p.96 right Alan & Linda Detrick; p.97 left Diane A. Pratt/Photo Designs 1998; p.97 right Crandall & Crandall; p.98 left P. A. Haring; p.98 right Jerry Pavia; p.99 Saxon Holt Photography; p.100 left Jerry Pavia; p.100 right Malcolm (Mike) Lowe; p.101 left Saxon Holt Photography; p.101 right Nor'East Miniature Roses, Inc.; p.102 both photos P. A. Haring; p.103 left Pamela Harper; p.103 right Malcolm (Mike) Lowe; p.104 Alan & Linda Detrick; p.105 left G. Mike Shoup; p.105 right Ben Phillips/Positive Images; p.106 left Alan & Linda Detrick; p.106 right P. A. Haring; p.107 left Jackson & Perkins; p.107 right Dency Kane; p.108, left Malcolm (Mike) Lowe; p.108 right P. A. Haring; p.109 left P. A. Haring; p.109 right Suzanne Verrier; p.110 left Malcolm (Mike) Lowe; p.110 right Bill Johnson; p.111 left Malcolm (Mike) Lowe; p.111 right P. A. Haring; p.112 left Jerry Pavia; p.112, right Malcolm (Mike) Lowe; p.113 left Jerry Pavia; p.113, right, Malcolm (Mike) Lowe; p.114 Malcolm (Mike) Lowe; p.115 left Alan & Linda Detrick; p.115 right P. A. Haring; p.116 left Jerry Pavia; p.116 right P.

A. Haring; p.117 left Bill Johnson; p.117 right Malcolm (Mike) Lowe; p.118 Malcolm (Mike) Lowe; p.119 left Malcolm (Mike) Lowe; p.119 right Albert Squillace/Positive Images; p.120 Malcolm (Mike) Lowe; p.121 left Jerry Pavia; p.121 right P. A. Haring; p.122 both photos P. A. Haring; p.123 Jerry Pavia; p.124 left Jerry Pavia; p.124 right Alan & Linda Detrick; p.125 left P. A. Haring; p.125 right Richard Shiell; p.126 Albert Squillace/Positive Images; p.127 P. A. Haring; p.128 left Alan & Linda Detrick; p.128 right P. A. Haring; p.129 left Malcolm (Mike) Lowe; p.129 right G. Mike Shoup; p.130 left Alan & Linda Detrick; p.130 right Bill Johnson; p.131 left Malcolm (Mike) Lowe; p.131 right Suzanne Verrier; p.132 left Derek Fell; p.132 right Jerry Pavia; p.133 G. Mike Shoup; p.134 left Alan & Linda Detrick; p.134 right P. A. Haring; p.135 left G. Mike Shoup; p.135 right P. A. Haring; p.136 left P. A. Haring; p.136 right Albert Squillace/Positive Images; p.137 left P. A. Haring; p.137 right G. Mike Shoup; p.138 P. A. Haring; p.139 left P. A. Haring; p.139 right P. A. Haring; p.140 left Dency Kane; p.140 right American Rose Society; p.141 left Richard Shiell; p.141 right P. A. Haring; p.142 left P. A. Haring; p.142 right Saxon Holt Photography; p.143 left Suzanne Verrier; p.143 right P. A. Haring; p.144 left Malcolm (Mike) Lowe; p.144 right P. A. Haring; p.145 left Richard Shiell; p.145 right Jerry Pavia; p.146 Alan & Linda Detrick; p.148 Saxon Holt Photography; p.149 Richard Shiell; p.151 both photos Crandall & Crandall; p.152 Ralph Byther; p.153 Storey Communications, Inc.; p.158 Crandall & Crandall; p.159 Allan Mandell; p.160 Terry Wild Studio; p.162 Richard Shiell; p.163 Jerry Howard/Positive Images; p.165 Crandall & Crandall; p.171 Saxon Holt Photography; p.173 Saxon Holt Photography; p.175 Crandall & Crandall; p.176 P. A. Haring; p.177 Karen Bussolini/Positive Images; p.178 Richard Shiell; p.180 Crandall & Crandall; p.181 Janet Loughrey Photography; p.183 Richard Shiell; p.184 Allan Mandell; p.185 Richard Shiell; p.186 Richard Shiell; p.187 Alan & Linda Detrick; p.191, p.193, p.194 Saxon Holt Photography; p.195 Richard Shiell; p.196 Storey Communications, Inc.; p.198 Margaret Hensel/Positive Images; p.199 top Crandall & Crandall; p.199 bottom Ralph Byther; p.200 left Crandall & Crandall; p.200 top right Crandall & Crandall; p.200 bottom right Ralph Byther; p.201 top left Saxon Holt Photography; p.201 bottom left and top right Ralph Byther; p.201 bottom right Crandall & Crandall; p.202 top left Jim Dill; p.202 bottom left Bill Johnson; p.202 top right Alan & Linda Detrick; p.202 bottom right Jack Clark; p.203 top left Daniel Gilrein; p.203 bottom left, top right, and bottom right Ralph Byther; p.204 top left Daniel Gilrein; p.204 bottom left Richard Shiell; p.204 right Ralph Byther; p.205 Saxon Holt Photography; p.206, p.207, Storey Communications, Inc.; p.210, p.213, p.214, p.217 Saxon Holt Photography.

Illustrations

Anna Dewdney, pages 33, 56, 155-157, 166-169
Beverly K. Duncan, pages 31, 32, 39, 150, 188-192